TURNING GERMANS INTO TEXANS

WORLD WAR I AND THE ASSIMILATION AND SURVIVAL OF GERMAN CULTURE IN TEXAS, 1900-1930

TURNING GERMANS INTO TEXANS

WORLD WAR I AND THE ASSIMILATION AND SURVIVAL OF GERMAN CULTURE IN TEXAS, 1900-1930

MATTHEW D. TIPPENS

KLEINGARTEN PRESS

Publisher's Cataloging-in-Publication Data

Tippens, Matthew D.
  Turning Germans into Texans : World War I and the assimilation and survival
of German culture in Texas, 1900-1930 / Matthew D. Tippens.
    p. cm.
  ISBN: 978-0-9843572-0-8
  1. German Americans—Texas. 2. World War, 1914-1918. 3. Texas—
History—20th century. 4. Immigrants—United States—History.   I. Title.
E184.G3 T57 2010
976.4—dc22

                                                              2009913361

Kleingarten Press
kleingartenpress.com

Dedicated to the memory of my friend, Troy Christian Chambers (1969-2004).

"Souls of men dreaming of skies to conquer
Gave us wings, ever to soar!"

Contents

Illustrations

Acknowledgements

The original inspiration for this book came from a conversation I remembered having with my maternal grandmother, Pauline Dorothea Maria Fischer. She told me of growing up in a small Kansas town founded by German pioneers. My grandmother attended the local Lutheran school (to my knowledge, the only school in town). Until the United States entered World War I against Germany in April 1917, half of her classes were taught in German and the other half taught in English. Following America's entry into the war, the German-language classes ceased immediately. As a result, my grandmother never mastered the German language like her parents and grandparents had. This always made me wonder how one event, occurring thousands of miles away, could have such a dramatic impact on Americans of German heritage. The war changed forever how German Americans and German culture were perceived.

Since this book grew out of my dissertation at Texas Tech University, there are many in Lubbock I wish to thank. The staff of the Texas Tech Library and Interlibrary Loan provided assistance in securing a wealth of materials. In addition, the Southwest Collection at Texas Tech University made available access to several resources, such as its oral history collection, church histories, and newspapers. In the history department, secretaries Peggy Ariaz and Debbie Shelfer helped to guide many a graduate student through the program. Dr. Gretchen Adams, as graduate advisor, directed the way through the mysterious institutional corridors. I am also grateful to the history faculty of Texas Tech University.

Further afield, the Center for American History in Austin contains a wealth of information on the history of Texas. Moreover, the center's collection of historic Texas newspapers is outstanding. Laura Saegert and the rest of the staff at the Texas State Library and Archives suggested numerous sources relevant to my subject. Reverend Luther Oelke, archivist at the Evangelical Lutheran Church in America Region IV—South Archives at Texas Lutheran University, proved generous with his time and ideas, especially concerning individual church histories and old copies of the *Lutherbote für Texas*. Thanks also to the following institutions: the Sophienberg Archives in New Braunfels, the Fredericksburg and Seguin libraries, and the Austin History Center. Several members of the German-Texan Heritage Society provided information and shared experiences from their own relatives during World War I. Lastly, I am appreciative for the advices of Frederick C. Luebke and Walter D. Kamphoefner. Dr. Luebke, the dean of German-American historians, cautioned me to avoid writing a filiopietistic account of ethnic history.

I am grateful to my colleagues and friends who inspired and supported me in so many different ways. I am most indebted Professor Paul Carlson. Dr. Carlson has mentored me from my first days as a doctoral student to the completion of my dissertation. His abilities as a historian, writer, editor, lecturer, and teacher are beyond compare. Dr. Donald Walker's generosity and intimate erudition of Texas history added many subtleties to this work. Dr. Stefano D'Amico, an incomparably knowledgeable Italian historian, introduced me to several micro-histories and works of urban history that, in many ways, served as a model for the book. Dr. Joseph King provided suggestions on including more of a national and international view of this study as well as possible economic motivators. I would also like to thank two former faculty members in the history department who have moved on to greener pastures. First, Dr. William Glenn Gray, who served as my advisor in German history. To Dr. Gray I owe a solid foundation in German historiography. He was a great help from the start of my efforts, supplying a wealth of material and encouragement from his own wide-ranging research and abundant knowledge. Second, Dr. Paul Deslandes showed me new and exciting ways in which history could be studied through a social and cultural paradigm. His graduate course on the history of London was exceptional.

I would also be remiss if I did not mention several of my colleagues from whose discussions I benefited. Thanks to Ron Power, Scott Buchanan, Travis Clayton, Damon Kennedy, Dana (Magill) Cooper, Jonathan Hood, Mike McNair, Leland Turner, Dino Bryant, and Patrick Maille. Special thanks goes to Son Mai, Jeff Wilhelm, and Tana Owens. I have also benefited repeatedly from the friendship and the insights of a triumvirate of graduate students. First, my former officemate David Weir, whom provided pleasant company and, along with his wife Becca, many good times. Second, Steve Short's broad knowledge on a variety of subjects supplied a fount that I could draw from again and again. Finally, Scott Sosebee and his wife Leslie Daniel showed my family what West Texas hospitality is all about. Scott, in particular, has been a mentor, a colleague, but most of all, a friend. I have no doubt that he will leave his unique mark on the history profession. Thank you all.

Last, but not least—family. To my Mom and Dad for their continued support of my education over the (many) years. My amazing and beautiful wife Leslie assisted me superbly as a part-time research assistant, late-night editor, motivator, and sympathizer during this project. No words can fully express how I feel about her or what she means to me. Thus, in my woefully inadequate Latin, I simply say, "*Te amo.*" You are tougher than the rest. Our two children have brought more joy into our lives than we could have ever imagined. Our son Lukas' infectious happiness and constant curiosity about all things are wonders to behold. Our daughter Hattie was not born yet when I first submitted the manuscript. She surprises us everyday with new words and sounds and many other fascinating things. They are truly blessings.

Introduction

On Tuesday morning, February 12, 1918, twenty-two year old Walter Drawe, clerk for the Germania Club in Fayetteville, Texas, hoisted the German flag over the two-story club equipped with a barroom at the corner of West Fayette and North Rusk streets. Displaying the German flag from the Germania Club had been customary for many years as a notice that a dance or other social event was to be given on the night of the day when the flag went up. When an American Red Cross rally occurred in the Germania Club, for example, the German flag appeared as a notice that such an entertainment would be given. At the time, however, the United States had been at war with Imperial Germany for ten months, and, no matter how innocent the act appeared, it sparked an immediate uproar.[1]

Observers alerted the authorities and Deputy Marshal E. T. Herring and Special Agent E. B. Sisk rushed to the Germania Club. A prior complaint had given federal agents the understanding that the Germans would shoot the first person that attempted to remove their insignia. The two men climbed to the gallery, chopped down the thirty-foot mast, splintering it from the head to the base, and tore the German colors from the nails that had been driven into the pole to hold it in place. A small crowd of townspeople gathered in the street, not knowing what the two men were doing. After the federal agents had removed the flag, they arrested six persons. In the meantime, they conducted a further investigation and had warrants issued for five more alleged to have been implicated. The agents arrested the town's mayor, W. C. Langlotz, at his blacksmith shop. In all, they had eleven men, including the directors and officers of the club, and charged them with a serious crime—violating the Espionage Act of 1917.[2]

Later on Tuesday afternoon, the federal agents made ready to bring their prisoners to Houston. The train arrived in Houston shortly before 10 p.m., and the feds brought with them the condemned red, white, and black flag. Patrol cars greeted them at the Katy station and the load of the accused was conveyed to jail. Assigned to a cell in the Harris county jail, the offenders were held all night and were brought to the federal building shortly after 9 o'clock Wednesday morning to face United States Commissioner A. L. Jackson. The eleven men were arraigned before the commissioner. United States District Attorney John E. Green, Jr. formally charged the men with violating sections of the Espionage Act and released them on a $69,000 bond after they had pled not guilty. Before letting them go, Green cautioned them, "If you make any attempt to find out who informed the government of your actions you may have to face more serious charges than those now against you."[3]

Even though a subsequent investigation revealed that the incident was the third time the German flag had been displayed in 1918 (even after the Germania Club's minutes, dated January 7, noted that they would display only the United States flag), the district attorney dismissed the charges against the men, in part, because the facts "fail to show any willful intent on the part of any of the defendants named to violate any law of the United States, or to manifest disloyalty to the government."[4]

Before freeing the men from the federal proceedings, Green delivered a stern lecture to the accused: "It is surprising and almost incomprehensible to me that citizens of the United States should become so accustomed to seeing a foreign flag that they would thoughtlessly permit its use during a time of war," the district attorney stated, "but I am convinced that such has been the case at Fayetteville and that the act was not due to disloyalty, but to thoughtlessness and ignorance." The district attorney ordered the

Fayetteville Germania Club to thereafter display the United States flag. He also took time to reprimand the Germans. They "are subject to severe censure," he said, "for being so utterly careless as to permit a German flag to be displayed in the city of Fayetteville on several occasions, in view of the present state of war between the United States and Prussian autocracy represented by the imperial German government." Green also hoped the incident would serve to educate German Texans: "I trust that this incident will be a lesson to Germans throughout Texas, whether they are naturalized citizens or alien enemies, and will in the future avoid all acts which might raise the presumption that they are disloyal. There is no doubt in my mind that there are many Germans who are thoroughly loyal." At the same time, the district attorney stated, "I am afraid that there is much disloyalty in . . . this district."[5]

The Germania Club incident shows the innocence with which many German Texans regarded their culture and heritage, and the ease with which the suspicions of the Anglo community could be raised. And the fact that the club suffered no serious consequences from the incident is perhaps representative of a somewhat more tolerant atmosphere in Texas than in many Midwestern locations, where the anti-German hysteria brought on by World War I proved to be the most severe. Nevertheless, during the war many Texans of German heritage did suffer as a result of the "Americanizers" attempts to turn Germans into Texans.

According to the United States Census, one in five Americans, some 58,000,000 people, claim full or partial German heritage, making German Americans the United States' largest ethnic group. Yet, German Americans have a remarkably low profile today, reflecting a dramatic twentieth-century retreat from their German-American identity. In this age of multiculturalism, why have German Americans gone into ethnic retreat? The most obvious answer owes a great deal to the anti-German backlash of World Wars I and II.

During the earlier of the two major wars, even before the United States declared war on Germany in April 1917, the patriotism of German Americans had already undergone two years of questioning. Then, American intervention in World War I, and the federal government's campaign to mobilize support for the war, escalated the suspicion into hysteria. The anti-German hysteria expressed itself in vigilante attacks and governmental actions that demanded explicit demonstrations of loyalty from German Americans and the suppression of symbols of German ethnicity. An emerging national security apparatus required thousands of German aliens to register with the police. By fostering the anti-German panic and demanding "100 percent American" loyalty, the war induced many German Americans to retreat from their European identity. In several areas of the country, the public expression of German ethnicity became virtually impossible during and immediately after World War I and remained problematic thereafter.

In Texas, as in other states, German Americans came under close scrutiny during World War I. However, unlike the states of the Midwest and the Northeast, historians have not dealt substantively with the wartime experiences of Germans in Texas. To this end, no major historical work has been completed concerning German Texans during World War I. In other states, there has been a fair amount written on German Americans during World War I. Carl Wittke's *German-Americans and the World War (With Special Emphasis on Ohio's German Language Press)*, published in 1936, documented "a violent, hysterical, concerted movement to eradicate everything German from American civilization." Although detailed in documenting real events, the work failed to analyze the impact of the war and the nature of the postwar German-American community.[6]

Writing in 1940, John Hawgood claimed in *The Tragedy of German-America* that the traumatic experience of the war had culminated in the completion of the Americanization of German stock. He asserted "the German-Americans, as German-Americans, did not emerge from the war at all." By the end of the 1920s, "the German-American era appeared to be definitely over and hardly likely to return."[7]

David Detjen in *The Germans in Missouri, 1900-1918: Prohibition, Neutrality, and Assimilation* chooses to trace the history of the German-American Alliance in Missouri from its beginnings at the turn of the century to its demise in 1918. The study focuses largely on St. Louis. The alliance, to the extent that it had a unifying purpose, opposed prohibition. Well-organized and aggressive prohibitionists, claims Detjen, sought to dry up the state and the ubiquitous German beer halls would not be exempt. With the outbreak of war in Europe in 1914, prohibition soon became a sideshow. The alliance was only one of a number of German-American institutions, including Lutheran and Catholic churches, to rally in sympathy for the German cause and, as a result, in support of American neutrality. What the alliance did manage was to bring the wrath of public opinion down not just on itself, but upon German Americans generally. When alliance leader Charles Weinsberg was arrested (though not convicted) in April 1918 under the Espionage Act the organization instantly vanished without a trace. Detjen concludes that the result of the war "was that the very German-American community and culture that the alliance had been created to preserve was destroyed."[8]

In the Wittke, Hawgood, and Detjen studies were the roots of what was to become the predominant conventional view: the disappearance of German Americans as an ethnic group. Such thought advances the notion that World War I caused, or contributed to, the demise, disintegration, and disappearance of German-American communities in the United States. Inherent in such a view is the assimilation assumptions of late nineteenth and early twentieth century America. The war, therefore, acted as a furnace on the melting pot of American society. Several works of German-American history have supported this view. The position asserts that the anti-German hysteria brought on by the war caused or contributed to the disappearance of German America.

A majority of the studies dealing with German Americans and World War I also maintain that anti-German hysteria brought on by the war quickly subsided with the signing of the armistice in 1918, or soon thereafter. The view has become the accepted one on the demise of the hysteria. The question has not been asked if nativism continued against the Germans into the 1920s, nor has there been an attempt to trace it. State histories provide nothing more than cursory coverage to the 1920s and cannot be characterized as case studies designed to test whether or not anti-German hysteria continued in the years following the war. In Texas, antagonism against Germans continued into the early 1920s as nativist fears against all things foreign persisted.

A small number of studies, however, stand in opposition to the previously mentioned ones concerning World War I and German Americans. Such studies argue that World War I did not lead to an ethnic disappearance. Although not as sharply articulated as the disappearance school of thought, the "survival" position contends that in localized studies of urban and rural German communities, valid grounds exist for questioning the notion that German Americans as an ethnic group with community institutions simply vanished, disappeared, and ceased to exist. The survival argument is the beginning of a serious and critical examination of the German element and one that is not based on assumptions of assimilation, nor written from the perspective of assimilation as the inevitable fate of all immigrant groups.

The survival school has already been applied to German Texans. In 1982, Dona Reeves wrote on the German-Texans' ethnic survival, stating that the German Texan "has resisted assimilation and held to his own special life style." Because of their strong statewide sense of group identity the German Texans, she argues, could be compared to the Pennsylvania Germans. Reeves writes: "As with other American ethnic groups, the German Texans represent a continuum, a self-renewing blend, which in spite of ecologic and cultural fragility and vulnerability to modern social and economic forces offers some promise for ethnic survival." According to Joseph Wilson, in German-Texan families German "was still the basic language of the home" as late as the 1940s and 1950s. Glen E. Lich notes that the "German Texans resisted the melting pot, although like other ethnic groups they contributed their own pieces of the mosaic of America—a nation of immigrants." Nevertheless, "much has been lost from the German tradition, but a good part of that heritage was strong." Gilbert J. Jordan found in 1979 that "much of

6

the nineteenth century German cultural heritage still remains and will continue to live on for many years."[9]

There are, above and beyond the studies cited thus far, a scattered number of references to the impact of war and the survival of German Americans as an ethnic group. Kathleen Neils Conzen strikes some of the notes in her article in the *Harvard Encyclopedia of American Ethnic Groups* where she writes of the "submergence" of German ethnicity rather than the disappearance, disintegration, or dissolution of such. Although her remarks on ethnic survival are confined to rural German Americans, Conzen nonetheless has identified some flaws in the idea of ethnic disappearance.[10]

In the best national analysis of the war, *Bonds of Loyalty: German-Americans and the First World War*, Frederick C. Luebke demonstrated clearly that although they were deeply affected by the war, German Americans and their community institutions survived. However, the war, in his view, accelerated assimilation in the long run. In relation to the postwar hysteria, Luebke has maintained that while the anti-German hysteria began to subside after the armistice, the "war" against German language and culture continued to be exploited by journalists and politicians.[11]

Several studies have, therefore, reported on and documented the survival of German ethnicity as well as German-American community institutions. The logical conclusion to such studies would be the rejection of ethnic disappearance in certain cases. The survival school is characterized by case and specialized studies of the German element by the state, regional, or local levels, rather than by general national surveys. In some case studies, despite being significantly weakened, the German element did survive the war. Thus, the example of Germans in Texas makes for a compelling argument in the survival school. In the years following World War I in Texas, German-language newspapers remained in print, German-language religious services continued, and many German Texans resumed following their German cultural organizations, albeit to a lesser degree than before the war.

If it survived World War I to some degree, where did German America go and how did Germans think of themselves after the war?

Attempting to answer these questions is Russell A. Kazal's *Becoming Old Stock: The Paradox of German-American Identity.* Kazal analyzes one major city, Philadelphia, concentrating on the years from 1900 to 1930 when the transformation of German-American identity was most abrupt. He recounts how fear and suspicion, fed by politics of the federal government, led to campaigns against all expressions of German language and culture in Philadelphia as elsewhere. Kazal acknowledges the role World War I played in suppressing German-American ethnic consciousness, but Kazal goes far beyond simple explanations, asserting that the way wartime hysteria reshaped German-American identity had long-term consequences for American pluralism and racial identity after the conflict.[12]

In the wake of World War I, Philadelphia's middle-class German Americans assimilated into simply Americans—"Old Stock"—as differentiated from blacks, recent immigrants from eastern and southern Europe, and other minorities. Through his exploration of pluralism's fate, Kazal links the German-American story to a larger national shift. He argues that the anti-German panic was really part of a broader attack on the ethnic pluralism characteristic of prewar America. Furthermore, Kazal notes, "the retreat from German-American identity during and after World War I played a key role in the demise of an earlier, more pluralist America and the rise of a more exclusive and conformist American nationalism." The conformist nationalism was both the product of the anti-hyphen and "100 percent Americanism" crusades of the war years and the rationale for the anti-radical and anti-immigrant campaigns that came later. In this sense, the anti-German hysteria of 1917 and 1918 was just a prelude to wider attacks on other ethnic and religious groups, and on pluralism itself, after the war.[13]

None of the aforementioned studies discusses German Texans' experiences and sentiments concerning the international war against Germany and the domestic war against everything German. Granted, German Texans were no longer a significant proportion of the Texas population as they were in such states as Wisconsin, Missouri, and Nebraska. The fact makes an investigation of the conflict in Texas more intriguing, for despite German Americans' relatively small presence in Texas, Texans worked furiously to limit the threat posed by the supposed "menace" in their midst.

In 1910, Texas had 48,032 residents born in Germany and 220,000 residents of German descent, placing the state fourteenth in terms of German-American population. California was the only state outside of the Midwest and Northeast with a larger German-American population than Texas and certain counties in Texas contained the highest concentrations of Germans anywhere outside of the Midwest. Still, German Americans represented a relatively small proportion of the Texas population. In 1910, only one percent of Texans claimed Germany as their birthplace, and first and second generation German Americans formed less than five percent of the Texas population. German Texans' limited demographic significance during World War I, however, and their adherence to many of the same values held by Texans of other northern and western European backgrounds did not make them immune from the pressures that German Americans in other areas of the country faced.[14]

Antagonism toward German Texans also may have been especially intense in Texas because the elites were less secure than were their counterparts in the East. Like many frontier societies, a paradoxical combination of toleration and conformism characterized the state of Texas. The lack of well-established social institutions, the absence of any ancient ruling class, and constant influx of newcomers created an environment that eroded tradition and became receptive to social and economic mobility and cultural diversity. Although a frontier society could not afford social rigidity, neither could it sustain cultural deviations that threatened a fragile social fabric. Recognizing the need for common values that would help to forge identity and foster social cohesion, Anglo Americans promoted fundamental practices such as the use of the English language and elevated simple symbols of patriotism such as the flag. In newly settled areas in which Anglos were scarcely more entrenched than their immigrant neighbors, Anglo Americans felt threatened by ethnics who refused to honor the elements of Americanism. On the other hand, in a county heavily populated by Germans, an Anglo-

Texan merchant might fear that he faced social and economic extinction.

Historian Frederick C. Luebke has also argued that Frederick Jackson Turner's sectionalist doctrines were based on methodology that was ideally suited for the study of ethnic minority groups in America. Far less celebrated than Turner's frontier thesis, his sectional work, Luebke states, encourages the study of ethnicity in its relationships, whatever they may be, to environment. Luebke believes that a study of any immigrant group must answer three questions: how a specific behavior of an immigrant group in any given place compared (1) to that of other groups in the same comparable environment; (2) to that of the same group in other environments; and (3) to what it became later in time. Adapting Luebke's analysis to Texas, the aim of the dissertation is to examine the process of change over time in German culture as it interacted with other groups within a specific physical and social environment.[15]

German Texans had settled in compact communities, establishing a strong presence in central Texas, especially in the area around Austin and San Antonio. The clannish appearance they projected through their concentrated settlement annoyed many Texans, as did their retention of German *Kultur*. In many communities, German was the language of religious, educational, and commercial affairs. As many as 75,000 to 100,000 German Texans may have still used the German language predominately or exclusively in 1907, and in 1914, twenty-four German-language newspapers in Texas claimed a combined circulation of over 70,000.[16]

German Texans, like most German Americans, remained proud of their ethnic heritage. Yet, to many Americans, cultural loyalty to Germany conflicted with political loyalty to the United States. German Americans' resistance to assimilation seemed a rejection of all things American, including the American government. There were legitimate reasons for concern over German Americans' support for the war against Germany. Throughout the period of American neutrality, German-American newspapers, including those in Texas, defended the Central Powers, denounced the Allies, and criticized President Woodrow Wilson's foreign policy. German Texans formed chapters of the German Red Cross and participated in humanitarian relief efforts to benefit the Central Powers.

After the U.S. entered the war, the response to German-American activities soon lost all sense of proportion to the danger. Simply being German or using the German language aroused suspicion. If the state could not rid itself of troublesome German Texans, assimilation, or "Americanization," would eliminate or at least punish the ethnicity that seemed to cause disloyalty. Mayors, ministers, school boards, legislators, businessmen, and students all participated in anti-German activities. Claiming that German Texans' ethnicity was equivalent to disloyalty, many Texans were determined to purge all traces of German culture from their state. The so-called "Americanizers" intended to turn Germans into Texans using whatever means necessary. They targeted German-language newspapers and German influences in the education system, and they enacted restrictions against instruction in the German language. The Americanizers even sought to eliminate the use of German from religious services, reasoning that it was immaterial if some church members knew no English. Not even pastors were above suspicion. To help prove their own loyalty to the U.S., many German Texans themselves participated in anti-German activities. If German Americans in Texas suffered during World War I, their fiercest assailants were sometimes fellow German Texans.

The effort to eliminate German culture was quite successful. German Texans anglicized their surnames, many churches eliminated German worship services, German-language newspapers ceased publication, and families made English the language of the home. German Texans were assimilating before the war began, and assimilation efforts during the conflict only hastened a process that many people had been encouraging for some time. Following World War I, the new generation of persons born of German descent was thoroughly Americanized; members of the new generation spoke almost no German and knew little of German culture. The appearance of Adolf Hitler on the world scene only intensified the tendency of German Texans to bury their ethnicity. By the second-half of the twentieth century, only the faintest traces of German ethnic life remained.

Yet, in many ways, the ethnic disappearance thesis does not hold true in the case of the Germans in Texas. The German-Texan community survived the war and did not vanish, disappear, or cease to exist. It did not go unscathed. On the contrary, the German-Texan community was deeply marked and permanently altered by the war experience. The changes together with the then prevalent notions of the melting pot were responsible for the misconception of the German Texan as a case of ethnic disappearance. It would have been impossible for German Texans in November 1918 to have returned to their status as of 1914. There was, therefore, a reorientation to the demands of the 1920s. The reorientation of German Texans should be placed in a broader context of the dramatic changes occurring in the 1920s in Anglo America. First, the revolution in morals, manners, customs, standards, and values repudiated and destroyed the ideological unity with the prewar period. Second, and especially in Texas, Germans were increasingly accepted as "Anglos" to differentiate them from African and Mexican Americans. During the 1920s, the anti-German nativism faded as the previously existing anti-Mexican American sentiment multiplied. By the middle of the 1920s, anti-German sentiment was no longer as prominent an issue in Texas as it had been during the war. Likewise, the attacks on the German language were replaced by attacks on the Spanish language.

Therefore, the book examines the plight of German Texans during World War I, the role the war played in speeding their assimilation, but, ultimately, despite such factors, the survival of a substantial portion of German-Texan culture. The central focus is on German Texans from 1900 to 1930. Such a focus will allow a comparison of German-Texan culture before and after World War I. There exists an ample body of historical literature on Germans in Texas. However, almost all of the literature concentrates on the nineteenth century, and of that, a majority of the work pertains to the pre-Civil War era. Twentieth-century literature on German Texans is almost nonexistent. In addition, historical literature on the state of

Texas during the Progressive era is also lacking. Thus, the book fills a void not only in the German-Texan literature, but also, to a degree, in early twentieth-century Texas history.

Germans were among the earliest white settlers in the state of Texas. Germans contributed greatly to the growth of the state in the fields of business, religion, music, agriculture, ranching, and cultural activities. Despite such accomplishments, German Texans became targets of the anti-German hysteria during World War I. Why was this? How did German Texans react? What role did the hysteria play in the process of German Texans suppressing their German ethnicity for an American one? What was the lasting legacy of the war for German Texans? Finally, if German-Texan culture survived the war, what was the state of that culture in the postwar years and beyond?

The German-Texan experience is unique. No other large immigrant group in twentieth-century Texas saw its country of origin go to war twice with the United States; none, correspondingly, faced such sustained pressure to forgo its ethnic identity for an "American" one; and none appeared to mute its ethnic identity to so great an extent.

2

German Texans to 1900

Germans began to settle in Texas during the 1820s. Most of the earliest were people who had been living in North America. Among them were some with German or German-sounding names from the German districts of Pennsylvania and other parts of the United States. In 1823, Baron de Bastrop, a Prussian-born associate of Stephen F. Austin, founded a community that bore his last name. Bastrop's town was located far into what was then regarded as the interior of Texas: 120 miles up the Colorado River. Some of the settlers of Bastrop were from the Duchy of Oldenburg in northwestern Germany. Austin took special interest in encouraging German settlers during the 1830s, but the effort at best resulted in very modest numbers of Germans coming to Texas.[1]

In 1831, Christian Friedrich Ernst Dirks of Oldenburg, Germany, known by his pseudonym "Friedrich Ernst," obtained land for a settlement in a remote part of Austin's colony. A postal clerk accused of embezzling funds from the Duchy of Oldenburg's postal service, Friedrich Ernst managed to flee with his family to America. Arriving from Europe in New York in 1829, he intended to go to the Missouri Territory. Changing his mind while in New Orleans en route to Missouri, Ernst went to Texas. As was typical of early German immigrants in Texas: before going to the region Ernst had, if only briefly, been in the United States. In Texas, his farm was located south of Bastrop between the Colorado and Brazos Rivers. His endeavor to publicize his settlement achieved much success when an open letter of his was published in North German newspapers. In

1838, he founded his own town, which he named Industry, located in present day Austin County. In the meantime, a sprinkling of other Germans had arrived in Texas, and some of them had started settlements of their own. By 1840, an American emigrant to Texas had remarked on the substantial number of Germans in Texas.[2]

German immigrants became more numerous during the last years of the Lone Star Republic (1836-1845). They were welcomed for various reasons. Texans saw them as counterweights to the numerous advocates of the incorporation of Texas by the United States. Other Texans found in the German immigrants sturdy farmers who would stand by Texas loyally in the event of the resumption of war with Mexico. To still others, they were greenhorns to exploit. The Congress of Texas passed a law in 1843 requiring the publication of the Republic's laws in German. A rapidly increasing number of handbooks for German emigrants during the 1840s praised, often at the expense of the United States, the virtues of Texas as a place to emigrate: immigrants could become citizens in a short time, the Republic gave settlers free land, and additional land could be purchase for ridiculously small sums. A number of handbooks even contended the propitious time to emigrate to the United States had passed – that Texas had far more to offer Germans.[3]

Despite an increasing German presence in the Lone Star Republic, the projects of the Association for the Protection of German Immigrants in Texas surpassed beyond all measure those of other endeavors to direct Germans to Texas. The association is generally known in English, as well as German, by the term *Adelsverein*, which refers not to its German title (*Verein zum Schutze deutscher Einwanderer in Texas*), but, sarcastically, to the heavy participation of noblemen, including members of the ruling houses, in the venture. Germans founded the organization in 1842, following a meeting in Biebrich in the Duchy of Hessen-Nassau, and then converted it into a joint-stock company two years later. Among the founders of the *Adelsverein* were ruling princes and high nobles from the states of Nassau, Hannover, Hessen-Darmstadt, Hessen-Kassel, Brunswick, Waldeck, Württemberg, Coburg, and Meiningen.

King Frederick William III of Prussia supported it discreetly without financing it publicly.

Among the *Adelsverein* purposes were: 1) to improve the lot of the working class who are without employment, thus controlling their increasing poverty, 2) to unite the emigrants by giving them protection through this Association in order to ease their burden by mutual assistance, 3) to maintain contacts between Germany and the emigrants and to develop maritime trade by establishing business connections, and 4) to find a market for German crafts in these settlements and to provide a market in Germany for the products of these colonies. In addition, many of its founders expected healthy profits from the organization, as well as the alleviation of overpopulation from their lands.

The *Adelsverein* resulted from speculation based upon inadequate information. It obtained a gigantic territory in Texas, a land grant of two million acres, but the grant was poorly situated in west Texas between the Llano and Colorado Rivers, largely unsuited for farming and wholly occupied by hostile Indians. Nevertheless, the association sought to settle thousands of Germans there. A colonist would pay a fixed sum and receive in exchange passage to America and the journey through Texas to the association's territory. The first emigrants under the protection of the *Adelsverein* reached Galveston in July 1844; in 1846, the last arrived. This attempt to create a new Germany abroad was similar to numerous other projects undertaken before the American Civil War.[4]

In Texas, however, the primary interest of the government was not the success of its German immigrants, but having more land settled and more white inhabitants of non-Mexican, non-Spanish origins. Therefore, the existence of the *Adelsverein* remained for a brief period of great use to the government of Texas. The association provided a counterweight to the force exerted on one side by Mexico and on the other by the United States. Support from Europe was welcome. The British government was interested in the development of the *Adelsverein*: the German settlers could create a new balance of forces in Texas that would help the British to keep Texas neutral in the event that Great Britain and the United States went to war, an event that remained a distinct possibility. Despite its apparent benefits, a mixture of speculation, romantic colonizing impulses, and profit-seeking schemes by noblemen ultimately defeated the *Adelsverein*.[5]

Prince Carl von Solms-Braunfels, the organization's commissar in the republic from 1844 to 1845, spent many months in Texas, where his aristocratic proclivities jeopardized the entire undertaking. Solms did manage, however, to establish New Braunfels, in part to isolate his German colonists from American influences. After several catastrophes, Solms returned to Europe in 1845, succeeded by a far more astute nobleman, Otfried Hans von Meusebach, who modestly referred to himself in Texas as John O. Meusebach. Meusebach was equipped for the position, technically and psychologically. He established the city of Fredericksburg, naming it in honor of Prince Friedrich of Prussia, northwest of New Braunfels. He also negotiated a peace treaty with the Comanches. Despite his success, Meusebach resigned from the *Adelsverein* in 1847, the year prior to its dissolution.[6]

Settlement in the *Adelsverein* grant also took place along the northern bank of the Llano River. Through an agreement, forty men (the "*Vierziger*"), actually thirty-six young men from Darmstadt, Germany, settled on the *Adelsverein's* grant with the intention of building a communistic colony. The group in October 1847 took up residence on a farm it named Bettina, in honor of Goethe's friend Bettina von Armin. "The Forty" proceeded to practice their principles, which included avoidance of any decisions not reached communally and voluntarily. But the settlers also lacked the agricultural training necessary to sustain themselves, and their colony lasted less than a year. Disillusioned, members drifted away, presumably melting back into regular society.[7]

The United States Census of 1850 found only 8,300 people in Texas who had been born in Germany, although Germans constituted by far the largest European-born segment of the population. Terry Jordan estimates the size of the "German element"—people born in Germany as well as all inhabitants with one or more parents born in Germany—in Texas in 1850 at 11,621.

The 11,621 German residents of Texas formed 7.5 percent of the white population and 5.4 percent of the entire population. However, the low counts of Germans by the middle of the century should not lead one to conclude that fewer than 10,000 German-speaking people had come to Texas, or that fewer than 10,000 lived there. Even taking into consideration the high death rate and the possibility that a number of Germans left Texas and went to other parts of America, Germans were apparently undercounted in Texas during the 1850 census survey. Furthermore, a sprinkling of peoples from Switzerland, Alsace, and the Hapsburg Empire, in addition to some German Americans from the United States, increased the ranks of German-speaking Texans.[8]

The Germans concentrated in certain parts of Texas, primarily in a belt stretching across the south-central part of the state from Galveston and Houston along the Gulf Coast to Kerrville and Mason in the Hill Country. Along this "German Belt," especially in and around such towns as New Braunfels and Fredericksburg, there were islands of non-southern social and cultural institutions that could not be found in other slave states, except perhaps in large cities, such as New Orleans. Some of these German residents disliked slavery, and many supported the Union. Nevertheless, they did not alter the essentially southern nature of the population, economy, and society of antebellum Texas. The Germans, however, through their political activities and their newspaper publishing, increasingly became a potent influence upon the affairs of the state. Such actions eventually led many Anglo Texans to gain a "historic distrust" of German Texans.[9]

The Hill Country community of Sisterdale became the center of an intellectual community, a perceived hotbed of "radical" German activity, and was prominent in Texas politics. German Baron Ottomar von Behr developed Sisterdale. In February 1848, he bought a large tract of land at the place and established a sort of communist colony. Behr became known for his hospitality, and his farm, until his untimely death in late 1855, became the nucleus of a growing community of similarly educated political theorists. Many were "forty-eighters," liberal minded, often idealistic refugees from

19

Germany's failed revolutions of 1848. By the early 1850s, Sisterdale boasted six barons (including Edgar von Westphalen, Karl Marx's brother-in-law) and nineteen settlers with university educations (including three Ph.D.s). Due to their lack of experience with agriculture and ranching on one hand and their abilities to conduct weekly meetings and conversations in Latin on the other, they were nicknamed "Latin farmers." In this period even San Antonio was hard-pressed to match Sisterdale's cultured assembly.[10]

In 1853, Sisterdalers organized the *"Freie Verein"* (Free Society), a political club with the goal of debating the social issues of the day and working for the full expression of German opinion in state politics. The club ignited a firestorm across Texas when slavery became the defining public issue of the times. The revolutionaries who were moderate in Germany became, because of the issues of slavery and secession, radicals in Texas. Ten miles up the river, a new town, Comfort, was established in 1854, which as a stronghold of *Freidenkers* (freethinkers) and abolitionists, quickly took on the character of Sisterdale's daughter colony. The political radicalism of the area found varying echoes in the San Antonio, New Braunfels, and Fredericksburg triangle. San Antonio, the old Spanish capital of Texas, was a thoroughly Mexican place in the 1850s and looked it. However, it was steadily acquiring Anglo and German residents, mostly merchants, artisans, and professional people. While the Americans commandeered political power, the Germans set about building institutions that served their interests. Sisterdalers frequented the city and there can be little doubt that the opinions of the Sisterdalers were closely followed in the German taverns and saloons of San Antonio before the Civil War.[11]

In March 1854, the Sisterdale *Freie Verein* blindly lit the fuse to a political time bomb. The society issued a statewide call to sister organizations to send delegates to a German political convention to be held in May after the German-Texan Singing Festival in San Antonio. Germans debated the issues in order to achieve a unified political stance in the upcoming presidential election so that German sentiments would be taken seriously in Texas. The convention was duly held and a platform of ideas approved. It contained a controversial plank: "Slavery is an evil whose ultimate removal is, according to Democratic principles, indispensable." The resolution unleashed a verbal debate across the state. The net result was to set most Anglo Texans against the Germans for meddling in an issue over which they were considered too recent arrivals for their opinion to carry any weight. It also set many Germans against each other, not necessarily over the issues of slavery, but over the wisdom of antagonizing the surrounding Anglo-Texas majority.[12]

The event constituted the defining moment in Texan-German political relations in the years leading up to the Civil War. It fixed the potentially false impression in Anglo minds that Germans would not support the Southern cause. Of course, not all German Texans were radical abolitionists, in fact, some Germans owned slaves but in a percentage far less than their Anglo neighbors. Recent research by Walter D. Kamphoefner has shown that German Texans had little role in slave ownership or support for secession. For example, in three counties of the Hill Country region not a single German owned slaves. Whereas, in the older settlements in Austin, Fayette, and Colorado counties, some sixty Germans owned slaves between 1840 and 1865. Still, despite the strong presence of Germans in the older counties, German Texans made up less than five percent of all the local slaveowners.[13]

Debating the volatile slavery issue were two newspaper editors: "forty-eighter" and revolutionary, Dr. Adolf Douai, and botanist Ferdinand Lindheimer. Called the earliest popularizer of Marxian ideas in the United States, Douai's outspokenness resulted in his near ruin on several occasions. Driven from New Braunfels as a teacher, he became editor of the *San Antonio Zeitung*, the only German paper in Texas that regularly published articles in English calling for the abolition of slavery. When he was drummed out of the state in 1856, Douai went to Boston. His first school there was destroyed after an allegedly atheistic commemoration of Alexander von Humboldt. Douai survived, however, to become known as the introducer of Friedrich Froebel's kindergarten system in America. Ferdinand Lindheimer, on the other hand, became not only the cultural, but also the political spokesman of the German majority. As editor of the *Neu-Braunfelser Zeitung*, he attacked German unionism, calling it impolite to antagonize the American settlers and dangerous to meddle in their affairs. Personally opposed to slavery and a hesitant supporter of secession, he nonetheless protested against men like Douai because of the reprisals Germans might suffer should they be perceived as opposing secession.[14]

The secession referendum of February 23, 1861, passed by a landslide across Texas with less than a quarter of the voters in opposition. However, returns show the heavily German counties unreceptive to secession. Two German frontier counties, Gillespie and Mason, led the state with a 96 percent margin against secession. In Kerr County, the German communities around Comfort (soon to become Kendall County) voted nearly two-thirds against secession, actually a surprisingly small margin considering its subsequent resistance to the Confederate cause. Bexar County, with the largest number of Germans in the state, witnessed a narrow secessionist victory, but the city of San Antonio turned in a razor-thin margin for the Union. Even older Texas German settlements farther east show little evidence of enthusiasm for secession. Germans voted against secession in Colorado, Bastrop, and Fayette Counties. Only in Austin County did even close to a majority of the Germans vote for Southern independence. The only western county that voted strongly for secession was Comal County, which included the city of New Braunfels. More than anything, the county's support for secession reflected trust in the advice of Ferdinand Lindheimer and his *Neu-Braunfelser Zeitung*.[15]

After the Civil War began and the national conflict grew ever more intense, the mistrust between Germans and Anglos reached deeper into excitable minds. The Hill Country paid a heavy price for the mistrust. Marauding state militia detachments seeking out German abolitionists ravaged the region and left Sisterdale, in particular, in virtual ruins. Several hundred male Unionists on the Fourth of July, 1862, organized a German battalion with companies from Kendall, Gillespie, and Kerr Counties. When letters were intercepted allegedly connecting the German officers with Southern Unionists, Confederates declared open rebellion in the three counties and placed them under strict martial law. Believing that a safe conduct had been issued, the German cadre assembled for movement into Mexico but a Confederate force, under the command of James M. Duff, ambushed them in the early morning of August 10, 1862. The Battle of Nueces, as it came to be called, effectively crushed the idealism of the German-Texan Unionists. In addition to the Nueces battle, Confederate troops killed Southern Unionists in October 1862, while attempting to cross the Rio Grande, and Confederates killed other Unionists elsewhere. Until after the war, no one even dared to gather the bones of the fallen, then relatives and friends transported the remains to Comfort and buried them under an obelisk that bears the inscription "*Treue der Union*" (loyal to the Union), along with the names of the victims. For years after the Civil War, the Battle of Nueces left hard feelings amongst the Germans.[16]

After the Civil War, immigration entered a new phase as increasing numbers of Germans filtered into the state. In fact, more Germans came to Texas after the Civil War, from 1865 to 1890, than came in the entire thirty years of immigration before the war. In contrast to the Germans who came in antebellum times, those arriving after 1865 came not as pioneers, but as secondary settlers who expected to continue the market-oriented agriculture they had known in Germany. The number of residents having German ancestry increased from 41,000 in 1870 to 125,262 in 1890, a gain of more than two hundred percent in two decades. In 1890, German Texans outnumbered Texans of Mexican ancestry, whose total population stood at 105,193. In 1900, there were over 50,000 foreign-born Germans in Texas, about two and one-half the times the total of 1860.[17]

The German immigrants who entered Texas after 1865 settled primarily in the eastern end of the German Belt. The decade of the 1870s, particularly, was one of extremely active rail construction in the region, and the state government granted the rail companies large tracts of land along their lines as a financial inducement. The railroads, in turn, recruited settlers, including many Germans, to purchase and colonize these lands. They printed brochures in German and distributed them in parts of Central

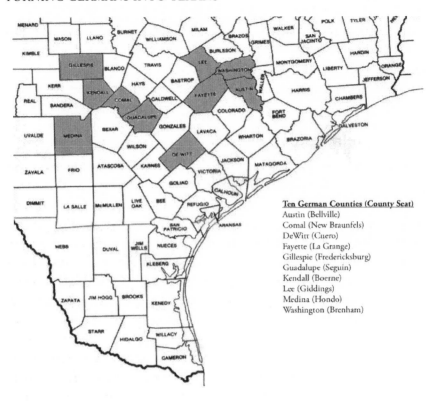

The ten "German" counties of Texas and their county seats.

Europe. The brochures extolled the virtues of the railroad lands for settlement, and agents of rail companies were on the docks at Galveston when immigrant ships arrived. In such a manner, Germans came to settle in and around towns like Schulenburg and Weimar on the Southern Pacific Line; Sealy on the Gulf, Colorado, and Santa Fe Railway; Giddings on the Southern Pacific, and many other smaller towns. In addition to the new immigrants, the eastern German Belt also expanded northward and southward. German immigrants also had a tendency to settle together with immigrants from Czechoslovakia. Terry G. Jordan suggests the German-Czech settlement pattern was due to the fact that the two immigrant groups must have felt a bond of kinship. Also, Bohemia and Moravia, the homeland of nearly all Texas Czechs, had for centuries been under

German cultural influence and had long been under the political control of Germanic Austria. Such influences perhaps explain the close German-Czech settlement relationship.[18]

The area of the old *Adelsverein* colony, stretching through the Hill Country from to New Braunfels to the Llano River Valley, received very few immigrants after the Civil War, perhaps because railroads bypassed the rugged, hilly area. An expansion of the western German belt occurred after 1865, but the indigenous German population was responsible for the expansion. By the 1880s and the 1890s an interesting contrast had developed between the eastern and western ends of the German Belt, a difference that persists to the present day. In the eastern areas, persons of German ancestry were more numerous than in the west, but in the western counties the percentages of Germans in the total population were higher. The disparity is explained by the fact that the eastern counties were much more densely populated.[19]

While the German belt extending across central Texas absorbed most of these later immigrants, a significant number of people settled in what Terry G. Jordan calls small German "folk-islands" scattered across wide areas of south, north central, and northwest Texas. The break up of large cattle ranches, such as the XIT, resulting in small units of land sold to individual families, led to many of the folk islands. Railroad lands created others. Immigrants coming directly from Europe rarely settled on the German folk-islands. Instead, German Americans from the Midwest or from the German Belt in south-central Texas dominated the settlements. By 1900, German folk-islands spread over a great deal of Texas.[20]

In some instances, a central authority, such as the Roman Catholic Church, private colonization companies, or the railroads organized and directed the settlement activity. A company operated by the Westphalian-born Flusche brothers attracted Germans to northern Texas. They bought tracts of land, recruited German Catholic settlers in the Midwest, and through the resale of land realized a modest profit. In this manner, the brothers founded the Catholic folk-islands of Muenster and Lindsay, both in Cooke County; Pilot Point; and Mt. Carmel. The Flusche brothers, devout

Catholics, always took care to concentrate sufficient numbers of colonists in each colony to assure the survival of religious and linguistic identity. The work of Father Joseph Reisdorff also impacted the Catholic German colonization of northern and western Texas. He purchased tracts of land presumably acting as an agent of the church, brought in German Catholics from the Midwest to settle, founded a church, saw it through the initial years, and then moved on to repeat the procedure in another location. Father Reisdorff founded Windthorst, Rhineland, Nazareth, Umbarger, and Slaton.[21]

Most of the German settlers were farmers. Although Germans in 1870 made up only four percent of all American farm workers, slightly over a quarter of all employed Germans worked in agriculture, constituting over 33 percent of all foreign-born farmers. In 1900, Germans owned near eleven percent of all American farms and accounted for almost ten percent of the country's agricultural employment. Contemporaries regarded the stereotypical nineteenth-century German farmer as stable, hard-working, dependable, and thrifty. Where Germans settled among non-Germans, such stereotypical behavior proved short lived, as local norms prevailed. But where fellow countrymen reinforced similar patterns of life and work, the traditional mind-set of the German peasant endured far longer, lending some truth to the stereotype and creating the only German-American ethnic cultures to persist into the middle of the twentieth century.

German clustering of sufficient size to influence cultural persistence occurred in Texas. The logic of clustered settlement was persuasive. A nucleus established in an area not yet fully settled could support German churches, schools, local governments, and familiar social patterns, and it lured other Germans to fill in the remaining land. When settlers moved on, German newcomers or the children of the pioneers took up the land; community norms discouraged sales to outsiders. The transfer of land to children during the parents' lifetime adapted German goals to American circumstances and fostered an unusual degree of persistence and expansion in many rural ethnic communities. Once established, such clusters in Texas usually endured, intensified, and expanded over time. The persistence of distinctive attitudes and social patterns revealed the strength of the ethnic culture, which was encouraged by isolation and frequently centered around the local church. In many rural areas the German language has persisted to the fourth and even fifth generations.[22]

Whether the practices of German farmers were judged to be first rate or merely odd, neighbors perceived the Germans as different from themselves. The Germans picked up English rather quickly and adapted Anglo customs to their own culture, but remained proud of their own language and traditions, and they kept them. They began to publish German-language newspapers only a few years after they arrived in Texas. They believed in education, and they saw to it that the early schools taught both German and English. They differed from their Anglo-American neighbors in another important way. Most Anglo-Americans moving west after the American Revolution moved as individuals. But the Germans did not come to the frontier solely as individuals. They came as a group, as a colony, and they were concerned with community. Only a few years after arriving in Texas, the immigrants began to construct a thick web of cultural organizations, not only agricultural associations, but also dancing and singing societies, drinking and shooting clubs, and what was to become an enduring social institution, the Sons of Hermann, a fraternal organization. At the outset, they fashioned organizations that cost no money; it would be a while before the pioneering generation could afford to augment the singing societies with brass bands. German Texans sang, drank, hunted, and played cards, and later they created rural festivals and parades that became the wonder of the region: the first county fair in Texas and the first *Schützenfest*, an event where German farmers with the products of the skilled German gunsmiths measured themselves against Anglo legends of frontier marksmen with their Kentucky rifles. As families and communities, the Germans congregated in celebrations that brought a unique and vivid quality to Texas life.[23]

"Willkommen zum Saengerfest" ("Welcome to the Singers' Festival") – photo taken in 1889 looking northward up Congress Avenue toward the state capitol in Austin.

The urban German element also developed rapidly in the period after 1865. Many of the immigrants had been engaged in nonagricultural employment in Germany, and it is not surprising that they sought to settle in the towns and cities and establish themselves as craftsmen, hotel keepers, brewers, and the like. In general, the cities and towns that boasted large German populations in the postbellum period were the same ones that had attracted immigrants before the war, that is Galveston, Houston, San Antonio, and other towns of the German Belt. The German-speaking population of the state's developing cities—Houston, Austin, San Antonio, and Dallas—also increased considerably during the final decades of large-scale German immigration to Texas. San Antonio, for example, was dominated both culturally and economically by a German element in

28

the 1870s, and, according to the city assessor, persons of German birth or descent comprised one-third of the population there in that decade. Between 1860 and 1890, the number of people of German descent in San Antonio more than doubled, indicating the importance of postbellum immigration.[24]

Urban Germans proved ultimately unable to isolate themselves like the farmers. In 1900, the fifteen cities with German populations of 15,000 or more contained over 36 percent of the total German-born population of the United States. A further thirteen percent lived in the 94 cities with 1,000 to 15,000 German-born residents. Such numerical concentrations permitted urban Germans to create virtually self-sufficient neighborhood communities based on shared activities, voluntary associations, and formal institutions. "Little Germanies" were common in many American cities. Yet the second generation of urban Germans assimilated quickly into the American mainstream.[25]

German Americans early won a reputation for political apathy. They failed to produce officeholders commensurate with their numbers and seldom performed as reliable cogs in the political machine. Language difficulty, lack of familiarity with democratic practices, and the narrowly economic motivation for their immigration to America offer some reasons for German political impotence. The Germans also appeared to be politically ineffective, at least in comparison to the Irish. Moreover, Germans were more likely than the Irish to settle on farms, where isolation from political activity was more or less inevitable in the nineteenth century. As a result, American politicians paid little attention to the needs and desires of their German constituents. Because they frequently spread across the socioeconomic spectrum, German-American voters rarely held uniform views on the political issues of the day. The German ethnic community with its rich and poor, its educated and uneducated, its skilled and unskilled workers, its urban as well as rural residents, and its Catholics and Protestants was diverse enough that unity in support of anything or anyone was rarely possible to achieve.[26]

29

Attempts to create a German-American political party met with failure. German Americans united politically only when it came to defending German *Kultur*. Issues capable of stimulating the Germans politically, such as prohibition, attacks on parochial schools, the German language, and so-called blue laws, were usually temporary. When the threat faded, so did the opportunities for political leadership based on German group interest. Moreover, the defense of German ethnic culture was essentially a negative enterprise. It was usually a question of what the Germans were against rather than what they were for. If he had no reason for existence other than the defense of ethnic culture, a German-American political leader inevitably sounded strident, uncompromising, and unattractive to non-immigrant voters.[27]

If German Americans had a unifying political issue, it concerned the role of government in questions of morality. Programs of coercive reform were offensive to large numbers of German Catholics and Lutherans. In their view, the central role of government was to guarantee the fullest measure of personal liberty consonant with law and order. For the government to legislate morality by means of prohibition or blue laws was to invade the authority of the church. They argued, for example, that a bottle of whiskey, by itself, was neither good nor evil. Sin lay in its abuse: it was not wrong to drink, but it was a sin to get drunk. Similarly, many Germans were appalled at the effect blue laws could have on their traditions of "continental Sundays," amiable conversation, convivial drinking, and innocent dancing in beer gardens or, for that matter, at church picnics. From their standpoint, women's suffrage was merely a political trick to double the prohibitionist vote. Worse, women's suffrage threatened the role of women as wives and mothers and thereby the centrality of the family.[28]

Following the Civil War, the Germans in Texas joined with the newly freed slaves to support the Republican Party. Because many of them had been adamant Unionists and thus could take the "Ironclad Oath," which therefore permitted them to participate in politics, they won election to a number of local, state, and federal offices. Because they connected Democrats with the Confederacy, the Germans became the backbone of the Republican Party in Texas and the cornerstone of the two-party system in the state. For many Germans who became prominent during the last part of the nineteenth century, Reconstruction was their introduction to business, politics, and public life. As the years past and the Republicans receded from power, many Germans joined the Democratic Party when Texas essentially became a one-party state.[29]

Germans in Texas tried to prevent assimilation through the use and teaching of the German language in schools. In the 1850s, the German American community of Austin deplored the lack of public education and established one of the first successful free schools in the state. Opposition to the free school emerged from the Texas Know-Nothing Party. The opposition may have been roused from the fact that the school was to make use of three languages; it was to be "a public school in which German, English, and Spanish would be taught." The proportion of non-English languages in the daily curriculum was never indicated directly, but the fact that it focused on German students and aroused nativist fears suggests that German and Spanish were not pursued as dry, academic studies. The state legislature approved the school's charter in 1858 without any mention of curricular content or language stipulation. The approval illustrates the implied sanction that the state gave to localities and ethnic groups interested in multilingual education as well as the prominent place of the German language in the early stages of public education in Texas.[30]

In the Hill Country region, Germans in the town of Fredericksburg attempted early to establish their own free, publicly financed school. In 1852, they levied municipal taxes for the purposes of funding such a school, but the state courts declared the method of using local taxation to fund public schools unconstitutional. Germans in New Braunfels lobbied for a special charter from the state legislature to allow them to "levy and collect a special tax" for their schools. A twenty-year charter was finally granted in 1858, and the school was named the New Braunfels Academy. Eventually, the academy transformed into a public school. Up to 1892, the school's board of directors kept the minutes in

German and translated them into English. German was not just reserved for board meetings. Study of the German language was mandatory for all students. In his annual accounting to the state for the 1886-87 school year, H.E. Fischer, the president of the New Braunfels Board of Trustees, dutifully reported of his school that "in addition to the English elementary branches, the German is taught." In New Braunfels, 100 percent of all grade school pupils received German instruction in 1900, two-thirds of them in public rather than parochial schools. In fact, the New Braunfels city council had only switched to English in 1890.[31]

In 1894-95, Judge J. T. Estill of Gillespie County, which contained the town of Fredericksburg, wrote that there were not any children of English-speaking parentage and that the children had difficulty speaking English. Other school systems also admitted to teaching German in a vague, unspecified manner, almost as if they did not want to indicate how it was taught. The German-English school of San Antonio, founded in 1858, was one of the state's most prestigious educational institutions during the late nineteenth century. According to its charter, German and English had equal status and it even succeeded in implementing a third language, Spanish, into its core curriculum. The school continued until the 1890s; its decline coincided with the decrease in German immigration (in 1880 only one in two-hundred students had been born in Germany). At the turn of the century, the city of San Antonio shut down the German-English school and turned the building into a public school.[32]

German was taught in other parts of Texas as well. Shortly after the Civil War, in the southeastern coastal plains of Austin County in the town of Shelby, a German teacher taught English as if it were a foreign language. In the 1880s, teachers still used German as a medium of instruction alongside English. In Bellville, an 1887-88 education report indicated that students learned the German language in all eight grades.[33]

School officials in Victoria County, home to the city of Victoria, had difficulty in keeping the German and Spanish languages from being taught in public free schools and asked that the law be amended so that only the English language be taught. More than anything else, however, the reforms of the 1880s and 1890s played the key role in the demise of German language education: first, English-only mandates embedded in laws governing teacher certification; and second, English-only instructional mandates in laws governing curriculum and school conduct. However, the English-only requirements were often circumvented and not enforced, especially in ethnic communities where German or other languages continued to be used in public schools, when possible, or in private schools, when necessary. German professor Joseph Wilson later wrote, "one might just have well passed a law ordering leopards not to be spotted." State Superintendent R. B. Cousins articulated the rising tide of nativism in his written comments following the 1907-1908 school years. "The German children continue to be German and to speak German, and frequently grow to maturity ignorant of the language of their country. Must Texas educate Germans? Are we not rather to educate Texans?—Americans?" Texas would finally get serious about English-only during the heyday of nativism centered against German Americans and Mexican Americans caused by World War I and the social disruptions on the United States-Mexico border, which, in turn had been influenced by the Mexican Revolution and the deteriorating economic and social position of Tejanos. As a fully enforceable mandate with specific criminal punishments, English-only arrived in 1918 in Texas.[34]

German Texans were vehemently opposed to prohibition. German voters never approved of the national prohibition movement. They voted it down in every election and ignored it when the amendment finally passed. Germans consumed substantial quantities of beer and other alcoholic beverages. Nearly every German town of consequence in Texas had at least one brewery; San Antonio had six major breweries and a number of smaller ones. Beginning in the 1840s, many Americans began to react against the damage to society and the individual caused by alcohol. There were two separate movements that crusaded against the problem. The temperance movement sought to persuade people to stop drinking, while the prohibition movement aimed to make the sale and manufacture of liquor illegal. Texas was home to many fundamentalist Christians who rallied to the prohibition cause, and the crusaders became known as the "drys." The Constitution of 1876 provided for "local option," which allowed individual communities to decide whether to allow alcohol sales. In 1895, 53 of Texas' 239 counties were dry and another 79 were partially dry.

In 1887, Texas prohibitionists tried and failed by narrow margins to get a statewide prohibition law passed. Important Democrats, such as Texas' United States Senators, John H. Reagan and Samuel Bell Maxey, supported prohibition, but others opposed. Prohibitionists viewed German Texans, correctly, as staunch opponents to the amendment, and often vehemently attacked them. They drank beer publicly, worshipped at Lutheran or Catholic churches, and German Texans or their parents had foreign origins. Perceived by many Texans as solid, respectable, middle-class citizens, Germans also posed many difficulties for the prohibitionists. A powerful political and social force in San Antonio and the Hill Country of Texas, Germans could trace their Texas roots back farther than most of the xenophobic reformers. One correspondent to the *Texas Baptist and Herald* summed up the prohibitionist dilemma when he described them as hardworking, industrious, and churchgoing, but also drinking, gambling, dancing, and heathen.[35]

As expected by the prohibitionists, Germans opposed the amendment. San Antonio's Turner Hall hosted numerous anti-prohibition rallies, sometimes conducted in German. Congressman William Crain, whose district encompassed much of the Hill Country, also opposed the amendment. Prior to the vote, citizenship applications from German immigrants in Texas cities dramatically increased. At least 6,000 Germans took out naturalization papers shortly before the election. The *Texas Baptist and Herald* printed the names of a number of applicants: "These foreigners did not love the country sufficiently to accept naturalization before, but when the votes for whisky were to be cast, they are brought to the front." Despite occasional reports of some German support for prohibition, drys made no effort to organize German voters. Jennie Bland Beauchamp, president of the Texas WCTU, appealed for the assistance in supporting Baptist missionaries who would undertake "Gospel temperance work" among German Texans, but she was not optimistic. "We can not do much for them until we get them from under the saloon influence," she wrote.[36]

On August 4, 1887, Texans rejected prohibition. Final returns gave prohibitionists fewer than 130,000 votes out of nearly 350,000 cast, more than had been cast in the contest for governor in 1886. San Antonio rejected the amendment by a vote of 4,861 to 507. In heavily-German New Braunfels, 409 votes were cast, every single one of them against the amendment. Cat Spring Germans voted down the referendum by a resounding 238-0. In a letter to the *New York Voice*, Senator Reagan reported that "prohibition was defeated by votes of the negroes, Germans and Mexicans." He also concluded that, "a majority of the native Americans and of the Democrats of Texas are for this reform movement" and that "without the colored and foreign vote yesterday, prohibition would today have 60,000 majority." Estimates of the size of the "German vote" were anywhere between 60,000 and 100,000. The crushing defeat did not destroy the prohibition movement in Texas, but it forced the issue into the background of state politics for the next twenty years.[37]

Abroad, the unification of Germany had a dramatic impact on German-American identity in the United States. In earlier decades, before the creation of the German Empire in 1871, few German immigrants regarded their home state in Europe with affection. Most German states had been authoritarian, repressive, intolerant of religious diversity, and unresponsive to the needs of the common people. But many German-American hearts swelled with pride as Otto von Bismarck whipped the French in 1871 and placed his Prussian king on an imperial German throne. Although thousands of Germans had emigrated to escape military service, their pulses quickened at the news of German victories on European battlefields. A new sense of German ethnicity developed as the number of immigrants from rapidly industrializing Germany declined, and ethnocentric publicists deliberately cultivated a new pride in things German to halt the erosion of the German-American community caused by assimilation. A united German republic had,

35

indeed, been the goal of many refuges of 1830 and 1848, and the failure to achieve it had been the cause that brought many of them to America.[38]

The unification of Germany had a great effect on the German Americans. It created a new sense of identity in being German American, not merely being from a given region or locality in Germany. There was not only unrestrained joy that the Fatherland had been united, but also a feeling that the status of the German heritage had been elevated. Public displays of elation knew few bounds. Parades and huge mass meetings occurred in New York, Chicago, Cleveland, St. Louis, and elsewhere. Also, German-American organizations collected large sums of money and sent it to the widows and orphans of soldiers who had lost their lives in the successful struggle for German unity. The victory celebrations held across American in 1871 were not only celebrations of German unity, but also celebrations of German heritage. The parade in New York, for example, aimed to display German-American contributions in the arts sciences, trades, agriculture, and industry, and it included veterans of the Civil War. At this time in New York the idea of a national organization for German Americans emerged. The *New Yorker Staats-Zeitung* proposed the creation of a national organization to promote German-American relations, to increase German-American political clout, and to preserve German heritage.[39]

German Americans praised unification and hoped that decades of peace might follow. They praised as well as the phenomenal progress Germany had made in the areas of business, industry, trade, the arts and sciences, social legislation, and international prestige. Germany was now a respected nation and German Americans felt they had proved and demonstrated their patriotism and their contributions to America. It had been an uphill struggle, but in 1871 they felt they had earned the right to celebrate the fact that they were now an integral and important part of the nation. Little did they know the repercussions that German unification would have for many of them some forty years later.[40]

The unification after Germany's victory over France in the Franco-Prussian War in 1871 inspired a great celebration in Texas. A

Exterior of Bismarck Saloon, Fredericksburg, Texas. *Courtesy of UT Institute of Texan Cultures at San Antonio, 075-0230. Loaned by Kilman Studio (Fredericksburg, Tex.).*

month after the capture of Paris in January, 1871, San Antonio's German community held a celebration with a torchlight parade, ball, and orations at the Casino Club to commemorate the event. In Fredericksburg, a saloon was named in honor of Otto von Bismarck, and in Comfort a father named his newborn son after the Battle of Sedan. Even twenty years later, German Texans celebrated German unification. During the 1890 *Volksfest* parade in San Antonio, a float commemorating the surrender of the French to Kaiser Wilhelm I at Versailles, entitled "The Kaiser Triumphant, 1870," was entered. On the float the "Kaiser" stood in white uniform and spiked helmet. Kaiser Wilhelm was surrounded by various troops in very recognizable contemporary German military uniforms, hats, and helmets. But while German Texans rejoiced at the long-awaited news of the new Germany, they sensed that the unification, achieved without them, left them no part in the old country. The land they had left no longer existed. It had become a new, modern nation, and for the German Texans there was no past to which they could return. They could only go forward into the future—as Americans.[41]

In the nineteenth century, German Americans seemed likely to persist. Their leaders could toy with the idea of creating a separate state; numbers and cultural consciousness enabled it to dominate large areas. Other Americans admired the skills, diligence, thrift, and family strength that seemed to make Germans ideal candidates for Americanization. Many Americans, however, deplored the clannishness and cultural traits of the Germans that kept them stubbornly apart. Others disapproved of German radicalism and anarchism, their resistance to prohibition, their insistence on retaining the German language, and their interest in an increasingly aggressive Kaiser. The German Americans, many people believed needed to be closely watched. Nevertheless, the very size of the German immigration, its religious, socioeconomic, and cultural heterogeneity; and its skills, time of arrival, and settlement patterns all combined to ensure a gradual process of acculturation and assimilation. The trauma of World War I only hastened the submergence of German ethnicity.[42]

Deutschtum and the Impending Crisis, 1900-1914

In 1900, there were approximately 190,000 persons of German descent living in Texas, a little over six percent of the state's total population. Yet, even in the years of the twentieth century preceding World War I, the German element in Texas, as a percentage of the total population, had already declined from its peak in 1890. During the period from 1900 to 1909, German immigration nationally saw its smallest number since the decade of the 1830s. At the same time, many Germans assimilated into mainstream Texas culture, and more English words entered the German vocabulary. Advertisements printed in the English language appeared in German-language newspapers, and, in addition, modern communications and transportation reduced the isolation of German communities. Some even forgot the German language of their youth.[1]

Nevertheless, there was still a considerable German influence in the state. At least 75,000 to 100,000 Texans used the German language and many churches worshipped in German. Schools taught German, merchants and customers conducted business in the language, and the publication of German newspapers continued and actually increased in number. Despite some assimilation by second and third generation Germans, many German Texans still clung to elements of German *Kultur* and sought to preserve them. Granted, it is hard to measure the level of *Deutschtum* (Germanness) in Texas at the beginning of the twentieth century and leading up to World War I, but elements of *Kultur* were present.[2]

As German-American communities formed, the settlements displayed some basic and readily discernable groupings, or subdivisions. The two groups have generally been referred to as the *Kirchendeutschen*, or "church Germans," and the *Vereindeutschen*, or "club Germans." The former refers to German Americans for whom their religious affiliation formed a central focal point in their lives, whereas the latter refers to those whose organizational affiliation occupied a central role. The two factions formed religious and the secular camps in the German-American community.[3]

The church Germans consisted of German Americans who belonged to any one of the numerous Protestant, Catholic, or Jewish religious faiths. They formed basically a conservative element in their communities. They established a wide variety of religious institutions, including their own hospitals, orphanages, homes for the elderly, seminaries, and societies. Most importantly, they established parochial German-language schools for their youth. Indeed, in some communities, the German parochial school system dwarfed the public school system. Also, many church Germans maintained German bookstores stocked with books, newspapers, periodicals, and other publications catering to the denomination in question. Some of the religious bodies held little in common with each other, hence, in the religious camp, there were additional subdivisions. The separation meant that there was a tendency for each group to grow and develop independently from others. Indeed, sometimes the editors of a group's publications would engage in theological, social, and political debates with the editors of the publications of other religious bodies. Some of the most heated debates in the nineteenth century, for example, occurred between German Lutheran and German Methodist editors. Politically, the church Germans could be characterized as staunchly antiradical, antisocialist, and anti-"forty-eighter." However, most did not officially or overtly engage in political affairs and issues except when it was an issue which directly affected their particular church body, such as, the issue of public laws relating to non-English language instruction.[4]

Religion and heritage were closely intertwined, and often German-American churches have been among the strongest institutional supporters of the German language and heritage in America. The church Germans used the German language and heritage to ward off heresy, maintain unity, prevent losses, and exclude internal influences. The allegiance promoted and supported their own identity and religious focus. Also, church Germans tended to come to America together in families and groups and then settle together, thus promoting a close-knit community structure. Many agreed with the basic notion that "language saves faith," which stressed the importance of the German language in relation to the preservation of one's faith.[5]

The German language thus nurtured, and was nurtured by, religious identity, and religious communities retained the strongest sense of German ethnicity. Also, it was no accident that in German-American literature, all American-born authors came from a German-American religious community. The fact reflects the success of such communities in preserving German heritage. The publications of the church Germans were often youth-oriented and were designed to keep young people within the fold, as well as to keep them from being unduly affected by Anglo influences in American society. One should keep in mind that the concept of church Germans is designed to cover a diverse array of religious groups, and the only real bond the groups held in common was a strong commitment to religious values and to German language and heritage, both of which were closely related.[6]

The secular camp, referred to the *Vereinsdeutschen* or the club Germans, was historically viewed as the liberal element in the German-American community. Its members' commitment to German heritage revolved around secular societies and organizations, *Vereine*. Like the religious element, club Germans were not a homogenous group either. They consisted of secularized workers recruited usually from the lower ranks of the white-collar class and

German County	1900	
	Persons Born in Germany	% of total population
Austin	1,973	9.54%
Comal	966	13.78%
DeWitt	1,551	7.28%
Fayette	3,055	8.36%
Gillespie	802	9.75%
Guadalupe	1,950	9.12%
Kendall	445	10.85%
Lee	1,122	7.69%
Medina	393	5.05%
Washington	3,281	9.96%
Ten German Counties Total || Ten German Counties Average	15,538	9.14%

Table 1: German population from the 1900 census. Note: the data listed for the 1900, 1920, and 1930 censuses does not include those of second, third, or fourth-generation German ancestry. Source: Historical Census Browser [http://fisher.lib.virginia.edu/collections/stats/histcensus/].

German County	1910				
	Persons Born in Germany	% of total population	Persons w/ Both Parents Born in Germany	Total of Persons Born in Germany + Persons w/ Both Parents Born in Germany	% of total population
Austin	1,317	7.44%	2,647	3,964	22.4%
Comal	667	7.91%	1,508	2,175	25.8%
DeWitt	1,502	7.94%	2,693	4,195	17.9%
Fayette	1,868	6.27%	3,560	5,428	18.2%
Gillespie	592	6.27%	1,749	2,341	24.8%
Guadalupe	1,257	5.05%	2,872	4,129	16.6%
Kendall	344	7.62%	710	1,054	23.3%
Lee	815	6.21%	1,465	2,280	17.4%
Medina	352	2.62%	983	1,335	10.0%
Washington	2,256	8.83%	4,567	6,823	26.7%
Ten German Counties Total || Ten German Counties Average	10,970	6.62%	22,754	33,724	20.3%

Table 2: German population from the 1910 census. The 1910 census was the only census between 1900 and 1930 to list German parentage. Source: Historical Census Browser [http://fisher.lib.virginia.edu/collections/stats/histcensus/].

German County	1920	
	Persons Born in Germany	% of total population
Austin	853	4.52%
Comal	407	4.61%
DeWitt	1,159	4.14%
Fayette	1,228	4.10%
Gillespie	393	3.92%
Guadalupe	851	3.07%
Kendall	239	5.00%
Lee	603	4.30%
Medina	142	1.22%
Washington	1,067	4.01%
Ten German Counties Total || Ten German Counties Average	6,942	3.89%

Table 3: German population from the 1920 census. Source: Historical Census Browser [http://fisher.lib.virginia.edu/collections/stats/histcensus/].

German County	1930	
	Persons Born in Germany	% of total population
Austin	514	2.73%
Comal	359	3.00%
DeWitt	842	3.07%
Fayette	865	2.82%
Gillespie	253	2.30%
Guadalupe	575	1.99%
Kendall	161	3.24%
Lee	412	3.08%
Medina	96	0.69%
Washington	893	3.52%
Ten German Counties Total || Ten German Counties Average	4,970	2.64%

Table 4: German population from the 1930 census. Source: Historical Census Browser [http://fisher.lib.virginia.edu/collections/stats/histcensus/].

the higher echelons of the blue-collar class. Financially, many of them were well off. Politically, club Germans followed an assortment of philosophies, ranging from radicals, freethinkers, and socialists to conservatives. Liberals often assumed leadership positions in the *Vereine* as well as in the German-American press. The club Germans formed societies patterned on the models established by the German middle and working class of the mid-nineteenth century.

The societies of club Germans fulfilled a social function. They built expansive halls and club houses for their members, some complete with beer gardens, bowling alleys, theaters, libraries, and other offices. Profits from the events, dances, picnics, and other activities of the societies, including the sale of food and drink, kept many a society on sound financial footing.[7]

Undoubtedly, the club Germans shared a commitment to German heritage, which centered on their support and involvement in an array of societies and organizations. Many German-American societies existed, such as mutual and fraternal aid societies, voluntary fire and militia companies, and educational, historical, literary, musical, cultural, social, and political societies. Some of the clubs and societies were based on the area of the origin of the members, such as Swabian, Bavarian, or Pomeranian. The various societies usually organized into regional federations, which in turn affiliated with national organizations. For example, local singing societies were affiliated with district organizations, which in turn affiliated with either of two national organizations. The numerous Turner societies, or *Turnvereine*, formed a national organization, *Der Turnerbund*, now known as the American Turner Society. They also sponsored national conventions known as *Turnfeste*. The club Germans valued the *Gemütlichkeit* of their *Vereine* and their various festivities. Some criticized them for their devotion to the societies, but this merely reflected the important social, cultural, and political role and function of the societies in the German-American community. The club Germans became the strongest advocate and supporter of public education and campaigned for the introduction of German instruction, as well as physical education or *Turnunterricht*. Indeed, German Americans in 1840 in Cincinnati were the first to introduce bilingual education in America and in the 1890s were responsible for the introduction of physical education into the curriculum.

Because of its numerous social, cultural, and political activities, and the many public kinds of parades and festivities, the club Germans were without question the most vocal and visible segment of the German-American community and came to define for many both within and without the German-American community what it was that constituted German Americans. Especially to non-German Americans, the club Germans represented and were seen as the German-American community, although in fact they represented only part of the equation.[8]

In areas of Texas where Germans constituted the ethnic majority of the population, Germans retained their culture, modified in various ways, for a surprisingly long time. At the center of that culture, more often than not, were the local churches and the *Kirchendeutschen*, church Germans. About two-thirds of the Germans who settled in Texas were Protestants, mainly Lutheran. German-speaking Methodist missionaries further intensified Protestant diversity in Texas through conversion. Published genealogies of German Methodist families suggest that, before conversion, most had been Lutherans, Catholics, or members of the State Church of Prussia. Even though the major Catholic strongholds in the Rhineland and Bavaria were not major contributors to the migration of Germans to Texas, perhaps as many as three in ten were Roman Catholic. German Protestants and Catholics coexisted peacefully from the very first, making no effort to segregate themselves by quarters within the towns or by districts in the countryside.[9]

Halftone of Zion Lutheran Church, Fredericksburg, Texas, c. 1910s. *Pioneer Memorial Museum (Fredericksburg, Tex.). ITC 073-0692.*

Because Lutheranism had its roots in Germany and continued to be part of the German cultural phenomenon in the country, the continued use of the German language in the United States by German immigrants was to be expected. As subsequent generations of Germans became assimilated, the question arose as to when and how to integrate the English language into German church life. The issue became more acute as immigrant children became more proficient in the use of the English than in the German language, especially at the turn of the twentieth century. The language question was also an issue in the realm of parochial school development. German was the language used most frequently in immigrant homes. As German Lutheran communities sought to establish schools, the question arose as to which language would be the primary servant of German pedagogy: German or English? Such an omission can be interpreted as a decision on the part of Lutheran Church officials in Texas to resist cultural and economic forces that might hasten assimilation of the German Lutheran Church into the non-German Texan culture. Several of the German-language Lutheran pastors feared for their pure Lutheran faith if English were allowed in the churches. They believed, that sectarianism would infiltrate more quickly through the English language.[10]

The strength of the Lutheran Church in Texas was contingent upon several factors, not least of which was its ability to communicate with its membership. Throughout the nineteenth and early twentieth century, the Lutheran Church attempted to maintain contact through the print media with a varying degree of success. Beginning in 1903, the Evangelical Lutheran Texas Synod published *Der Treue Zeuge.* The paper was the voice of German Lutheranism until 1915, after the outbreak of World War I. That same year the First Texas Synod featured a new publication, the *Lutherbote für Texas.* Of all the newspapers published by Lutherans in Texas, it was the only one with articles in the English and German languages. In fact, the first edition in 1915 contained English articles, the number of which increased until 1933 when the number of articles appearing in both English and German were approximately equal. In 1921, the paper had three thousand subscribers. The extent to which the use of the English language had permeated the Lutheran Church in Texas by the twentieth century is not something readily identifiable by subscription rates or other types of similar quantifiable data.[11]

For most German Lutherans, ethnicity and religion were inseparably intertwined. German became for Lutherans what Latin had been for the Catholics since the early centuries. Lutherans used German as a bulwark behind which they felt secure. True Lutheranism used the German language to guarantee communication, and such use allowed access to the original writings

The entire school body of Trinity English-German Lutheran School, Houston, Texas, 1914.

of Martin Luther, the reformers, and his interpreters. While English became the mundane or secular language, Lutherans raised German to the level of an ecclesiastical or spiritual language resulting in the printing of all religious books in German.

Roman Catholics, on the other hand, did not have the reliance on the German language that Lutherans did. Catholics were used to hearing Latin during church services, accepting a foreign tongue as a carrier for salvation. While the Evangelical Lutherans in the United States printed church materials in German, books for the Catholic Church were either printed in English or imported from Germany. Several factors favored English language use by the Roman Catholic population of German-language origin. First, Catholic schools oftentimes did not maintain the original languages of immigrants, forcing them to use English in an educational setting. Second, the internationalism of Catholicism accelerated integration processes that aided "Americanization." Finally, the fact that many

Catholics took an anti-prohibition stance resulted in anti-German language attitudes among non-German speakers who favored prohibition.

The activities of the so-called *Vereindeutschen*, or club Germans, in Texas declined before the twentieth century. San Antonio's *Volksfest* parade, for example, which started in 1882 as a German-Texan sponsored festival, took place seven times during the 1880s and 1890s, bringing together San Antonio's German community. The festival, however, did not survive into the twentieth century following the pattern of urban Germans whom assimilated much more quickly than rural ones. Although some German-Texan organizations would contribute floats to a few Battle of Flowers parades after 1900, the last *Volksfest* occurred in 1893 and the festival succumbed for three reasons: the lack of new German immigration and the assimilation of German Texans into the Anglo population, the inability of Germans to mount enough of a "civic force" to continue the festival, and the lack of rich businessmen who could afford to back such an elaborate event.[12]

Many of the German *Vereine* in Texas did not keep directories or official records and many had only short life spans. On the other hand, some *Vereine* located in rural areas had extremely long life spans. For example, the Cat Spring Agricultural Society, the oldest agricultural society in Texas, was founded on June 7, 1856, and recently celebrated its 150th anniversary. Also, many German Texans were members of several clubs, associations, and societies, possibly active in some and passive in others, situations that may have led to inflated membership numbers. Some clubs had as many as 250 members. Others might have only sixteen members, but an accurate average cannot be established. Membership numbers fluctuated during the years from 1880 to 1910, and they represented only a fraction of the total immigrant population.[13]

In Texas, festivals or celebrations were inclusive, welcoming outsiders to the affairs. A specific *Verein* usually organized the celebration, but participation was generally open to the public. Samples might be the *Schützenfeste* (shooting festivals), *Sängerfest* (singing festival), or similar celebrations. The participation by the general public required the use of the English language or a type of entertainment that could be understood regardless of the language used. Thus, the inclination for publicity promoted the use of the English language into the *Vereinsleben* (daily activities of a club).

The *Vereine* also served functions in the spheres of politics, benevolence, health care, faith, defense, local economy, and education. In a few instances, self interests of individuals were recognized but usually the *Vereine* served interests of the whole community or of population groups within the community. Texas' German immigrants came from different German states, German-language countries, and countries with German-speaking minorities, thus inherently harboring different national and ethnic backgrounds. Their so-called German *Kultur* was therefore based on a common denominator or included only those aspects that they all had in common or accepted as common.[14]

When the state of Texas finally assumed the responsibility for education and decided to prevent what was perceived as the "Germanization" of education, the *Vereine* became sanctuaries and outlets for cultural and ethnic elements that were considered worthwhile for preservation. All those who wanted to speak or listen to the German language could do it in a variety of clubs. The different clubs were not advocating forms of German nationalism to the exclusion of American democracy or the spreading of the German language as a replacement for English. But they may have appeared to support German *Kultur* over American traditions. Still, as responsibility for education became that of the state and secondarily the community, the German *Vereine* did not influence or change the curriculum of Texas' public school systems in regard to the German language. The mere fact of *Verein* membership, the vocal practice of spoken German, and the exposure to German-language materials passively influenced the language maintenance processes of the German Texans, especially those who actively participated in the *Vereine*.[15]

Still, at the beginning of the twentieth century several of the German *Vereine* maintained a significant presence in Texas. Among them were the *Turnvereine* (athletic clubs and later bowling societies), numerous singing clubs and choirs, literary associations, *Schützenvereine* (shooting clubs), the *Volksfest* association, Texas Farmers' *Verein*, and the *Deutscher Krieger Verein* (for former soldiers of the German Empire). One of the largest memberships belonged to the Sons of Hermann.

Organized in 1860 in Rochester, New York, the Sons of Hermann was one of the nation's oldest fraternal societies. The following year, 1861, Germans organized the first Texas lodge in San Antonio. By 1902, the city had ten lodges. In 1907, the Sons of Hermann had 264 lodges across Texas with a total membership of 11,000. As late as 1910, members used the German language during meetings and entertainments. The spirit was strongly influenced by the initial founders who wanted a United States-wide association that would become a gathering ground for those German-language elements who had fled a suppressed homeland and who supported liberty. The initial founders of the order had selected the name Hermann in memory of the Germanic tribal leader (Hermann der Cherusker) who succeeded in freeing the northern and central areas of Germany from Roman occupation. Membership to the Sons of Hermann was reserved for those being of German-language background. Although it welcomed the unification of German states, the order did not advocate returning to Germany, nor a close relationship with the Fatherland. Nor did it advocate the establishment of a "new Germany" in the United States.[16]

Among the *Vereine* still popular at the beginning of the twentieth century were the German singing societies. In Texas, they were founded and developed without any significant association with other groups in the United States. Almost every town with a considerable German population had a singing society. Eventually, German Texans formed the Texas State *Sängerbund*, an association of German singing societies. By the late nineteenth century, the German musical influence had grown significantly, and non-Germans began to take in the growing music festivals, the pinnacle of which was the state *Sängerfest*. At the beginning of the twentieth century, the festivals were being held at two-year intervals, rotating among Dallas, San Antonio, Houston, Austin, and Galveston. With minor variations, they continued the celebration until World War I, when they ceased.[17]

Despite the continued success of some German organizations, a number of German Americans sensed a mounting crisis in German-American life at the turn of the century. Many Germans moved to stem the erosion of German *Kultur* in the United States. They began a movement that within a few years spawned a nationwide league of German-American *Vereine*, an organization that numbered among the largest ethnic organizations in American history: the National German-American Alliance. The alliance, or *Deutsch-Amerikanischer National-Bund*, sought to save the nation's *Deutschtum* from the forces of assimilation, in particular by striving to keep the younger generation of German Americans within the ethnic fold. It pursued this goal by attempting to foster what today would be called "ethnic pride." Alliance leaders saw the key to this effort in a campaign to shape the nation's understanding of the place of German Americans in the nation's history. By encouraging historical research on German immigration, agitating for recognition of "German achievements," and initiating a spate of monuments to notable German Americans, they hoped to solidify a claim that their ethnic group shared with Anglo-Americans a role in the nation's founding.[18]

The National Alliance originated in the city of Philadelphia in 1899. Activists meeting in the city that year founded the German-American Central Alliance of Pennsylvania, inviting Charles J. Hexamer to serve as the new group's president. The organization appears to have begun as a venture to preserve existing *Vereine* in eastern Pennsylvania. In short order, it organized in other states. From the early efforts emerged the National German-American Alliance, which held its constituent convention in Philadelphia in October 1901. Structurally, the new National Alliance was composed of individual *Vereine* grouped together into city alliances or branches, which in turn were federated into state alliances; the state alliances together made up the National Alliance. In a real sense, the National Alliance represented an attempt at a nationwide, rationalized organization of America's *Vereine*.[19]

Charles J. Hexamer, who served as president of the Central Alliance until 1915 and held the same position in the National Alliance from its founding until 1917, was also president from 1900 to 1916 of the German Society of Pennsylvania. He was the Philadelphia-born son of Ernst Hexamer, a veteran of the failed Revolution of 1848 who had fled Germany in 1856 and pursued a career as a civil engineer. While assimilating into middle-class American society, Charles and Ernst Hexamer also maintained their German traditions. Even though Ernst and his wife spoke English, German remained the language of the home, and Ernst insisted that while Charles was an American, his son should never forget his German heritage. Charles Hexamer's education was extensive. In 1886 he received both a Ph.D. in Civil Engineering and a Doctorate of Laws. At the age of twenty-four, he had achieved a level of education possessed by very few individuals of the time.[20]

Charles J. Hexamer's National Alliance, like the Central Alliance from which it grew, incorporated a variety of impulses. As the Central Alliance's original constitution—adopted largely unchanged by the National Alliance—stated the organization aimed "to awaken and to promote a feeling of unity in the population of German origin in America" and to use its power, "once centralized," to defend its "legitimate desires and interests." The document also pledged the group to fend off "nativist encroachments" and to safeguard "good, friendly relations" between the United States and Germany, while demanding "the full, honest recognition" of the contributions made by German immigrants to America.[21]

The National Alliance thus functioned at once as a vehicle to bring together a declining and fractured German America and as an organization tending to protect its interests. One of those interests was what alliance activists called "personal liberty"—in essence, the right to drink beer and wine. The defense of this "right" against a rising tide of prohibitionist sentiment came to dominate the group's political activity. Indeed, Clifton Child, in an early and influential interpretation, argued that the alliance "rose to power as a defensive organization" battling prohibition. Restricted by its 1907 congressional charter from engaging in politics, the National Alliance worked nonetheless through state and local alliances to approve "wet" candidates for office and rally votes against "dry" measures and politicians. Beginning in 1913, the organization drew heavy subsidies from the brewing industry to help finance its antiprohibition campaigns. In the years leading up to the First World War, Child maintained, prohibition was "the sole *raison d'être*" of many local branches.[22]

In 1914, the National alliance claimed a membership of two million. While its greatest strength lay in Pennsylvania, Wisconsin, New York, Ohio, Indiana, Illinois, and Iowa, it had well-organized branches in thirty-three other states, including Texas.

The Texas alliance was formed by a federation of existing German-American organizations. Locally, the organizations included county alliances or branches that sent delegates to the state organization. The county alliances in turn were federated into the Texas state alliance, and the states collectively constituted the National Alliance. Each branch set up committees to formulate its policy and to carry out its decisions, the most important generally being the legislative committee, which represented its interests before the various departments of local and state governments. The level of influence that the National German-American Alliance had in Texas is unclear. Records are scarce, but its main influence seemed to be in fighting prohibition and supporting wet candidates. The Texas state branch of the German-American National Alliance was formed in 1909 in San Antonio, naming Hugo Moeller, editor of the *San Antonio Freie Presse*, president, and Paul Meerscheidt of San Antonio vice-president. The same year, Charles J. Hexamer, president of the National Alliance, spoke in Houston during that city's German Day activities.

The Texas alliance listed its primary purpose as fighting "the so-called blue laws." It also promised to refrain "from all interference in party politics, reserving, however, the right and duty to defend its principles, also in the political field, in case these should be attacked or endangered by political measures." Other objectives of the state alliance were to recommend "the introduction of the study of German into the public schools," the opposition of "any and every restriction of immigration of healthy persons from Europe," and the abolition of "antiquated laws no longer in accordance with the spirit of the times, which check free intercourse and restrict personal freedom of the citizen." Minutes from the 1911 National German-American Alliance convention declared that the Texas branch was "in a flourishing condition."[23]

Meerscheidt, in his testimony before the Senate in 1918, discussed some of the Texas alliance's prewar activities. He stated that one of the goals of the group was to get Germans elected to the local school boards. The Texas-born Meerscheidt estimated that one-half of the population of San Antonio was German (clearly, an exaggeration), yet attempts were being made to eliminate the teaching of German in public schools. He believed it best that students study German in addition to the English language. The problem was, according to Meerscheidt, that the younger generation, including his own children, did not want to take German. He nonetheless insisted they do because "they are better off in this world if they know German."

Politically, the Texas alliance remained loyal to the Democratic Party. Meerscheidt, however, seemed to contradict the testimonies of other alliance members before the committee. For example, he contended that the National Alliance took little interest in Texas politics and prohibition, stating on the prohibition issue that "they know how every German there is going to vote, and there is no necessity of doing anything." He also claimed to be ignorant of many of the political goals of the National Alliance.[24]

Meerscheidt saw the Texas alliance primarily as a social organization, not a political one. In politics and business, he believed that Germans and Americans were the same. However, socially they were different. Germans, he said, "like to have their dances and entertainments, and have their clubs and dances, which the Americans have not, and keep those up, the songs and singing societies, and in that way they are separate." He also stated his belief that German *Kultur* was the highest state of civilization. Even though he contended it would be best for the Germans to assimilate into American culture, Meerscheidt saw no harm in the two groups remaining separate for social purposes. When asked of Hexamer's statement resisting assimilation because Germans "were not going to drag down the civilization of Germany to Americanism," Meerscheidt replied that he did not agree with Hexamer on the subject.[25]

The prohibition issue again forced German Texans back into the political realm. Almost without exception, Germans supported wet candidates. In fact, temperance was either an issue totally ignored or treated lightly in the German-Texas community. To support temperance was to abandon one's cultural identity. The views of continental Europeans, and thereof primarily the German-language populations, in regard to consumption of alcoholic beverages was always more liberal. Beer was considered a form of nourishment if consumed in moderate and regular fashion. Catholic monasteries had assumed the task of beer-brewing for several centuries in Southern Germany and Austria, partially as a source of income, but also as one way to control quality and alcohol content. During Lenten and fasting, beer was a substitute for nutriments.

Prohibitionists, since their defeat in 1887, concentrated on local option elections and met with enough success, especially in North Texas, that in 1901 alarmed liquor interests formed the Texas Brewers Association. In response, drys in 1903 organized the Texas Local Option Association and in 1907 a state chapter of the Anti-Saloon League. The two antiliquor groups merged in 1908 and demanded that the legislature call a referendum on a statewide prohibition amendment, the first such proposal to be placed before voters in twenty years. Legislators rejected this call in 1909, but voters in the 1910 Democratic primary strongly endorsed the referendum and elected a majority of dry representatives and senators, thereby virtually ensuring that it would win approval once the legislature met in 1911. Curiously, the prohibitionist success did not carry over to the governor's election, which was won by Oscar B. Colquitt, a Georgia-born wet politician who since 1902 had served on the Railroad Commission. The Texas branch of the National German-American Alliance had representatives from every German society and from every lodge of the Sons of Hermann to support Colquitt. The Texas *Staatsverbund*, whose object was to promote the interest of the German Catholics in the state, advocated temperance, but opposed prohibition. Colquitt overcame several weak, dry opponents by appealing to antiprohibition sentiments in South and Central Texas and winning over conservatives with a promise of political peace and legislative rest. In the Democratic primary, Colquitt carried 40.5 percent on the statewide level, but nearly twice that in the ten German counties.[26]

Prohibitionists quickly put aside their disgust at Colquitt's victory because early in 1911 the legislature lived up to its expectations and submitted a constitutional amendment to voters. The campaign, which culminated in July, took on more the air of a moral crusade than a political contest. Drys and wets raised money, held rallies and torchlight parades, and sponsored speakers to take their message to the people. Evangelical Protestant churches "locked shields" against the liquor interests and led the campaign. Drys drew strength from racial prejudice in that blacks were identified with wets. Texans of Mexican and German descent came in for their share of criticism also, as did the big cities for their temptations and allurements. Antiprohibitionists argued that the drys constituted a threat to personal freedom that knew no bounds. "Civil liberty will give way to military despotism to appease fanaticism on this subject," said Governor Colquitt, in 1911. The wets had their own Anti-Statewide Prohibition Organization of Texas, financed in large measure by the local and national brewing interests. The executive committee operated out of Houston under the direction of Jacob "Jake" F. Wolters, an attorney for the Wholesale Liquor Dealers Association. Wolters, a third-generation German Texan, had led the Democratic party antiprohibitionist forces in defeating a prohibition amendment in 1908. Wolters argued that prohibition would increase taxes, would be harmful to the public schools, and would be detrimental to the principles of government.[27]

In 1911, Texas had 167 dry counties, 61 were partially dry, and only 21 were wholly wet. In the wet counties, however, were located the larger cities and greater voting strength. Of the ten German counties of Texas, five were "wet" and five were "partially dry," with none being "dry." On July 22, 1911, more than twice the number of voters who had gone to the polls in the previous year's gubernatorial election turned out and defeated the amendment by a narrow margin of 6,297 votes. South Texas, the Germans, Mexican Americans, African Americans, and the major cities were instrumental to the wet victory. The German counties of Texas were critical in defeating the measure. Out of 25,335 total votes cast in the ten German counties, 21,507 were cast against prohibition. Comal County voted over fifty-to-one against the prohibition amendment. Drys insisted that the manipulation of black voters had produced the wet victory and vowed to fight on. The issue could not be killed simply by one defeat.[28]

Like the antiprohibition movement, an extensive German-language press also disseminated *Deutschtum* and German-Texan culture. The part played by German language newspapers in the life and Americanization of the German element in Texas from its beginnings to the present has not been subjected to a thorough investigation, but publication of German-language newspapers in Texas dates from the establishment of the Galveston *Zeitung* in 1846. At least eight other German newspapers joined the *Zeitung* before the beginning of the Civil War. The most prominent was the *Neu-Braunfelser Zeitung*, edited by Ferdinand Jakob Lindheimer. It inaugurated its long and eventful history on November 12, 1852, and it became the longest running German-language newspaper in Texas. The outbreak of the Civil War interrupted the expanding field of German-language journalism in Texas. Only four of the prewar newspapers survived the war period. Following the Civil War, as the number of German immigrants to Texas increased so did the growing demand for German-language newspapers. Before 1870, five new journals joined those that had survived the war, bringing the total to nine. As the tensions of Reconstruction lessened, the establishment of new German newspapers in the state continued to grow. By 1907, the number of German newspapers and periodicals published in the state had reached an all-time high with twenty-nine, even though the number of German-language newspapers nationally was declining. In 1914, at the outbreak of World War I, there were still twenty-six German-language publications in Texas.[29]

In 1910, the United States conducted its final census before World War I. The census showed a German element in Texas numbering approximately 220,000 people. The percentage of Germans among the state's population, however, continued to decline, dropping from 6.2 percent in 1900 to just 5.6 percent in 1910. The number of Texans born in Germany also declined from 53,350 in 1900 to 48,032 in 1910. The drop in the German element in Texas parallels the drop in the German element in the United States at large during the period. Yet, despite the declining numbers, in certain counties in Texas, Germans still made up a considerable percentage of the population. Washington, Comal, Kendall, Austin, and Gillespie counties, all had German populations in excess of twenty percent of the total population of the county. The five counties had some of the highest percentages of Germans in any county in the southern United States prior to the war. Bexar County had a German population in excess of 11,500 people. Once the U.S. entered the war, the German counties, at least from the point of view of non-German Texans, created concerns about the loyalty of their German population.[30]

4

German Texans and American Neutrality, 1914-1917

On June 28, 1914, Serbian nationalists assassinated Archduke Franz Ferdinand, heir to the Austro-Hungarian throne, and his wife in the streets of Sarajevo. To many Texans and Americans, Europe was a far off place at the time and the possibility of war in Europe was of no concern. Yet, many German newspapers in the United States fully realized the serious consequences that might follow the assassination. The German papers initially echoed the reaction of the American people and the United States' traditional policy of isolation and neutrality, but as the events of July 1914 unfolded and Europe moved closer and closer to war, Germans in the United States accepted and vigorously defended the official German explanation of the origins of the war.

Not long afterward and two days after German troops had marched into Belgium and drawn Britain into a general European war in 1914 both the *Fredericksburger Wochenblatt* and the *Neu-Braunfelser Zeitung* placed blame for the war on the Allied Powers and expressed confidence in an eventual German victory. The German-language papers advanced a pro-German viewpoint due to freedom of the press and because of the United States' official position of neutrality. Yet, the German press likely was more pro-

German in its position than many German Americans and German Texans may have been. A number of Fredericksburg residents, for instance, criticized the *Wochenblatt's* editor, German-born Robert G. Penniger, as being too pro-German. Indeed, their position provided an alternative viewpoint on the war than from what was available in the English-language press. To many Americans, however, the German press was the best indicator of German-American opinion, regardless of the degree of divergence between the German press and its readers. In an attempt to calm differences that German Texans and their Anglo-Texan neighbors may have had about the war, some of the German-language press felt it their duty to explain the pro-German viewpoint. In October 1914, for example, the *Giddings Deutsche Volksblatt* contained an article the reader cut out and handed to his English-speaking neighbor in order to answer the question, "I do not see why the Kaiser wanted war."[1]

The restraint German Texans mustered in early August 1914 proved fragile and fleeting. The European war unleashed passions among the state's ethnic groups that spurred their political mobilization. Many Germans rallied to the homeland cause. Men and women of the state's *Vereine* launched war relief campaigns, and German newspapers defended Germany's actions. A group of German Texans from Victoria, known as the "German-American Rough Riders," volunteered their services to the German army. Through August, representatives from German associations mobilized to pursue the twin goals of war relief and the rhetorical defense of Germany. Charles J. Hexamer, president of the National German-American Alliance, announced a nationwide campaign to raise $2 million in war relief. In Texas, German associations collected money to aid the German and Austrian Red Cross. Indeed, the fighting in Europe brought a measure of ethnic unity long sought by German spokesmen. Thus fortified, some German-Texan leaders moved aggressively to defend Germany's honor, to lobby for an approach to neutrality they felt would not favor Britain, and to forestall American military intervention on behalf of the Allies.[2]

Yet the war also rallied partisans of the Allied cause, especially among those of English background. Some declared their sympathies immediately. Others initially sought a neutral stance, in the spirit of President Woodrow Wilson's call for impartiality "in thought as well as action," only to be alienated by Germany's conduct of the war and, to some extent, the aggressive tone taken by German-language newspaper editors and alliance leaders. Hexamer and the National German-American Alliance pursued a remarkably unsubtle campaign to shape American neutrality, one that, whatever its merits, struck many non-German-American observers as a dangerous injection of ethnic passions into foreign policy at a moment of particular peril for the United States. Hexamer took an ethnic movement that began with goals of cultural maintenance and attempted to make it a force in high politics. The step instead helped prompt a mounting series of attacks on German-American activists and eventually on German Americans in general as disloyal "hyphenates" who put their ties to Germany above America's best interests.[3]

The reaction, reflected during the neutrality period in campaigns for "anti-hyphenism," "Americanization," and military "preparedness," did not stop at denouncing ethnic group activity in the political sphere. Its demands for national unity culminated in an attack on the very legitimacy of cultural ethnic separatism and a call instead for a "100 percent Americanism." The National Alliance proved both a victim of and—to some extent—an inadvertent catalyst for a new kind of American nationalism, one with far less room for culturally pluralist conceptions of the nation and "hyphenated" ethnic-American identities. Such American nationalism would reach full force in the anti-German panic that followed American intervention in the war. But its elements took shape during the neutrality period, enough so that by 1916 the *Dallas Morning News* would write that "this nation cannot be content with less than the full and undiluted loyalty of those whom it decorates with its citizenship, a loyalty of the kind that prejudices the mind and heart in its favor." Those who cannot show that "kind of loyalty are hyphenated citizens, regardless of their blood."[4]

As Europe lurched into war in late July and early August 1914, Texans could see all about them echoes of the nationalistic fervor that was sweeping capitals across the Atlantic. The editors of

Texas' major English-language newspapers urged caution, however, and preached neutrality. The *Houston Post* blamed antagonists on both sides. The *Dallas Morning News* blamed previous and current European leaders and urged the United States to act as a mediator between the warring nations. The *San Antonio Express* hoped that the war would be one of comparatively short duration. President Woodrow Wilson echoed the thoughts when he announced his position in a widely publicized statement on neutrality on August 4, 1914. The proclamation warned Americans against siding with any belligerent nation.[5]

In spite of calls for neutrality, German Texans voiced their anger over newspaper coverage of the war. Persons of German descent composed part of the readership of all of the major daily newspapers in the eastern and central part of Texas. San Antonio witnessed the greatest debate. The *San Antonio Express* carried the messages of protest of the city's large number of German Texans, including an influential mercantile sector. A mass meeting at the Hermann Sons' Hall in San Antonio on August 15 issued a condemnation of the Allied bias in news stories. "Germans and Austrians have full right to defend their existence," they proclaimed. The American press printed "falsehoods, which bring prejudice against the German nation and the German citizens in this country." The *Dallas Morning News* misreported that German residents of San Antonio started their own German-language newspaper, the *Freie Presse*, to combat news "of an anti-German character" and "to handle war news from a German standpoint." (In actuality, the paper existed for eight decades and was published as a daily from 1875-1918; the report being an example of the misinformation and suspicions present in the Anglo press.) Indeed, the atrocity tales in connection with the German occupation of Belgium were most difficult to combat. Although practically all were disproved by later investigation, they were, without doubt, the most effective weapon in Allied propaganda.[6]

While some people had doubts about how Germany was being portrayed in the press, the most vocal German Americans closed ranks to defend the German government and people. Charles

J. Hexamer, president of the National German-American Alliance, on August 3, 1914, issued an appeal to the German-language press nationally, outlining how "the German name" could be defended "against the animosity and ignorance of a minority in our own country." He was prompted in part by fears of one-sided and negative coverage from the nation's English-language press of Germany's conduct. By mid-August, editorials attacking the German cause had become common. Likewise, the cutting of the German transatlantic cables after Britain entered the war virtually ended the transmission to American newspapers of German accounts of the conflict. To a degree, however, Hexamer's appeal predated these developments and amounted to something of a preemptive move. He called on alliance branches in every city to sponsor press agents who could refute, in English, "all hateful attacks" of "irresponsible reporters from English newspapers." Hexamer further declared that alliance branches should take up collections for German war relief. Both the *Neu-Braunfelser Zeitung* and the *Fredericksburger Wochenblatt* blamed the English-language newspapers' reliance on Allied news releases for their pro-British and anti-German reports. The *Katholische Rundschau* (San Antonio) was less diplomatic, it called for a positively pro-German foreign policy.[7]

From the beginning of the war in August 1914, the *San Antonio Express* carried many front-page stories, photos, and commentary about Germany and the Central Powers. On August 1, the *Express* lead story carried the headline "Kaiser Is Ready to Wield Sword." The daily's first special section devoted to the war contained lengthy feature stories of enthusiastic, gleeful Germans parading in New York City with a "raging war spirit." The *Express* reported in a front-page story the addition of a cable wire service that included war specials from London, Paris, Berlin, and the capitals of all the major contestants. Shortly thereafter, the paper began a series of articles detailing the experiences of a German army officer. In an editorial entitled "Let There Be Justice," *Express* editors criticized censored war news, which, they argued, resulted in "one sided, ex parte reports." The newspaper issued a call for independent, impartial war correspondents who would provide reports "regardless of whose arms may be victorious and whose vanquished in each and every fray." The large German commercial sector, combined with the substantial presence of German immigrants in Central Texas, maintained a strong influence with the San Antonio newspaper until the U.S. declaration of war in 1917.[8]

Other Texas dailies attempted to balance their coverage in reaction to complaints of bias toward Great Britain and France. The *Dallas Morning News* and the *Houston Post* carried stories within the first weeks that dealt with press censorship and complaints by the German government that Germany was being unjustly blamed for the war. Germany belatedly attempted to label Britain the aggressor. The *News* editors, however, stated that should Germany lose the war, "one of the very considerable causes of its misfortune was the violation of its own agreement to observe the neutrality of Belgium." In another editorial, the *News* predicted the war would "exhaust all participants." The editors noted the need for "an international supreme court which would pass judgment on controversies that threaten the world's peace."[9]

The *Houston Post* expressed "surprise" in the first weeks of the war that German Americans were not pleased with the news coverage. The *Post* editorials explained that no ban existed on German news and the daily maintained "no prejudice against the German people or the people of any nation involved in the war." The rulers of the belligerent nations shouldered the blame. The editors noted, however, that the Associated Press had admitted that the only official news of the war came from England and that government censorship possibly "colored, perhaps exaggerated" the information published about the war. Editors urged patience and scrutiny of all war news. Throughout the early months of the war, banner headlines, photos, and extensive articles about the war in Europe dominated pages of daily newspapers in Texas and the nation. At the end of August, some editors, having read the official British and German explanations for the war, moved to a position decidedly hostile to the Central Powers. From 1914 to 1917, the *Dallas Morning News* evolved as the leading pro-Allied publication in Texas while the two

Houston newspapers maintained a more balanced position during the period.[10]

Most Americans believed the United States could avoid becoming involved in the European conflict, but immediate concerns arose among businessmen and farmers about the war's impact on the nation's commerce. Then, as German troops rolled into Belgium and France, hope for immediate economic gains for Texans vanished quickly. Britain embargoed cotton shipments to Germany and Austria-Hungary and, as a result, alienated some Allied enthusiasts in the state. In 1914, Texas produced more than four million bales, one-fourth of the nation's cotton crop. Prices fell. To alleviate the falling prices in the state, Governor Oscar Colquitt called an emergency session of the Texas legislature and asked legislators to create a state warehouse and banking program. His ambitious plan gained little public or legislative support. Nevertheless, the sudden fall in cotton prices sent political shock waves through the Wilson administration. When President Wilson failed to recognize immediately the problem and derailed protective legislation in Congress, critics quickly labeled him pro-British.[11]

Meanwhile, problems over election outcomes were predicted at the polls in November 1914 because staunch Texas Democrats would vote for the Republican or Socialist ticket if things did not change. As outgoing governor in 1914, Colquitt, in a *New York Times* interview, described the Wilson administration as "the greatest failure in the history of the Presidency." After leaving office, Colquitt, in part to preserve his base of support among the Germans, supported Germany in quarrels over neutrality, and he continued to scold the president.[12]

At the same time, Texas Progressives looked forward to the summer 1914 gubernatorial primary. The drys rallied behind Thomas H. Ball, a Houston attorney. The wets favored James E. Ferguson, a Central Texas banker, who had never before held an elective office. "Farmer Jim" promised to veto all prohibition legislation: "I will strike it where the chicken got the axe." Ball's advisors turned to the Wilson administration to stave off defeat. Wilson, Secretary of State William Jennings Bryan, and Postmaster

General Albert S. Burleson issued public statements for Ball in mid-July, a tactic that moved Ferguson to denounce federal interference in state affairs. Despite the presidential action, Ferguson combined the wet vote with farmers concerned about tenancy and achieved a 45,000-vote majority in the Democratic primary. Ferguson also dominated the German vote, beating Ball 17,307 to 2,958 in the ten German counties. It marked the beginning of a long period of cooperation between German Texans and Ferguson. In the November election, Ferguson won easily in heavily Democratic Texas, with the runner-up being the Socialist Party candidate, German-Texan E. R. Meitzen. Meitzen, who operated the Socialist newspaper, *The Rebel*, received, despite his heritage, little of the German vote.

Relations between Ferguson and Wilson improved in the aftermath of the primary, and it lasted until the spring of 1917. In contrast to Governor Colquitt, who openly bickered with Washington over Mexican policy, Ferguson deferred to the Wilson administration in his public statements and confined dissent to private correspondence. A similarly cooperative attitude marked the governor's actions on neutrality after World War I had begun.[13]

Ferguson's victory inflicted a serious setback on the progressive Democrats. The new governor was a master campaigner, a deft manipulator of wet and rural sentiment, and a clever opportunist with an eye on the state treasury and other sources of personal profit. His ability to muddy differences over prohibition perpetuated the confused condition of state politics. Drys and progressives faced the gloomy prospect of four years of antiprohibitionist leadership in Austin. As World War I progressed, however, ties between Ferguson, the National German-American Alliance, and national brewers became a severe liability. Furthermore, after 1915, the performance of Ferguson as governor severely hampered the entire antiprohibitionist cause.[14]

The National German-American Alliance later confessed that it had been "very much interested" in the election of Ferguson in 1914, and had sent men to Texas to distribute propaganda against prohibition. A 1915 report of the propaganda and organization committee of the alliance detailed the group's efforts to combat "anti-Germanism" in Texas. "Our next look we directed to Texas, where fanatics had declared war upon Germanism to the hilt," said the report. "We found there a glorious thorough-going, self-conscious Germanism, both in the second, third and also the fourth generations, which was for the most part centralized in a mighty order of the Sons of Hermann." The National Alliance seemed most pleased with Ferguson's election to the governor's mansion: "Most comforting was the result of the election, in which the German vote in Texas made itself felt more strongly than ever before made, and it was undoubtedly the factor which saved Texas from a Puritanical yoke."[15]

Meanwhile, German newspapers continued to take up Germany's cause. Toward the end of 1914, the National Alliance mounted a campaign for an embargo on arms exports from the United States, a step that newspapers followed. Many editors believed that an embargo on arms from the United States was the best way of preserving American neutrality, since British control of the seas meant only the Allies could benefit from the arms trade. The *Fredericksburger Wochenblatt* criticized the Wilson administration's trade policy and the *Katholische Rundschau* attacked the United States for prolonging the war by supplying the weapons with which to fight, and it stated that Wilson's policy played "into the hands of England."[16]

As the war continued, German culture increasingly came under attack, and German-American churches wondered what would happen if they lost their means of communicating with their members—the German language. The Lutherans wanted to maintain the German language and culture of their church. The Lutheran Church-Missouri Synod, the largest and most conservative of German Lutheran organizations, at the onset of the war adopted in its official publications a neutral stance. It was essentially anti-war. Not all German Lutheran editors and publishers were as strongly neutral. Some attacked Britain, others filled their pages with pictures of the Kaiser, the German army in action, German battleships, and German military leaders. With views similar to those of Charles J.

Hexamer, they called for a united German-American stand against the pro-Allied American press. Although there were exceptions, as a whole, the Lutheran churches did not allow their publications to become agencies of pro-Germanism.

What pastors, professors, and editors did as private citizens was another matter. Some became very active for the German side in 1914 and 1915. Several German Lutheran pastors from Philadelphia, for example, jointly sent a letter to the Kaiser to express their hope for a German victory. Members of Lutheran congregations collected relief money for German victims of the war, yet the amount accumulated was not significant. On the other hand, there were publications that were sharply critical of Germany.[17]

The reaction of German Catholics to the war in Europe is harder to measure because they were a minority group within the Roman Catholic Church. The pro-German reaction of German Catholics seems to mirror that of German Lutherans. Catholic bishops of German heritage were careful not to adopt pro-German positions during the neutrality period. Nonetheless, many of the clergy, as many as a third of which had names of German origin, sympathized with Germany. Some German-Catholic publications espoused the benefits of a German victory to Catholicism. Likewise, the German Roman Catholic Central-*Verein* of North America, a union of German Catholic organizations across the country, increasingly involved itself in the activities of the National German-American Alliance. As with the Lutherans, the German Catholics sometimes had a difficult time separating the idea of German cultural maintenance from German nationalism.[18]

Buoyed by an unprecedented degree of ethnic unity, Hexamer and the National Alliance moved to shape America's policy of neutrality so as to keep it truly neutral, at least in their eyes, and to avoid a war with Germany. Alliance leaders and branches played a major role in the arms embargo agitation; they likewise took the initiative in opposing the raising of an allied war loan in the United States.

As they pushed these political efforts in late 1914 and 1915, relations between the National Alliance and President Woodrow

Wilson steadily deteriorated. The British had imposed a blockade on German ports, which in certain respects clearly violated American neutrality. Wilson's ultimate acquiescence in the blockade compromised his neutral stance, essentially confining access to American munitions to the Allies. Wilson's opposition to an embargo and his overall neutrality policy increasingly drew the wrath of German-American activists, whose arguments held merit. The president, of course, did not see things in such a way. Wilson's irritation at such criticism contributed to his public questioning of the loyalty of his critics. Thus, in the spring of 1915 the shadow of "disloyalty" began to fall on activists in general.[19]

Germany declared a "war zone" around the British Isles, within which German submarines would destroy enemy vessels without warning. Wilson then warned that he would hold Germany to "strict accountability" for the destruction of American ships and lives. The question remained as to what the United States would do to protect the alleged right of Americans to travel in safety on British passenger liners. On May 7, 1915, a U-boat precipitated a full-scale crisis by sinking the *Lusitania*, with a loss of nearly 1,200 people, including 128 American citizens. Until the end of August, when the Kaiser ordered the abandonment of unrestricted submarine operations against passenger ships, war with Germany seemed a very real possibility, despite the fact that the German Embassy had placed warnings in U.S. newspapers for Americans not to travel on British ships. In the meantime, supporters of the Allies could argue with some justification that Berlin already had carried the war to American soil. Beginning in February, reports surfaced of sabotage carried out by agents operating from the German embassy in Washington. At least some of the stories may have been genuine, and they included reports that described foiled attempts to destroy American factories and to carry bombs aboard American ships.[20]

Initially, Texans and the English-language press condemned Germany. The *Dallas Morning News* stated the *Lusitania* attack was a "crime against civilization" while the *Houston Chronicle* described it as "a blow to national dignity." State Senator J. C. McNealus of Dallas made front-page news when he called the assault "unparalleled in modern times in the wantonness, the cruelty and the disregard of all civilized human promptings." The Texas Senate passed a resolution urging the United States to declare war against Germany. In the days that followed, questions about the incident appeared. Governor James Ferguson urged caution and said people should not be "swayed or excited by the passions of the hour." The *Houston Post* warned readers "not to be hasty in their judgment" and place their confidence in President Wilson's "wisdom, courage, and patriotism."[21]

Not every Texan blamed Germany for the *Lusitania*'s sinking. Popular reaction in the following weeks illustrated the divisions that existed in the state. A letter to the *Houston Chronicle* said "the loss of American lives rests entirely and exclusively on the British government." Another reader wrote that American ammunition resulted in great losses to Germany on the battlefield. Before condemning those responsible for the *Lusitania*, the nation needed to confront its role as munitions supplier to the Allies. "We . . . should not be too hasty in out judgment of those who face death in dealing death, for home and native land." Others placed the responsibility directly on the German government. The ill-fated liner and loss of life was "an act of cruelty that will never be forgotten or forgiven."[22]

The German-language press, understandably, defended the actions of the German Empire. The *Giddings Deutsche Volksblatt* argued that Americans who lost their lives on the *Lusitania* were not victims of German aggression, but of British subterfuge; the British government had acted unscrupulously by designating the *Lusitania* as a passenger ship when it had been armed for war and carried munitions and contraband. Instead of denouncing Germany for sinking the ship, Americans should have directed their criticisms toward England for its failure to keep innocent people off its ships during the war. The *Katholische Rundschau* praised Secretary of State William Jennings Bryan for his efforts to warn Americans to avoid travel on belligerent ships, a warning that other neutral governments had made but which the Wilson administration refused to make.[23]

The major English-language newspapers in Texas pursued a cautious position. They condemned the attack while they supported

President's Wilson's policy of negotiating with Germany. After its reaction to the horror of the passenger liner's sinking, for example, the *Houston Chronicle* sympathized with the German-American community in Texas. In an editorial entitled "Our German American Citizens," the *Chronicle* urged readers to consider those on which the "brunt of the crisis falls most heavily." The editors said the attack should not lead to a break between America and Germany and noted the community worked to "lessen antagonistic sentiment in this country." Such an attitude "does not mean that their loyalty is in doubt should eventualities come to pass." A month later, the *San Antonio Express*, still critical of Britain, continued to advocate neutrality while defending Germany. The reasons for neutrality "were as plentiful as blackberries." The *Express* also praised Wilson's leadership, stating, "All of us realize that there is a careful and judicious pilot at the helm of the ship of the state." Many historians consider the *Lusitania* a turning point in American public opinion. Texas English-language newspapers, however, maintained a neutral course in spite of the dramatic coverage of the *Lusitania* crisis.[24]

Nevertheless, the German-language press in Texas seemed to realize that, in the wake of the *Lusitania* sinking, American opinion was slowly turning against them. Those Americans who began with the intention of maintaining a neutral stance, became alienated by Germany's conduct of the war. In response, the German-language newspapers in Texas urged an even stricter policy of neutrality, unlike what many German Texans perceived as a pro-Allied version of neutrality that would eventually result in the United States' entry into the war against Germany. To prevent such a progression, the German press in Texas focused on the factors its editors felt were bringing the United States closer to war. Economic interests, the editors argued, acted as a barrier to peace because many corporations were benefiting from aiding the Allies. The *Fredericksburger Wochenblatt* added that the true battle for humanity was the struggle against Wall Street and that America's road to ruin was paved with British gold. The *Katholische Rundschau* was puzzled by the fact that, despite America's neutrality, American bankers could participate in the war. The *Lutherbote für Texas* sarcastically claimed that the purpose of J. P. Morgan's visit with British Ambassador Cecil Spring Rice was to discuss neutrality.[25]

In addition to the reprehensible behavior of Wall Street, the German press in Texas felt that munitions manufacturers were just as culpable for their indirect participation in the war and their influence upon U.S. policy. The *Fredericksburger Wochenblatt*, for example, criticized the profits of Bethlehem Steel, derisively asking what share of them should be owed to Bethlehem's patriotism. The paper found it interesting that the "clang of metal" always seemed to accompany cries of patriotism and preparedness. The *Lutherbote für Texas*, in a parody of Matthew 2:6, prophesied to Bethlehem, Pennsylvania, "you who are small among cities in America, out of you will come the tools of destruction, through which thousands in Europe will be condemned to death."[26]

As the likelihood of the United States' entry into the war increased, the German-Texan press made desperate attempts to reverse the undesirable direction of American foreign policy. In addition to blaming the Allies for starting the war for dishonorable goals, the German press through mid-1917 maintained confidence in the eventual success of the Central Powers. Germany's use of submarine warfare and zeppelins, the difficulties of the British and Russian governments in recruiting troops, the effectiveness of the German military in France, and the great strength of the German navy meant inevitable success for Germany even if the United States should enter the war. Admittedly, the German Texas papers believed that discounting the potential impact of the United States on the outcome of the war would undermine any sentiment favoring American entry into the war; additionally, such a position would have been undoubtedly more popular with their readers than one which suggested that the Central Powers were on the verge of defeat. The papers failed to realize that praising the success of the Central Powers would only intensify support for U.S. actions to halt "Prussian autocracy" among those to whom the German government and its militaristic actions were abhorrent.[27]

By the fall of 1915, worries about the allegedly divided loyalties of "hyphenated" Americans had escalated into a nationwide "anti-hyphenate" campaign. Former president Theodore Roosevelt stood at the head of the "Swat-the-Hyphen" movement, and President Wilson lent it moral authority. Wilson was careful not to name German Americans specifically in his attacks, in part perhaps because he meant his attacks to apply as well to Irish Americans. His speeches, however, revealed a conception of American nationality that had less and less tolerance for ethnically based cultural as well as political differences. "You cannot become thorough Americans if you think of yourselves in groups," Wilson told an audience of newly naturalized citizens in Philadelphia, three days after the *Lusitania* sinking. "America does not consist of groups. A man who thinks of himself as belonging to a particular national group in America has not yet become an American." In the fall, he denounced divided loyalties with even greater force, when Roosevelt joined him. In an October 12 speech, Roosevelt the former president, an aggressive proponent of intervention on behalf of the Allies, depicted as treasonous the actions of "those hyphenated Americans who terrorize American politicians by threats of the foreign vote."[28]

An onslaught of anti-hyphen speeches, editorials, and political cartoons followed. While they tended to decry the "disembodied category" of those immigrants with divided loyalties, the speeches, editorials, and cartoons were understood to target those whom Roosevelt termed "professional German-Americans." Around the country, continued revelations of alleged spying and sabotage reinforced the image of German American activists as subversives and conspirators. Once thought of as the most assimilable and reputable of immigrant groups, German Americans were now clearly under attack. By the end of 1915, the *Fredericksburger Wochenblatt* already understood the upcoming crisis when it declared "the coming period will decide the future of *Deutschtum* in the United States."[29]

The "anti-hyphenate" campaign that overtook the United States in 1915 both fed on and fostered two other movements: the push for the Americanization of immigrants and for military preparedness. The Americanization campaign nationally had prewar roots in the settlement house movement, the drive for patriotic education in the public schools, and efforts of patriotic societies such as the Daughters of the American Revolution to reach adult immigrants. Such societies, motivated by fear of immigrant radicalism, preached to newcomers "a loyalty that consisted essentially of willing submissiveness" to the law. As John Higham argued, the emerging Americanization movement incorporated both this stress on conformity and national unity and the settlements' "immigrant gifts" approach of valuing Old World cultures to ease immigrant adjustment. But Americanization as a movement aimed at adult newcomers lacked mass support until the war, when fear of divided immigrant loyalties brought it into the public spotlight. The May 1915 reception for new citizens that President Wilson addressed became a model for similar ceremonies held on July 4 in cities around the country under the rubric of "Americanization Day." The group created to organize that event renamed itself the National Americanization Committee and began to shift from a social welfare emphasis to one of promoting naturalization, English-language training, and "undivided loyalty to America." On July 5, the city of Dallas held its Americanization Day, with 10,000 people turning out to hear former mayor W. M. Holland tell the crowd that "every unnaturalized citizen of this country should today forget his bias for or prejudice against any country engaged in the horrible slaughter in Europe" and that "unnaturalized citizens should thank Almighty God that they are permitted to dwell in the United States." The extent to which the crusade against hyphenates had merged by early 1916 became clear at the committee conference held in January in Philadelphia. Roosevelt closed the gathering with a call for "an intense sense of national cohesion and solidarity" and cast "hyphenated Americanism" as its opposite.[30]

The preparedness campaign, the third movement, sought a stronger national defense. It increasingly helped define the terms of the Americanization movement. After the sinking of the *Lusitania*, President Wilson sought to expand the nation's land and naval forces. The president's "preparedness" campaign appeared to some Americans to be a logical response to increased tensions. Critics saw the move as a step closer to war. Despite the fact that several members of Texas' congressional delegation opposed Wilson's foreign policy, polls showed that as a whole Texans overwhelmingly supported it. The *Dallas Morning News* pointed out that a large number of German Texans lived in the districts of Wilson's critics. A preparedness rally in Dallas drew thousands of people who supported the president's actions. Indeed, Theodore Roosevelt, who backed all three movements (anti-hyphenate, Americanization, and preparedness), used his Americanization conference speech to argue for universal military training, a larger navy, and national regulation of business—all meant to provide the "proper type of preparedness to protect the nation."[31]

Not to be deterred from the general public's approval of Wilson's preparedness campaign, Texas congressmen continued their opposition. They believed that the nation faced no real threat from Germany and that the federal budget adequately covered military expenditures. Other Democrats, however, viewed the resistance as disloyalty and recruited opponents to run against the anti-preparedness congressmen in the 1916 Democratic primary elections. Nevertheless, some Democrats alleged that the president's policy placed the nation on a path to war. In response, Texas Congressman Atkins Jefferson "Jeff" McLemore sponsored a bill that required the president to warn Americans of the risks they assumed if they boarded an armed merchant ship. The Wilson administration viewed the McLemore resolution as a challenge to the president's authority over foreign policy. McLemore's proposal languished in committee for weeks and then lost in a floor vote by a two-to-one margin. At the time, opposition to the president's policies in Texas seemed to be more of a threat than German torpedoes.[32]

During 1916, with President Wilson leaning toward the Allied side, politicians in Texas had to negotiate a difficult course. Because America's official policy was one of neutrality, the politicians could not appear to be favoring one side or the other. Into this mix walked former Governor Oscar B. Colquitt. Colquitt made headlines in his 1916 Senate race against incumbent Senator Charles Culberson. In April, the *New York World* reported a "national campaign under the direction of well known German-Americans to control elections on the United States." Featured most prominently was U.S. Senate candidate Oscar Colquitt. The *World* charged that Colquitt's solicitation of German support made him "more loyal to the Kaiser and the German nation than his rival for the Senatorship." With the close race in Texas, the *World* predicted the sizable German-American vote in the state could elect Colquitt to the Senate. Colquitt's campaign centered on his opposition to Wilson and prohibition, "which brings him great favor with German-American voters." The *World* reprinted letters from Colquitt's campaign to Alphonse Koelble, a leader of the National German-American Alliance, and Bernard H. Ridder, editor of the German newspaper *New Yorker Staats-Zeitung*. In the letters, Colquitt requested support and complained of attacks he had suffered due to his opposition to the president's handling of problems with Mexico. He also requested that supporters write letters to the editors of Texas newspapers printed in German. The names of twenty-three German-language newspapers and their editors were enclosed in the letter. Many Texas daily newspapers carried the *World*'s story.[33]

Despite accusations of pro-Germanism, Colquitt appeared to be on his way to the U.S. Senate. He finished ahead of Culberson with 120,000 votes in the six-man July primary, drawing strong support from the German counties and anti-prohibition voters. Colquitt spoke during the Cat Spring Agricultural Society's 60th Anniversary Fest with W. A. Trenckmann. Despite the conflict in Europe, Trenckmann gave his talk in German. Colquitt's support for intervention in Mexico also served him well among many voters concerned with increased hostilities along both sides of the Rio Grande. In the runoff election with Culberson, German organizations in the state openly endorsed Colquitt for the seat. The *Hermannssohn in Texas* urged Germans of the state to support Colquitt. "German citizens! Unite your 60,000 votes on Senatorial Candidate Colquitt!" Colquitt continually criticized Wilson's pro-Allied position, a stance that gained him support in the German counties. The *Dallas Morning News* described the runoff as a "question of support or opposition to the Wilson administration." Culberson supporters were asked "are the people of Texas going to stand by President Woodrow Wilson or the German Kaiser?"

Thanks to the aggressive actions of Culberson's friends and the Wilson administration, the incumbent managed to overcome Colquitt in the runoff election. Governor Ferguson, himself an antiprohibitionist and friend of German voters, even parted company with Colquitt and declared for Culberson. Colquitt received his usual support from the German population with seventy percent of their vote, but managing only thirty-four percent in the remainder of the state.[34]

Meanwhile, the ongoing feud with President Wilson led some National German-American Alliance activists to discuss ways to work for his defeat in the Presidential election of 1916. Charles Hexamer and many officials of state and local alliance branches subsequently threw themselves into the campaign for the Republican presidential nominee, Charles Evans Hughes. The National Alliance, under the terms of its congressional charter, could not participate in the 1916 election, so the Central Alliance, now with John Mayer as president, stepped in to assume the mantle of leadership for alliance activists nationwide. In May, the Central Alliance issued invitations to a wide range of German associations, including other state alliances, for a conference in Chicago on the U.S. presidential race. Paul Meerscheidt, vice-president of the Texas alliance, attended the conference. The gathering made no formal endorsements, but its consensus was understood to favor Hughes. Mayer emerged as chairman of a conference committee charged with marshaling a united German-American vote and mediating between German associations and political party leaders. By the fall of 1916, then, Mayer, Hexamer, and other Germans had contributed mightily to making the "German-American vote" an issue in the presidential election.[35]

The alliance's increasing involvement in national politics was echoed locally in Texas. Despite the fact that Wilson won reelection during the 1916 presidential race, a majority of German Texans voted for the Republican Hughes, despite the fact that in the gubernatorial election they voted for James E. Ferguson, a Democrat, by a two-to-one margin over his republican opponent R. B. Creager. The results alluded to the fact that many German Texans resented the aggressive stand taken by President Wilson against the submarine policy of the Germans in the European war and by his references to "hyphenated Americans."[36]

Texas and the rest of the Southwest posed a unique situation in the years of American neutrality. In 1915 and 1916, many Texans believed that if it were to go to war with a foreign country, the United States would have been at war with Mexico, not Germany.

The feeling related to the Mexican Revolution that had started in 1910. The uprising was the first of the twentieth century's long list of remarkable national revolutions. The initial rebellion began against the authoritarian regime of General Porfirio Díaz, who had ruled the nation since 1876. Francisco I. Madero, a wealthy Mexican landowner, plotted to overthrow Díaz. Madero's revolt began in November 1910 and soon enlisted the support of other leaders, notably Francisco "Pancho" Villa, Emiliano Zapata, and Pascual Orozco. Their forces openly attacked government forces, and on May 25, 1911, Díaz abruptly resigned and left for Europe. Madero assumed the presidency, but revolts continued, even among his most notable supporters. Both the United States and Germany supported General Victoriano Huerta, who ordered the successful assassination of Mexico's popular but besieged revolutionary president. The unpopular Huerta, who like Madero, failed to quell popular revolts, resigned as president in July 1914, and departed Mexico on a German ship. Venustiano Carranza eventually succeeded Huerta, but news during 1915 and 1916 of clashes between the forces of Villa and Carranza in northern Mexico and battles between the Mexican army and Zapata in the southern part of the embattled nation frequently appeared on the front pages of Texas newspapers. Because of its proximity to Mexico, Texas became both a sanctuary and a source of arms for various factions involved in the Mexican Revolution.[37]

The problems on Texas-Mexico border country focused on Mexican nationalism, German intrigue and sabotage, and later American draft dodgers. Even before the war in Europe began, Texas Governor Oscar Colquitt declared that American casualties and property losses in the Mexican Revolution were being seriously neglected by Washington and President Wilson. In February 1914, Colquitt sent four National Guard companies to "defend and protect the people of this state, whom I consider the national government to be neglecting." To many Texans the war in Europe still appeared to be a distant conflict compared to the real violence on their state's southern border. Raids continued north of the Rio Grande as armed men attacked ranches, railroads, and small communities. News accounts attributed the attacks to Mexican raiders. In 1915, Governor James Ferguson told President Wilson of the "perilous and grave" conditions in South Texas.[38]

In addition to the escalating violence along the border, Texans increasingly saw Mexico as an area of operation for German agents. In April 1914, the United States attempted to stop a German arms shipment to the Huerta government in Veracruz, Mexico. After Huerta's resignation in 1914, Germany, in an attempt to provoke war between Mexico and the U.S., tried to have Huerta returned to power in Mexico. Germany believed that if the United States and Mexico went to war, the conflict would prevent the U.S. from entering World War I against Germany. Germany's restoration plan was foiled, however, when Huerta died in El Paso on January 14, 1916. Later, after the United States entered the war, American secret agents were successful in infiltrating the German spy ring in Mexico.

Among the American agents was William Neunhoffer, a Texan of German parentage. In May 1916, Neunhoffer, a practicing San Antonio lawyer, had been mobilized with his National Guard unit and sent to the Mexican border. His mastery of the German and Spanish languages attracted the attention of the Department of Justice, which then made Neunhoffer an agent. Neunhoffer traveled to Mexico City in June 1917 to investigate the activities of German nationals in Mexico. In 1918, Neunhoffer's efforts led to the arrest of German agent Lothar Witzke, who was arrested as he crossed the border into the United States. Witzke revealed all he knew about the German secret service, and the U.S. government sentenced him to death; only to be free him several years later.[39]

Meanwhile, Huerta's death hardly deterred Germany from trying to provoke war between the United States and Mexico.

Germany now turned to Villa, who seemed to offer a good prospect for provoking war. On January 10, 1916, at Santa Ysabel, in the province of Chihuahua, Villa's gang attacked a train carrying seventeen American mining engineers, killing all but one. The massacre threw the U.S. into an uproar and evoked a thunderous demand for intervention. So great was the rage of Texans when they learned of the massacre and what had been done to the bodies that martial law had to be declared in El Paso to keep vigilantes from crossing the border and killing Mexicans wholesale. Ex-president Theodore Roosevelt, receiving a petition from the border, called for the regular army to march into Mexico at once. Unbeknownst to Roosevelt, two German businessmen from El Paso had circulated the petition. President Wilson, in spite of the petition and uproar, refused to intervene in Mexico and give in to German desires.[40]

Wilson could not ignore Villa's next move. On the night of March 9, 1916, Villa and a group of five-hundred men entered Columbus, New Mexico, ransacking the city and killing sixteen Americans. Killing Americans in Mexico was one thing, but taking Americans lives on U.S. soil left Wilson with little choice. Following Villa's raid in New Mexico, President Wilson quickly ordered General John J. Pershing and ten thousand U.S. army troops into Mexico "for the sole purpose of capturing the bandit Villa." Interestingly enough, Pershing was of German descent, his family's name had been Pfoerschin before it was anglicized. The border crisis had pushed even the strongest Texas opponents of national preparedness to support intervention and the armed escalation. Wilson's aggressive actions with Mexico in the months prior to the general election certainly added to his popularity in Texas. After nine months in northern Mexico, Pershing's force early in 1917 returned to Fort Bliss in El Paso without Villa. Troops stationed along the border remained until 1920, long after American soldiers returned from Europe.[41]

As a result of the ongoing conflicts with Mexico, Texas well in advance of America's entry into World War I became a central training center for the nation's military. Texas businesses enjoyed the prosperity that resulted from the military buildup. Attitudes

Cartoon from the front page of the *Dallas Morning News,* March 2, 1917, following the revelation of the Zimmermann telegram.

sharpened among Texans as tensions along the border increased and newspapers focused on the upheaval in Mexico. Thus, by 1916 the Mexican Revolution had become the dominant issue in Texas. On the front pages of Texas daily newspapers and in the minds of everyday Texans, events associated with Mexico overshadowed the war across the Atlantic.

Once U.S. troops rolled into Mexico, the press in the German capital of Berlin was ecstatic. Germany now had the diversion it desired to keep the U.S. out of the European war. The most important effect of the Villa raid and the subsequent U.S.

intervention was the fact that Mexican President Venustiano Carranza adopted a pro-German position. Throughout the rest of 1916, Carranza attempted to cement his relations with Berlin with offers of Mexican-German cooperation. By the end of the year the German government was convinced that the only way it could win the European war was by waging unrestricted submarine warfare against Allied shipping, a tactic Berlin believed would bring the United States onto the Allied side. With Pershing still in Mexico and Carranza desperate for German aid, Berlin decided the time was right to goad the United States into a wider war with Mexico. German Secretary of State Arthur Zimmermann's solution was to offer the return to Mexico of "the lost territories of Texas, New Mexico, and Arizona" if Mexico and Germany would "make war together." Unfortunately for Zimmermann, the telegram was intercepted and deciphered by British intelligence.[42]

On March 1, 1917, President Wilson released the contents of the Zimmermann telegram to the U.S. press. By this point, Germany had resumed unrestricted submarine warfare and the telegram only added more fuel to the fire. The story hit the streets of Texas with the force of a political hurricane. Public indignation and alarm erupted across the state. The *Dallas Morning News* devoted its entire front page to the telegram. A front-page illustration entitled "The Temptation" pictured a horned German figure offering a bag of money to a man with a sombrero. The devil character pointed to a map picturing Texas, New Mexico, and Arizona. Shortly after the Zimmermann revelation, the *News* declared "this country is in reality at war now." The years of revolutionary activity in Mexico that produced fear and anxiety in the state now encouraged Texans to forsake their misgivings about intervention in foreign affairs. Instead of harboring reservations, Texans were now predisposed toward the idea of intervention against a foreign power. In some ways, the Zimmermann telegram did for Texas what the *Lusitania* sinking had done for the rest of the country.[43]

President Wilson, who campaigned in 1916 on his ability to keep the nation out of the European conflict, reversed his stance and in April 1917 asked Congress to declare war on Germany. The president listed the Zimmermann telegram and its threats against U.S. security among the reasons to abandon neutrality and enter the war. The president listed many other reasons, but the one that mattered to most Texans dealt with Germany's ties to the government in Mexico City. Many believed that Germany, based on its record in Mexico, posed a real threat as both an external and internal enemy. The *Dallas Morning News* said, "Germany had made war on us at home with torch and bomb." Texas newspapers interpreted anti-American sentiment in Mexico and among Mexican Americans as pro-German partiality. The newspaper articles reflected the prejudice toward Mexico and all persons of Hispanic descent that most Texans held. Even as the nation began to mobilize for the battle overseas, Texas editors urged people to keep a sharp eye on the Rio Grande: "War upon the fields of Texas is not beyond the powers of the imagination. Home guards may be needed."[44]

To those German Texans still opposed to the war, the *Houston Post* carried a stark warning. "German subjects or sympathizers," it said, "who speak in terms of contempt of the government and country whose hospitality they enjoy must expect unpleasant treatment." Disparaging remarks against the war effort, the paper implied, invited retaliation. When war came in April 1917, the desire for fighting was far from unanimous. Six senators, the most vocal of whom was Robert La Follette of heavily-German Wisconsin, and fifty representatives voted against the war resolution. Congressman Atkins Jefferson McLemore, the only Texan to vote against the war resolution, received tremendous criticism from Texas daily newspapers, which championed America's entry into World War I as a "defense of liberty." Nearly a million Texans volunteered for military service or entered the draft and several hundred thousand saw active service, including German Texans.[45]

Because of the events in Mexico and along the Rio Grande, Texans needed little persuasion to support the overseas war effort. For many German Texans, however, the next two years subjected them to tremendous scrutiny, attacks on the German language and culture, charges of disloyalty and treason, and violence.

5

The Anti-German Hysteria in Texas, 1917-1918

In 1917, two days before President Woodrow Wilson asked the United States Congress to declare war on Imperial Germany, Detroit Tigers' outfielder Ty Cobb, one of the great baseball players of his era, played an exhibition game in Texas. During the contest, Cobb slid into second base with spikes high and badly slashed Charles Lincoln "Buck" Herzog of the New York Giants. Cobb leaped on top of the bleeding Herzog and pounded him with his fists screaming, "German! German!" The incident was only a precursor of things to come in Texas and around the country.[1]

After President Wilson received the declaration of war he was seeking, the suspicion to which German Texans and German Americans had been subjected escalated into hysteria. The growing anti-German panic expressed itself in vigilante attacks and governmental actions that demanded explicit demonstrations of loyalty from German Americans and the suppression of symbols of German ethnicity. German Texans who failed to buy a Liberty Bond or to show sufficient respect for the war effort could expect to lose their jobs, be turned into the police, the federal Bureau of Investigation, or the Texas State Council of Defense. Bands of armed men broke into the homes of German families who were rumored to have a picture of the Kaiser on the walls. An emerging national security apparatus required thousands of German aliens to register with the police. As the panic took hold, the line between perceived disloyalty and ethnic cultural expression dissolved. At best, German Texans were seen as unsupportive of the war effort; at worst, they were saboteurs and agents of Imperial Germany working for Kaiser Wilhelm II in the United States.

The onslaught rendered virtually impossible the public expression of German-Texan ethnicity during and immediately after the war. Spoken German receded from Texas' streets. Associations suspended celebrations, including the Texas State *Saengerfest*, the most popular of German musical events. The National German-American Alliance itself collapsed in 1918. Public expressions of a German-Texan identity would only become possible again, in a limited way, in the early 1920s. By fostering the anti-German panic and the demand for unhyphenated "100 percent American" loyalty, the war induced many German Texans to retreat from an ethnic identity while helping to set the terms for a search for an alternative identity.[2]

Demands mounted that Germans as well as other Americans provide positive demonstrations of their loyalty. Behind the demands lay the frustration that government officials and patriotic groups felt with the state of public support for the war. The two parties knew that in April 1917 American public opinion was far from unified. The Allies might have garnered the sympathy of most Americans during the neutrality period, but actual participation in the conflict was another matter. Irish Americans as well as German Americans and pacifists as well as socialists had all loudly voiced their opposition to intervention. A substantial number of citizens were indifferent, if not hostile, to American entry when it came, and a majority, while willing to defer to their president, likely did not see the war in Wilsonian terms as a crusade for democracy. Enthusiasm was lacking in a country 3,000 miles from the scene of battle.[3]

The Wilson administration, therefore, "was compelled to cultivate—even to manufacture—public opinion favorable to the war effort." In early April, Wilson created the Committee on Public Information (CPI) to coordinate the government's domestic propaganda, and, in essence, sell its war aims to the American people.

Under the leadership of muckraking journalist George Creel, the CPI produced and distributed pamphlets, posters, short films, and press releases and recruited 75,000 citizens to serve as "Four-Minute Men" who would deliver brief, patriotic speeches in movie theaters, churches, and union halls. Texans felt the full force of the propaganda barrage.[4]

Initially, the CPI took a relatively liberal approach in its propaganda, seeking to persuade, in the best Progressive manner, by force of fact rather than fear. With time, however, the committee began to spread images of the German enemy as monstrous and bestial. The CPI supported films, made in full conjunction with Hollywood producers, with titles, such as *To Hell with the Kaiser!*, *The Prussian Cur*, *Wolves of Kultur*, *The Claws of the Hun*, and *The Kaiser, the Beast of Berlin*, that dehumanized Kaiser Wilhelm II and his people. A widely distributed committee poster that made its way to Texas in time for the Third Liberty Loan campaign of April and May 1918 depicted an American doughboy shielding a woman and child from a German soldier. Above this scene ran the appeal "Halt the Hun!" By the same token, CPI propaganda increasingly stressed a loyalty that left no room for political dissent. The loyalty messages reflected the views of Wilson, who tended to see wartime criticism of his administration as verging on disloyalty.[5]

For those left unenthusiastic by Creel's campaigns, there was always the remedy of coercion. Wilson had promised in April 1917 that, "if there should be disloyalty, it will be dealt with the firm hand of stern repression," and the government's repressive means mushroomed during the war. In June 1917, Congress passed the Espionage Act, which provided for $10,000 fines and twenty-year prison terms for those who obstructed recruiting, attempted to cause "insubordination, disloyalty, mutiny, or refusal of duty" in the armed forces, or made or conveyed "false reports or false statements with intent to interfere with the operation or success of the military or naval forces of the United States or to promote the success of its enemies." Another provision allowed the postmaster general, Albert Sidney Burleson, a Texan, to ban from the mails any matter "advocating or urging treason, insurrection, or forcible resistance to

91

"Halt the Hun!" American soldier pulling German soldier away from mother and child.

any law of the United States." The act's wording enabled federal officials, in effect, to punish both criticism of the administration's war policies and "individual casual or impulsive disloyal utterance." The repressive powers were then made explicit in a May 1918 amendment know as the Sedition Act. It outlawed "any disloyal, profane, scurrilous, or abusive language about the form of government of the United States, or the Constitution of the United States, or the flag of the United States," or language that might bring them "into contempt, scorn, contumely, or disrepute."[6]

The burden of enforcing the new statutes fell on the Justice Department, its relatively new Bureau of Investigation (BOI, later the FBI), established in 1909, and the United States attorneys who represented the department around the country. While it had several hundred agents, the BOI's director in the spring of 1917 had gladly accepted a businessman's offer to supplement the force with a "citizens' auxiliary" that would help to monitor enemy aliens. Quickly afterward, the American Protective League (APL) came into existence, and it eventually boasted a nationwide membership of 250,000 volunteers. U.S. Attorney General Thomas Gregory, also a Texan, described the APL as a "powerful patriotic organization" and "well-managed." In practice, APL "agents" spied on neighbors and fellow workers, opened mail, committed burglaries, and illegally arrested other Americans. Always operating under a cloak of secrecy, the agents became in 1918 the chief commandos in a series of extralegal and often violent "slacker raids" against supposed draft evaders.[7]

A variety of "patriotic" organizations also worked alongside federal authorities. These ranged from the National Security League (NSL) and the American Defense Society (ADS) to the Patriotic Order Sons of America and the Military Order of the Loyal Legion. The NSL and ADS in particular came to embody a "100 percent Americanism" that sought a "universal conformity organized through total national loyalty." Such loyalty was to be expressed through visible service and the abandonment of ethnically based cultural differences, especially German or German-American ones. By the summer and fall of 1917, the German *Vereine* and the German language became special targets of the patriotic groups. The NSL charged German-American organizations that had not publicly adopted resolutions against the German government's actions with aiding the enemy. The NSL and ADS both were agitating by the fall against the teaching of German, which the latter group said was "not a fit language to teach clean and pure American boys and girls."[8]

During the first six months of American involvement, Wilson, his administration's propaganda and investigatory arms, and the patriotic groups functioned together to intensify the "spy hysteria," and then added to it a hysteria over a malevolent German culture. Arguments in mass circulation magazines and newspapers for the suppression of the German-language press fueled the merging national climate of fear and hostility. By the fall of 1917, a "fierce hatred of everything German pervaded the country." Place names, food names, and musical offerings were altered to eliminate any trace of German content: Berlin, Iowa, became Lincoln; sauerkraut became liberty cabbage; and Beethoven was banned in Pittsburgh. German-language training was eliminated from school curricula in communities across the nation, patriotic ceremonies featured the burning of German books, and several states restricted the freedom to speak German in public. Acts of violence against German Americans mounted during the winter of 1917-1918 and peaked in April 1918 when a mob in Collinsville, Illinois, killed by hanging Robert Prager, an immigrant miner.[9]

As Prager's murder suggests, the anti-German panic flared most intensely in the Midwest, the region with the highest concentration of German immigrants and their descendents. Texas also endured extreme manifestations of the hysteria. In the state, people tarred and feathered, beat, and whipped German Texans.

The state councils of defense aimed to ensure that German Americans remained loyal to the United States during the war. The state councils were part of the Council of National Defense, created in August 1916 as a component of the preparedness movement. The Council itself comprised the secretaries of war, navy, agriculture, commerce, labor, and interior. The Council's original purpose was to coordinate relations between business and government for the production of food and munitions. The Council directed its first efforts to organizing itself and encouraging in every state the formation of defense councils, which in turn were to foster county councils. The latter, in turn, would bring about "the creation of community councils of defense in the [local] school district or a similar…unit of such small size that all the citizens in that locality can be reached through personal contact." After the United States entered the war in April 1917, the Council's organizational structure, as well as its original mission of economic coordination, was seen as obsolete. Instead, the resulting state councils, now largely reduced to propaganda organs, fostered vigilantism against local dissenters and "slackers."[10]

The state councils varied in function and authority. In some states, the governor simply appointed a panel of prominent citizens but gave them no authority commensurate with their assignment. In other states, especially in the Midwest where the German population was frequently perceived as a genuine threat to national unity, legislatures enacted statutes creating the councils and granted them sweeping legal powers, including the authority to subpoena witnesses and to punish for contempt. Council activity frequently centered on food and fuel production and conservation, mobilization of labor, and sanitation and public health problems. The network of local councils usually promoted the sale of government war bonds, collected contributions to the Red Cross, and coordinated activities of the Committee on Public Information on that level.[11]

In several states, however, the councils of defense were the direct agents of "superpatriotism." Subcommittees of the councils dealing with patriotism, "Americanization," and disloyal activities persecuted allegedly disloyal German-American citizens. The superpatriots notoriously used vigilante methods in their pursuit of "slackers" and "Kaiserism." Thousands of Americans learned firsthand the meaning of guilt by association, accusation by secret informers, the loss of free speech, terrorism, and violence.[12]

Governor James E. Ferguson appointed the Texas State Council of Defense in May 1917. Given only minimal funds by the state legislature, the state council relied upon dues assessed to each county council to fund its operations. O. E. Dunlap, the son of a large Mississippi slaveholder, and the president of a Waxahachie bank, was named the state chairman. Dunlap's activities, however, were minimal because state council secretary Judge J. F. Carl maintained the majority of the correspondence with the county councils. Carl had worked as a lawyer, teacher, and judge before becoming the only full-time officer of the Texas State Council of Defense. He expressed part of the council's mission when he said, "We must nip in the bud any expression of Kaiserism." By October 1917 Carl could boast that the "State Council of Defense has been doing good work in this direction. We have apprehended thirty-six German spies." The Texas council may have lacked the sense of direction that characterized state councils in the Midwest. Nonetheless, it was active through the work of its county councils.[13]

With over 240 county councils and about 15,000 community councils at its disposal, the Texas State Council of Defense carried out a wide range of activities. Some county councils advocated relaxed immigration restrictions in order to maintain agricultural production, as farmers feared production would decline without the labor of Mexican nationals during the war. Other county councils assumed the role of moral crusaders, monitoring the social conditions in communities near military bases. In West Texas, county councils focused on drought relief. Throughout the state, investigating and securing the loyalty of German Texans was a major concern, regardless of the means by which it was accomplished. The individual county councils often controlled the intensity and direction of their efforts against Germans, independent of the danger that members of the German-Texan community actually posed. Since county judges appointed the county council members, individual communities could not control the character of their councils. Nor did German surnames on the council ensure that German Texans would be free from pressures, though councils without members of obvious German heritage tended to be more intolerant. Regardless of their initial focus, the county councils soon became the suppressors of opposition to the war through a program of "Americanization."[14]

The Texas State Council of Defense in May 1917 alerted the Department of Justice to the activities of the Farmers and Laborers Protective Association (FLPA), resulting in the arrest of fifty-five men. The organization, established in 1915 for the advancement of farming and laboring men and for the cooperative purchase of various supplies, had several thousand members in north central and northwest Texas. In addition, several members of the FLPA belonged to the Socialist Party and the Industrial Workers of the World (IWW). Numerous Americans who viewed socialists and IWW members as "slackers" attacked both groups throughout the country due to the socialists' and IWW's opposition to the war.

Compounding the problems of many of the arrested FLPA members was the fact that some of them were of German descent. The accused were charged with conspiracy to resist the authority of the United States, to commit treason, to incite rebellion and insurrection, and to disrupt interstate commerce. Details soon emerged about a startling plan. According to witnesses, in the event that conscription became law, FLPA members planned to burn the city of Abilene, execute conscription officers, blow up railroad tracks and bridges, and seize telephone and telegraph wires. Members were instructed to fight conscription to the death, not allow foodstuffs to reach the government, seek union with the IWW, and organize Negro lodges. Moreover, there was an allegation that FLPA members had even threatened to assassinate the President of the United States.[15]

A trial for the fifty-five arrested FLPA members followed. Shocked by the allegations, many Texans looked forward to the trial, which was held in the U.S. District Court at Abilene during the fall of 1917. Defense attorney William Hawley Atwell would later call the six-week trial "one of the most remarkable trials held in America." Potential jurors who had read *The Rebel*, a Texas socialist newspaper operated by German-Texan E. R. Meitzen, or any other socialist paper, were dismissed. Clearly, the prosecution viewed the FLPA and its members as part of a national socialist effort to disrupt war preparations. At the pretrial conclusion, Judge George Whitfield Jack told the jury, "Either we must fight Germany and Europe now, or in American later."[16]

Defense lawyers attempted to counter the charges against the FLPA members. They called witnesses to the stand who testified to the good character and general reputation of many of the defendants.

William Bergfeld of Weinert, a government mail carrier, became the key FLPA defendant during the trial. Born in Seguin, the twenty-eight-year-old Bergfeld testified that his father was German and had come to the United States in the 1870s. At no time, Bergfeld claimed, did he advocate rebellion against the United States, opposition to its laws, or resistance to conscription. Most importantly, Bergfeld denied that he had said the President ought to be killed. At the conclusion of the trial, the jury brought in a verdict of acquittal for Bergfeld and all but three of the defendants: the FLPA organizer, the group's president, and its secretary. The three received sentences of six years at Leavenworth federal penitentiary in Kansas.[17]

The anti-German hysteria of World War I also injected itself into Texas politics and German Texans paid a political price. German Texans had been a visible group of Governor James E. Ferguson's supporters and had backed him in the 1914 and 1916 elections, largely because of Ferguson's opposition to statewide prohibition. Ferguson's German supporters, however, proved a liability to him and Ferguson to them. In 1917, Ferguson faced impeachment charges due to his ongoing battle with the University of Texas and problems over his personal finances. Ferguson had vetoed practically the entire $1.6 million University appropriation because the board of regents had failed to remove several faculty members who the governor found objectionable and because the board had failed to carry out the governor's suggestion to abolish fraternities and sororities. A Travis County grand jury indicted Ferguson in connection to his university dealings and, in addition, his misapplication of public funds. In July 1917, a special session of the state legislature convened for the purpose of the impeaching the governor. After investigation of the charges against Ferguson, including the revelation that the governor had received $156,500 from a secret source that he refused to reveal, both the House and Senate voted for impeachment. When the charges were formally submitted on August 25, Ferguson left office and lieutenant governor William P. Hobby became acting governor.[18]

Not to be deterred by his ouster, Ferguson immediately announced his candidacy for governor in 1918. But first he wanted to rest. Soon after he left the governorship, Ferguson moved his family back to Temple where he established the *Ferguson Forum*, a small newspaper that he used as a mighty club against his enemies. Prohibitionists dubbed the paper "The Ferguson For Rum," charging it was merely a device for getting campaign funds from breweries.

The impeachment trial and its aftermath helped to reveal ties between the governor, the German-dominated brewers, and the National German-American Alliance. Wild accusations flew during the 1918 campaign concerning the source of the $156,500 loan Ferguson had received. The backers of Ferguson's opponent, William P. Hobby, claimed that the $156,500 loan had been given to Ferguson by the German Kaiser in return for opposition to the war effort. Cartoons soon showed the Kaiser and his advisors pointing to a map of Texas saying, "Yah, yah. Our German-American Alliance helped elect a Governor of that province in 1914."[19]

Other literature connected Ferguson's friends, such as former University of Texas professor Lindley M. Keasbey, to the German cause. Fired by the university in 1917 because of his anti-war activities, Keasbey, a former student claimed, had entered into a plan with Ferguson in 1914 to "Germanize the university." In return for originating Ferguson's land tenant plank and securing his election as governor, Keasbey was to have been made president of the University of Texas. From that position, it was alleged that Keasbey intended to hand down German *Kultur* to the people of the Southwest. Called a "Master of the Official German View Point" and decorated by Kaiser Wilhelm II, Keasbey was to further schemes of "*Kultur*" in Texas through its educational institutions, which the German-American Alliance sought to control, and through the Kaiser himself by the German leader's "exchange professor" scheme. In his accusation, the same former student also said that the safety of the nation "must be guarded against the insidious German propaganda." We must

Cartoon showing Kaiser Wilhelm II pointing to a map of Texas (Note the Zimmermann Plot rolled up).

"loyally devote ourselves to the cause," he concluded, "and banish every sinister German influence from the state, barring from office those who are tainted with Germanism and all who welcome its political support in Texas."[20]

Ferguson's association with German Texans during the crucible of war posed other problems for the former governor. In addition to being opposed by prohibitionists, Ferguson also came under fire from women voters, largely due to his statement: "Women's place is in the home," but also because of Ferguson's connection with Germans. Texas women warned that a victory by Ferguson in the 1918 Democratic primary backed by the "German brewery" would result in "a reign of political anarchy" and that Texas would become "a land despoiled and helpless" because the "beer barons of German name and sympathy will have elected their friends." In March 1918, the state granted women suffrage in the primaries and many of the suffragists found the German vote particularly appalling. "The Hun" was "the worst of our foes" said Austin suffragist Jane Y. McCallum. Governor Hobby remarked, "While the brave American boys were fighting the Huns in Germany with bullets, the brave American women were fighting the Huns in Texas with ballots." Former governor Thomas M. Campbell, speaking on behalf of Hobby, said "upon the women of Texas rests the duty of overcoming" the "evil influence of German propaganda." Campbell believed that "Every slacker and every pro-German will vote for James E. Ferguson." The people of Texas should be able to "lie down and sleep at night," he added, "without fear of awakening next morning to find that Texas had been delivered to the German Kaiser."[21]

The Democratic primary in 1918 was one of the most colorful in the state's history. Both Hobby and Ferguson tried to use the anti-German panic of World War I to their advantage. Speaking in Sweetwater on June 17, Hobby told the crowd, "No pro-German in all Texas is going to cast his vote for me, and I do not want his vote. If I can not be elected by the votes of true blue Americans I do not want that office." Three days later in Cisco, Hobby said, "the German-American Alliance made no mistake when it interested itself in the election of Ferguson in 1914 as sworn testimony shows it did." Again and again, Hobby reminded voters that Ferguson had accepted $156,500 from a source he refused to reveal.[22]

Ferguson countered Hobby by attacking the loyalty of German Texans, apparently in a move to distance himself from charges of "Kaiserism." Speaking in Sherman on July 18, Ferguson criticized Governor Hobby for appointing Jake Wolters, a "full-blooded German," as brigadier general of the state militia and for being introduced to South Texas audiences by Senator F. C. Weinert, "another full-blooded German." Both Wolters and Weinert were members of highly respected German-Texan families that were noted for their patriotism and loyalty. Wolters and Weinert resented the fact that the former governor would attack them. Wolters fired back in a statement: "I was taught from infancy to hate the Hohenzollern dynasty and all of the Prussian autocracy. . . . Jim Ferguson's criticism of Governor Hobby and his statement about Senator Weinert and myself are an insult to every American of German extraction in the United States." Wolters added, "Men of Texas" the "support of Jim Ferguson means the support of the Kaiser. . . . No American of German extraction" can "claim to be an American and give his support to Jim Ferguson." The remarks suggest that Ferguson's election ploy backfired as afterward Wolters brought many German friends into the Hobby camp.[23]

The Democratic primary went as expected. With drys, women, alumni of the University of Texas, and some Germans against Ferguson, Hobby easily won. He carried 234 counties and received 461,479 votes, nearly seventy percent of the state's total vote. Ferguson carried twenty counties, mostly the smaller counties of South and Southeast Texas, and received 217,012 votes. Despite his negative comments towards German Texans, Ferguson still carried six of the traditionally German counties and garnered more votes than Hobby in the German counties combined, suggesting that a majority of German Texans were still not ready to vote for a prohibition candidate. A week following the primary, sources revealed that Ferguson's $156,500 loan had come from two Texas brewers, L. A. Adoue of Galveston and Otto Wahrmund of San Antonio, and not as some people suspected from the Kaiser or the German-American Alliance as was alleged. The two brewers testified that they had loaned Ferguson the money because he needed it and because he had promised that there would be no change in the prohibition status in Texas. The revelation, however, came too late to help Ferguson.[24]

In the weeks and months immediately following the United States' declaration of war on Germany, Texans of German descent attempted to show that they were loyal to the United States. The *Katholische Rundschau* told its readers to stand by the President.[25] The *Neu-Braunfelser Zeitung* stressed that the United States' entry into the war applied to all American citizens, regardless of the fact of whether or not they were of German origin.[26] In April 1917, The *Giddings Deutsches Volksblatt* printed the *Star Spangled Banner* on the front page and told its readers that the time had come for German Texans to sever their ties with Germany.[27] German-Texan Jake Wolters, who had supported Hobby for governor, urged Germans to stand by the President. The *Fredericksburger Wochenblatt* urged its readers to silence those who wished to criticize the American government.[28]

On April 9, 1917, the citizens of Austin held a loyalty parade. Several German Texans participated including two hundred marchers of the Sons of Hermann and the Austin *Saengerrunde*. Judge Rudolph Kleberg of German descent expressed loyalty to the President of the United States and ventured to say that practically all American citizens of German extraction were of the same sentiment: "I don't think that there are any traitors in Austin," he said. "It is the duty of every American citizen to uphold the banner of liberty. I am proud of my German descent but still prouder of my Americanism. We have a duty to perform," Kleberg concluded, "and we should act coolly, courageously, and manly."[29]

Both New Braunfels and Fredericksburg, cities founded by German Texans, showed support for the American cause by holding loyalty parades in May 1917.[30] *Das Wochenblatt* reported that the funeral of a German-Texan soldier ended with the singing of *America*.[31] In Westphalia, Texas, Germans even burned German-language books to show their allegiance to the United States.[32]

German Texans proved their loyalty through the toughest test of all—the battlefield. On March 5, 1918, a German Texan from Fredericksburg, First Lieutenant Louis J. Jordan, became the first American officer to die in battle. He lost his life near Ludesville, France. When he learned of his assignment to Europe, Jordan supposedly vowed, "I will bring back the head of the Kaiser on a platter." He distinguished himself in other walks of life as well. He was a great football player. Considered one of the best linemen in the South as a guard at the University of Texas from 1911 to 1914, Walter Camp named Jordan to the All-American team. Jordan also served as the team's captain one year. He earned an engineering degree in 1915. Immediately following his death, the Texas House passed a resolution of sympathy for Jordan's relatives.[33]

German Texans had their supporters as well—oftentimes other, more prominent, Germans. San Antonio lawyer C. A. Goeth wrote, "I am firmly convinced the criticism and suspicion to which [German Texans] are subjected . . . is not well founded, is harmful, and is in the way of bringing about the much desire complete harmonizing of the citizens of German descent with that of other descent." Goeth believed it was "very important that our country refrain from continuously treating and addressing them as a separate class." He argued that the "great mass of citizens of German descent living in Texas are native Texans" and "they have never been in Germany, and have no reason to form an attachment for the German government." Furthermore, German Texans were "meeting the very rigid test of their Americanism."[34]

William A. Wurzbach wrote to J. F. Carl, secretary of the Texas State Council of Defense, concerning the patriotic activities of the Sons of Hermann in San Antonio. He boasted that the Sons of Hermann "have already invested $1600 in war savings stamps, and a great majority of them are members of the Red Cross. . . . They are good and loyal citizens."[35]

Despite public displays of their loyalty, German Texans soon came under attack from their neighbors. The Guadalupe County Council of Defense (CCD) advised Secretary Carl on the peculiar situation in Seguin: "The majority of our population are of German parentage, but with the exception of a very few, they know nothing of their father's country, and are loyal Americans, and they are quite sensitive when they are called anything but Americans." The Guadalupe CCD felt that "some who are of English parentage are taking advantage of just such an occasion as we have at present, to say the most insulting things about those of German parentage thinking and feeling that they have the U. S. Government back of them in

Falls County men, on train, departing for induction in the military, Marlin, Texas. Graffiti on side of train reads: "To Hell With the Kaiser." *Institute of Texan Cultures at UTSA, 103-0323. Loaned by Kenny Parnell.*

using such expressions, and of course, as no one dares to stop them." In addition, "one of our weekly papers," the council noted, "takes advantage of the seeming protection of the government and persists in writing articles . . . that no one of German blood is an American or a true American." The council concluded by calling the condition in Seguin "deplorable."[36]

Secretary Carl, in his response to the council, noted: "The position of citizens of German descent, or of German birth, is a very trying one at this time; for the thoughtless, suspicious, and irresponsible people too often take advantage of the situation to vent their personal prejudices or spleen. This should never be done." Carl added, "There is no better citizen than the loyal American citizen of German birth or descent, and the man who would take advantage of the war situation and the prejudices necessarily resulting from it, to injure, harass, or mortify the man of German descent is himself not a good citizen."[37]

Regardless of Carl's assurances, the Americanizers were dead set on eliminating any trace of Germanism from Texas culture. The

Victoria CCD compared Germanism to a children's game saying, "take it off or we'll knock it off."[38] One informant stated that if the agents of the government knew how some of the Germans in Coryell City talked "they would hang a hundred of them." The informant wanted the German Texans investigated saying, "let us show no leniency, there is no ground for double dealings in times like this" and "right now there is evidently something going on among the Germans."[39] The Bell CCD thought it could bring all "except the Kaiser-struck Germans" into line.[40]

In some cases, German Texans even came under attack from other ethnic groups within the state. Because his community contained several pro-Germans, a Czech man from Fayetteville sought a position on his local county council. Ed. W. Knesek, a member of the Czech fraternal benefit society, S. P. J. S. T. (Slavonic Benevolent Order of the State of Texas), said, "My wish is either to make [the Germans] good Americans or have them put behind bars."[41]

Lockhart sources reported Charles Kreuz (founder of Kreuz's market, named in 2006 one of the outstanding barbeque restaurants in Texas, according to *Texas Monthly* magazine) to the Texas State Council of Defense for several comments Kreuz had made in September 1917. Noting that several ministers in town had insulted the German race, Kreuz asked to be removed from the rolls of the local Presbyterian church. He also felt that America had no right to make war on "his people," the German race, since Germany had not invaded the United States. Kreuz said that he had little sympathy for the Americans who lost their lives on the *Lusitania* because they had been warned not to take passage. Kreuz said, "if he were in Germany he would be accorded more freedom than in this so called Free America" because in the United States, Americans "could talk as they please about the Germans" and the Germans "dared not open their mouths in defense." Furthermore, Kreuz stated everything printed in the "*New York Herald, New York Times,* and the *San Antonio Express* is all a pack of lies" and the only "true and correct news" is in a German-language newspaper printed in the United States. In addition, Kreuz said, "all of the American daily papers of any note are owned by English money and that the English allow nothing printed in them except with their approval and that everything pertaining to the war is censored by them." Records do not indicate what, if any, action the Texas State Council of Defense took against Kreuz.[42]

County councils of defense from across Texas reported almost daily on what they perceived as pro-German or disloyal activity. They reported, for example, German-Texan farmers who fed wheat to livestock, refused to sell wheat, and plowed up good wheat.[43] A German pastor in Castro County, one council stated, had three brothers in the German army.[44] Authorities in Kerrville arrested a German ranchman for threatening to kill President Wilson.[45] A city marshal arrested a former soldier of the German army in Taylor. The heavily armed German had a rifle, 150 rounds of ammunition, two German swords, and three pistols in his car. Police then took the German veteran to Austin and turned him over to federal officers.[46] A man from Karnes County indicated that within the county "pro-German sentiment is in evidence to an alarming extent."[47] The Bosque CCD reported that Germans were holding secret meetings near Clifton.[48] Likewise, officials investigated reports of secret meetings among Germans in Mason.[49] In South Texas, a fellow German Texan reported that Germans from Karnes City and Kenedy were supposedly holding meetings and making maps "for an ill purpose."[50] A captain in the Texas Rangers wrote that the section of the country around Karnes City, Texas, "is full of Germans who are not loyal to this government."[51] In addition, the Karnes CCD turned in several Germans from the county for disloyal utterances towards the government.[52] Some German Texans caused suspicion by "riding the trains day and night," so much so that a county food administrator felt they needed "a detective put after them." The administrator added, "We are going to bust up this rotten bunch."[53] The Aransas CCD and Bell CCD wanted to know if displaying a portrait of the Kaiser in a business or residence was a sign of disloyalty.[54] The Grimes CCD recommended that all Germans who wanted to travel should have to get certificates from their home authorities or else "lock them up." The council further advised there ought to be "men at the depots throughout the country to attend to

this matter vigilantly."[55]   The Aransas CCD was concerned that
Germans were planning on placing bombs in the shipyard in
Rockport.[56] It is not clear how many of the cases led to formal
prosecutions, but the experience of being investigated could be
intimidating enough.

The anti-German hysteria spread from the superpatriots to
affect the entire state. Many Texans believed and reported that
German spies were everywhere—working in secret, planning acts of
sabotage, and gathering intelligence for Imperial Germany. German
Texans, who only a few years earlier had been accepted members of
American society, were now supposedly employing diabolical
ingenuity in the United States on behalf of Kaiser Wilhelm II.
Nurtured on the belief that that Texans had to loathe Germany in
order for the nation to be fully mobilized, anti-German feelings had
been fostered more or less unconsciously by government policies, but
intentionally by many private persons and local county councils of
defense. Texans were encouraged to make war on German culture
and to watch the Germans and their institutions carefully for signs of
subversion. Suspicion was heightened by the fact that German spies
and disloyal German Texans were everywhere but could not, in fact,
be found anywhere.

Not surprisingly, cities in Texas founded by Germans
received special attention. A men's tailor from New Braunfels
reported "a strong pro-German feeling among the people of this
county," but he believed that in the course of another year "the
greater part of the German people will be solidly behind our
government."[57] Someone reported a German teacher that resided in
New Braunfels for calling the American flags displayed on the stage of
a theatre "rags."[58] Someone informed on another German in New
Braunfels for having a German flag stretched over an American flag
in his parlor.[59] Curiously enough, the reports from New Braunfels
came from persons with German surnames.

The Kendall CCD, likewise, described the condition of their
county: "This county is largely German. . . . When the war broke on
the world [the Germans here] all whooped for the Kaiser and the
'Fatherland.' There was no doubt as to where their sympathies lay.

Everything that emanated from pro-German propaganda sources was true. Everything else was a lie." The council added, "When America entered the war . . . everyman of German birth or origin was fighting for Germany. . . . Some of them are still pro-German." One member of the county council, himself a German Texan, summed up his feelings, "To be truthful my heart is with Germany, but, my mind tells me I must be for America now, for America is my country."[60] The council chairman later tendered his resignation to Secretary Carl of the state council because someone in the county remarked to him, "the people in the county of German origin have the idea you are against them."[61]

Some county councils from heavily German counties came under fire for not being active. A district judge from Johnson City suspected the Blanco, Mason, and Gillespie county councils of defense of being indifferent to the war and inactive.[62] The Llano CCD indicated that a "disloyalty spirit" was dominant in portions of Mason County, most notably in the town of Mason.[63] The Martin CCD found itself in an embarrassing situation for allegedly appointing two pro-Germans to its council: "These men have made themselves obnoxious as German sympathizers." According to the local council, the men refused to sign Food Cards (for food conservation), discouraged the purchasing of Liberty Bonds, and made a joke of patriotic demonstrations. Removing the Germans proved difficult because they were two of the most prominent businessmen in the area and many people were afraid to challenge them. Yet, the council said, "They must be removed. Our council is hopelessly crippled until they are."[64] After their removal, a council member continued to struggle with the decision. They "have been my friends for fifteen years. But I believe I am ashamed to tell young men that it is right for them to go to the trenches and fight the Germans there if I am going to be afraid to fight the intrigue at home."[65]

The American Defense Society wanted to know what Secretary Carl and the state council of defense was doing to stamp out German propaganda in Texas. The ADS felt by making public what was being done "would be a potent stimulus and incentive to patriotism." The ADS asked, "what measures . . . have been or will be taken by you in your state for the removal of German from your schools, suppression of the German newspapers or other steps for the extermination of the German propaganda?"[66]

Names were the most obvious evidence of German ethnicity and soon a name-changing campaign swept Texas. A lawyer from Houston thought the state council of defense should take up the matter of changing the names of German-sounding communities. The lawyer said the communities "bear the trademark 'Made in Germany'" and should be given "names that are thoroughly American." The communities that came to mind were Germantown, Rhineland, Hochheim, and Pflugerville. "The names are suggestive of the German-American Alliance," he said, "and the residents of these towns themselves, would no doubt welcome the change suggested."[67] Indeed, several German communities, businesses, and other items bearing a German name changed during the war. At the request of its German citizens, for example, the northwest Texas town of Brandenburg changed its name to Old Glory. In Houston, German Street became Canal Street. During the war, King William Street in San Antonio changed its name to Pershing Avenue, but, of course, changed it back after the war. The Goliad CCD recommended that Germantown, Texas, change its name to Schroeder after Paul Schroeder the first person from that community to die in France during the war. Schroeder, a second-generation German-Texan, is about as German a name as the Germantown it replaced.[68]

Yet, if it was somewhat less harsh in Texas, the anti-German panic was harrowing nonetheless, traveling an arc similar to that of the hysteria nationally. In Port Arthur, a group beat several men at a German *Verein* Club then forcibly closed the facility, painting over the door, "Closed Forever."[69] In Palestine, fellow employees severely whipped a German-born man and made him kiss the United States flag.[70] A German Methodist preacher escaped a lynching in Shamrock for allegedly baptizing an infant in the name of Kaiser Wilhelm II.[71] In Bishop, Texas, German Lutheran pastor, A. E. Moebus, got whipped with a leather strap for supposedly, but very

110

unlikely, holding a German "revival service" on the same night as a Liberty Loan rally.[72] A mob sought to tar and feather a German-Texan farmer picking cotton in the field but retreated when they found he had thoughtfully included a shotgun in his pick sack.[73] Rioters took six farmers of German descent in Brenham from their wagons and flogged them for refusing to join the Red Cross. After the whipping, the Germans reconsidered and joined the Red Cross.[74] A neighbor shot and killed a prominent German farmer from Mart, Texas.[75] In Gonzales, Texas, people took a German merchant and flogged him with buggy whips from his own store because he refused to hang Red Cross signs.[76] Citizens took a pro-German man in Lufkin to the main street crossing, tied him to a post, and whipped him. In the same town, an alien enemy asked to be put in jail for protection after townspeople threatened him with a whipping.[77] After making derogatory comments about the Red Cross, a German Texan was "given a good drubbing," yet the Austin CCD felt "they should have beat him to death."[78] In Luling, citizens tarred and feathered a man for making disparaging remarks to Red Cross solicitors and gave him twelve hours to get out of town. In Fayette County, two assailants shot and killed a German Texan, pulled his wife from the car, and beat her. The dead man had told his mother not to buy Liberty Bonds. Two of the killers were from the same German-Texan community, obviously eager to prove their loyalty.[79]

Despite these violent, vigilante actions, the Austin CCD complained that the councils of defense were not being tough enough on Germans. If "we are not to handle these unpatriotic pro-Germans without gloves," it announced, "we had as well close shop and wait until the end of the war."[80]

The shock of the violence had a lasting legacy. Not only did it threaten the lives of individual German Texans, but the violence, or threat of violence, also created a situation that rendered any public expression of Germanness impossible during the war, and problematic thereafter. Granted, in some areas of the state, German Texans went virtually untouched, but in others, Germans faced an almost daily possibility of intimidations, threats, or violence. Some German Texans huddled in fear and complied with all humiliating demands. A few Germans attacked German music and art. Many German-Texan parents decided that from then on they would speak only English in their family circles. Nevertheless, as it became apparent that law enforcement agencies and courts were not likely to protect victims of the violence, some vulnerable German Texans prepared to defend themselves. According to historian Frederick C. Luebke, as early as December 1917, many leaders of the German-American community realized that they had to fight back if their identity and institutions were to be preserved.[81]

The situation in Texas became serious enough that in June 1918 the Council of National Defense cautioned the Texas State Council of Defense in the matter of handling the German element in the state. "While we must not condone in the slightest any seditious or disloyal utterances or actions," the Council of National Defense said, "we must be careful to avoid an unreasonable and drastic procedure which will turn into active hostility sentiments which might be at worst passive." We do not want to be "stampeded into the very methods which we are fighting so desperately to drive out of the world."[82]

The German-language newspapers in Texas desperately tried to fight back against what they considered unreasonable harassment. The *Fredericksburger Wochenblatt* criticized the selectiveness of the attack on all things German. Americanizers could ban the performance of German music while utilizing German contributions to medicine.[83] *Das Wochenblatt* denounced politicians who questioned the loyalty of German Texans in order to advance their political careers.[84] The paper also grew tired of the political atmosphere in which some German Texans felt that it was necessary to denounce the German people to prove their patriotism.[85]

In an attempt to reason with the German population of Texas, some authorities called upon prominent German Texans whose loyalty was without question to speak to those of German descent. In April 1917, a leader of a loyalty day rally asked Rudolph Kleberg, a German-Texan, to speak at a celebration drawing on the populations of Yorktown, Nordheim, and Kenedy. The requestor wrote, "As you know our people are largely German either by birth or extraction, and are unanimously of the opinion that you are the man to make us talk."[86]   In May 1918, others asked Kleberg, a "Four Minute Man," to speak in Milam County since sections of the county were "largely populated by German emigrants and their descendents" and the county "has never met its quota on any Liberty Bond issue" or Red Cross quotas.[87]   Kleberg spoke again in Schulenburg on June 16.[88] Kleberg's actions soon drew the admiration of his friends. One wrote, "I watch with pleasure and note with pride the noble work you are doing in this great struggle and I know your efforts are being appreciated, especially by Americans of German name and of German birth."[89]   Kleberg wrote in a letter appearing in the *Austin American-Statesman*, "We are not fighting the Germany of Goethe, Schiller, Heine, and Kant" but the "Imperial German Government . . . which is fighting for its existence against the hosts of democracy."[90] Rudolph Kleberg perhaps best summed up the conflict that many German Texans were feeling during the war when he said, "I . . . am proud of my German ancestry and hope that Germany will emerge from this world struggle with honor and glory; but I am prouder still that I am an American."[91]

Wealthy German Texans who refused to buy Liberty Bonds upset the councils most of all. "These people plead poverty; this is a lie," a council stated. "They have over three hundred acres of the finest kind of land." Councils would assign quotas for the amount of Liberty Bonds residents should buy despite the fact that the purchase of bonds was, in theory, voluntary. In the case of German Texans, those who did not fulfill their quotas were considered disloyal or worse traitors. A German from Valley Mills claimed he had no money to subscribe to Liberty Bonds, but the local council indicated that the German had between $300 and $400 in the bank and that "this scoundrel needs attention badly."[92] Informants turned in a German man who owned "two thousand acres of land" yet only gave five dollars to the Red Cross.[93] The Austin CCD stated that a prosperous German farmer assigned a quota of $700 spent "not one damn cent" on Liberty Bonds. The council further complained that if their citizens knew that subscriptions to Liberty Bonds "were entirely voluntary the amounts of bonds sold wouldn't buy a decent loaf of bread." The council went on: "If a man is able to help this government and does not do so within the full limit of his ability, he can profess his Americanism all day long but he will never make me believe he is a loyal American."[94]   The Anheuser-Busch Brewing Association, attempting to show its loyalty, subscribed to a million dollar Liberty Bond, and placed $25,000 of it in Waco.[95] Authorities on the Texas Gulf coast reported two German-Texan farmers and stockmen living near Seadrift, Texas, for giving small amounts to the government. The source stated that both men were "very wealthy" but one had *only* purchased $250 of Liberty Bonds and the other purchased *only* $100 of War Savings Certificates.[96] Distressed over a poor harvest that would leave him unable to purchase the subscribed amount of Liberty Bonds, a German-Texan farmer in Fayette County shot himself to death.[97]

The Council of National Defense investigated a report that German-language newspapers were telling Germans they did not have to buy Liberty Bonds. The Council admitted that the "statement is, of course, true in the strictest sense; there is and should be no compulsion of the individual to buy Liberty Bonds."[98] Yet, German Texans who did not agree to purchase bonds, or who advised others not to buy them, faced the threat of violence or the fact that they would be reported to authorities. One man told a Liberty Bond solicitor, "There was no use of him buying Liberty Bonds as Germany would win this war and the bonds would not be worth anything and he would therefore lose his money." An African-American cook stated, "The negroes would be free and equal to white people when Germany won this war."[99] Goliad County officials stated that a German man advised people to continue to use the German language, told German Texans not to buy War Savings Stamps, and led Germans "in the ways of the Kaiser."[100]

The Bosque CCD turned in the heavily German community of Womack to the United States Bureau of Investigation because the residents did not participate in the U.S. Family Pledge Card Campaign. The council further remarked, "the German element is so strong that we found it impossible to get an American to handle the Federal business in connection with the Food Administration's work."[101]   A council later reported that the same Germans in Womack gave a big ball in honor of the Kaiser.[102] The council then placed four Germans from Womack under oath and questioned them about disloyal acts, the hording of grain, and restrictions on their tenants' crops. The Germans agreed to take out more Liberty Bonds, increase their acreage in wheat, and allow their tenants to sow more grain.[103]

Typical of many county councils of defense was a questionnaire distributed by the Bosque CCD. In order to obtain information for the government, every loyal citizen was to answer such questions as: "Did you subscribe to the first issue of Liberty Bonds? How much?" "Have you bought any Thrift or War Savings Stamps and will you continue to buy?" "Have you contributed to the Red Cross? Estimated amount?" "Do you know of any disloyal acts or statement by anyone?"[104]   Even when they purchased Liberty Bonds or War Savings Stamps, many councils accused German Texans of being unpatriotic and just buying them out of necessity. The Martin CCD indicated that Germans purchased Liberty Bonds "for the same reason that a drowning man grasped the straw."[105]

One manifestation of the anti-German sentiment of the times was ridiculing German Texans who had not purchased sufficient Liberty Bonds by painting their businesses, homes, or in some cases the Germans themselves yellow. Americanizers painted yellow two stores of men who refused to buy bonds in Denison. The vandals wrote, "If you are not with us you are against us" in large black letters.   They also placed placards on the storefronts with the inscription, "He says he will not help our government. He says he will not buy a bond. Shall he?"[106]   Austin suffragist Jane Y. McCallum recalled painting a German-Texan attorney's premises yellow after he refused to participate in the Third Liberty Loan drive.[107] In Palestine, men painted a "slacker" yellow.[108]

Despite the seriousness of the times, some of the things that councils reported German Texans for bordered on the ridiculous. The Fayette CCD turned in a man for not attending a Bastille Day celebration in La Grange.[109]   In Ozona, a German man needed "looking after" because he had studied at a German university yet worked as a "common blacksmith" and had a "very peculiar walk."[110] The Denton CCD informed on a German Texan because he looked "like a royal prince."[111] One man felt it necessary to enclose that an alien enemy German Lutheran preacher had a "cork leg."[112] Lipscomb authorities indicated that a German man became indignant when someone played the anti-German song, "Swatting the Hun," on their Victrola.[113] A man informed on a German from Waring after he called George Washington a drunkard.[114] Someone alerted authorities about a German Texan who supposedly buried explosive mines all over West Texas.[115] The Kleberg CCD revealed that a German businessman wore a watch "with all kinds of German characters upon it."[116] Two German women from San Antonio were allegedly getting tablets from a German doctor in Houston. According to the source, the "tablets were to be used on the young men of this country."[117]

In February 1918, Secretary J. F. Carl wrote to Governor Hobby requesting that candidates for office be required to take a loyalty pledge. He felt this would cut off "some of these fellows in thickly populated German communities who make themselves popular by obstructing the government and its methods." The governor replied that he felt the pledge would not be necessary for everyone, "but in event where one is challenged this should be required."[118]

In early 1918, the state legislature began debate on House Bill 15, which would make all criticism, even a remark made in casual conversation, of America's entry into the war; of America's continuation in the war; of America's government in general; of America's army, navy, or marine corps; of their uniforms; or of the American flag; a criminal offense punishable by terms of two to twenty-five years—and would give any citizen in Texas the power of arrest under the statute. Furthermore, a person could not display, or have in possession, a flag of any nation with which the United States was at war (i.e. Germany). With fist-waving crowds shouting in the House galleries above, legislators raged at the Kaiser and at the Germans in Texas whom they called his "spies" (one legislator claimed that the American flag had been hauled down in

Fredericksburg Square and replaced by the German double eagle) in an atmosphere that an observer called a "maelstrom of fanatical propaganda." Sam Johnson, father of future president Lyndon Baines Johnson, made a speech—remembered with admiration fifty years later by fellow members—urging defeat of Bill 15. The speech did not hurt Johnson politically, it could only increase his popularity among the Germans of his Gillespie County district. Almost singlehandedly, he succeeded in persuading the committee to delete from it the section that would have given any citizen the power of arrest. W. A. Trenckmann, editor of Austin's *Das Wochenblatt*, later wrote: "At a time when hate propaganda . . . was at its worst . . . he showed courage and fidelity to the trust which [we] put in him. [He] proved himself a true friend in those dark days when so many who had owed their success in public life to their German fellow citizens proved to be their worst enemies." Despite Johnson's opposition, in March 1918, the Thirty-Fifth Texas Legislature passed House Bill 15, it became known as the "Hobby Loyalty Bill."[119]

To enforce the Texas Loyalty Bill, Adjutant General James A. Harley, under the direction of Governor Hobby, appointed a special force of one thousand "Loyalty Rangers" for "the sole purpose of ferreting out disloyalty in Texas and making arrests when evidence justifies." Consisting of at least three men from each county in the state, the Loyalty Rangers acted as a secret service and received no pay, but the adjutant general said the "work is a patriotic duty and privilege." One man from Kenedy applied to be a Loyalty Ranger, saying "I am surrounded by Mexicans and some Germans who some of their neighbors believe would gladly commit overt acts of disloyalty if they only dared do so." A Houston man was willing to serve because "many Germans live in this part of the city and a few are pro-German sympathizers." A La Grange man wrote to Governor Hobby pleading, "Give me the right to help our country run down the disloyalty among the German speaking people of Fayette County. I have heard a good many remarks that if an American would say in Germany he would get shot for." The Loyalty Rangers concentrated on the Texas-Mexico border and German areas of the state. Because

117

of the vigilante and undisciplined nature of the force, the Texas legislature quickly after the war abolished the Loyalty Rangers.[120]

Perhaps the single largest group of German Texans to encounter difficulties during the war were German immigrants who had not naturalized. Operating on constitutions written in the frontier era, seven western states, including Texas, still permitted aliens to vote on the mere declaration of intention to become citizens. With the declaration of war, however, such people technically became "alien enemies." President Woodrow Wilson invoked the sole surviving provision of the Alien and Sedition Acts of 1798, which gave him the power to regulate, arrest, and deport unnaturalized subjects of a hostile power during wartime. By his proclamation, alien enemies were technically barred from coming within one-half mile of forts, arsenals, and munitions plants. In April 1917, University of Texas President Robert Vinson recommended to the Board of Regents that all German aliens be dismissed from the university. Vinson's policy led to the immediate resignation of one professor and the subsequent investigation of several others suspected of being alien enemies.[121]

In the fall of 1917, Wilson tightened restrictions, now requiring all German aliens fourteen years of age or older to register and forbidding them to move without permission. In accordance with the new government order, registration of male alien enemies in Texas began on February 4, 1918; those aliens who had not registered by March 1, faced the possibility of internment if arrested. In addition to registering, German aliens provided four photographs of themselves and fingerprints. By the end of the registration period in 1918, over 6,000 German alien males had registered in Texas. Later that year, laws required female alien enemies to register as well. In October, authorities arrested a German alien from Rogers for disloyalty and failing to register.[122] Government officials sent aliens found to be a "danger [to] the public peace and safety" to one of four internment camps located at Fort Oglethorpe, Georgia; Fort McPherson, Georgia; Fort Douglas, Utah; and Hot Springs, North Carolina. The Department of Justice in 1918 arrested a physics teacher at Waco High School. The Berlin-born teacher lost his job

118

and found himself interned at Fort Oglethorpe until the spring of 1919. In Kingsville, a presidential warrant called for the internment of an alien German from Milwaukee who had traveled to Texas without notifying authorities. Nationwide, by the end of 1918, federal internment camps held more than 6,000 enemy aliens, most of them Germans.[123]

The registration of German alien enemies had unintended consequences. The Texas Legislature dismissed Rudolph Tschoepe, a German alien enemy from Seguin who represented the Guadalupe County district. Tschoepe had come to the United States with his parents as a small child, had served in the Confederate army, but had never taken out the proper naturalization papers. Thus, he was not considered a United States citizen. Despite a resolution affirming confidence in his loyalty and regret over his dismissal, the legislature did not move to reevaluate the law that led to Tschoepe's removal.[124]

Property owned by German aliens was also subjected to governmental control. Laws required aliens to surrender records of their businesses to the custodian of alien property, who then determined if the continued management of the property by enemy aliens endangered the United States, in which case the property would be surrendered to the care of the custodian for the duration of hostilities. A reasonable law, it became the vehicle for superpatriotic sentiment when President Wilson appointed A. Mitchell Palmer as custodian. Although he did not have the power of confiscation, Palmer adopted aggressive policies designed to eliminate German-owned businesses in the United States. He was especially determined to use his authority against German-owned breweries because they had obstructed the prohibition movement.[125]

In Texas, the state council of defense told the various county councils it was their "duty to put forth your best efforts to ascertain the character, kind and place of all alien property, or property owned by alien enemies and transmit that information."[126] Soon reports of alien property flooded in from across the state. In Belton, the local council advised looking into the property of a wealthy German widow who had moved back to Germany.[127] The Kendall CCD described alien enemy property in Comfort.[128] The most amazing claim came from Waco. There, a land transaction took place identifying the seller as none other than Theobald von Bethmann-Hollweg, the chancellor of the German Empire. The report also indicated that the chancellor might still hold a significant amount of local property.[129]

Bethmann-Hollweg had inherited the property in 1897 upon the death of his brother, Baron Max von Bethmann-Hollweg, a longtime resident of Falls County. A Waco land developer bought the land for $7,700 through Bethmann-Hollweg's agent in Texas, Otto Rau, a banker from Riesel. The timing of the land sale indicates that Rau tried to retrieve the most land value possible for the German chancellor. Had Rau waited any longer the property might have been surrendered to the custodian of alien property. In fact, Bethmann-Hollweg had one remaining parcel of land in south Waco. Because there was little doubt of Bethmann-Hollweg's enemy status, the property in August 1918 transferred from Rau to the control of custodian A. Mitchell Palmer. Palmer also received a $5,000 promissory note, which represented the unpaid balance of the earlier transaction between Bethmann-Hollweg and the Waco land developer.[130]

Anti-German sentiment reached into higher education. The University of Texas in 1918 cut its German department staff from nine instructors to five. Sam Houston Normal Institute (now Sam Houston State University) accepted the resignation of German-Texan Conrad William Feuge, who taught German, mathematics, and coached football and basketball. Feuge taught at Sam Houston for fifteen years prior to the war. His colleagues warned him that his life might be in danger if he continued to work at the school. Following their advice, Feuge resigned and accepted a job near San Antonio, a town more welcoming to German Texans than Huntsville. He later moved to his hometown of Fredericksburg, where he spent the rest of his career as a teacher of mathematics and superintendent of schools. Anti-Germanism at Baylor University forced the resignation of Dean J. L. Kesler in March 1918.[131]

The National German-American Alliance could not escape the enmity it had earned during the neutrality period. Across the country alliance branches began to fold or change their names. In January 1918, Senator William H. King of Utah introduced a bill to repeal the National Alliance's congressional charter of 1907. From late February to mid-April, a subcommittee of the Senate Judiciary Committee held hearings on the measure. In 1918, the prewar argument, that the organization sought to maintain German America so that it could contribute its culture to an evolving America, no longer held weight. The outcome of the hearings was a foregone conclusion; on July 2, Congress repealed the act that had given the National Alliance its charter. By then, however, the alliance had ceased to exist. The executive committee met in April and agreed to dissolve the national organization, turning its assets over to the American Red Cross. Charles J. Hexamer, former leader of the National Alliance, did not take part in the decision. In failing health, he had resigned in November 1917 from the presidency of the alliance. His world collapsed; Hexamer came under surveillance, found himself expelled from organizations he had belong to for years and even refused service in stores. He retreated into seclusion and in 1921 died a broken man.

The Texas alliance branch never met again after the United States entered the war. In the summer of 1918, United States Secret Service agents seized the records of the Texas alliance in Austin. The seized materials revealed the plans and plot of a city known as "New Berlin" and destined some day to become the capital of "the province of Texas." Physical evidences of a plan existed in Burnet County, stakes and stones marked streets for an *"Unter den Linden."* The papers also revealed that Texas Congressmen had indulged the German-American Alliance, telling the organization that they were going to find a way to make the United States' entry into the war with Germany "difficult, if not impossible."[132]

The reports of pro-German Mexicans along the Texas border continued to concern many Texans.[133] The border area was described as a "hot-bed of German spies and German propaganda."[134] The special investigator for the Adjutant General of Texas wrote, "if they can be made to believe that Germany has any chance to win, we may expect trouble from them." He also warned of pro-German

121

newspapers, use of wireless radios by German agents, German officers in the Mexican army, and German banks in Mexico.[135] In December 1917, United States soldiers in El Paso shot and killed Charles H. Feige attempting to cross the Rio Grande into Mexico. Believed to be a German spy, Feige had a camera, a notebook, and drawings of Fort Bliss and other fortifications.[136] German propaganda infiltrated the border area urging Texans to fight registration and refuse conscription. Authorities arrested two German Texans in Mercedes, Texas, and charged them with treason for helping a German army reservist escape into Mexico. Reports continued to describe the lack of security on the border: "There is no question but that Germany is getting all the information she wants through Mexico." An investigator recommended that the telephone connection between the United States and Mexico be severed. "The Germans and their sympathizers are getting bolder every day, and their newspapers are full of German lies," he said. "There are four Germans, one a German professor in the Valley above here who need working over." The investigator felt the professor "should be interned on general principles. He is a dangerous man just now and smart as a whip."[137]

Agent Charles F. Stevens stated, "It is my opinion that there has been considerable German money spent in this section of the country for German propaganda and spy work." Stevens arrested a German horticulturalist alien enemy. "I suspect him to be one of these German agents," he wrote, "and a part of a chain of spies who are operating through our country from the east, into Mexico, getting news to the German agents in Mexico. He is a smooth man, and after questioning him for two days, I could not get him to incriminate himself on any of his statements, so I could make charges against him." He concluded, "It is my opinion that all such fellows in this community are dangerous men to our country and should be interned."[138] In a letter two weeks later Stevens wrote: "Trying to break up this German spy work was of great interest to the nation."[139]

The county councils of defense reported not only German Texans for having pro-German views, but also Mexican Americans. The Jim Hogg CCD sent a list of slackers to Judge Carl, embarrassed "that this list should be so large." The council also stated, "We have further evidence to prove that many Mexicans still remaining among us are strongly pro-German in their views. Some of them are aliens and others citizens of this country." The council made sure to mention a former Mexican resident of the county that now directed a bank in Laredo. His "integrity was never rated very high in this section," C. W. Hellen wrote, and "we were advised from a reliable source that he did entertain and express recently pro-German sentiments."[140]

The need to ensure loyalty during World War I reached into every state department and institution. The Texas Legislature in 1917 created the Central Investigating Committees of the House and Senate due to the general public suspicion and distrust of state government aggravated by the entry of the United States into the war, the resulting distrust of German Texans, the impeachment of Governor Ferguson, and charges of corruption and collusion made against officials and employees associated with or appointed by Ferguson. Governor Hobby suggested that each department be audited and each institution visited. One of the concerns of the investigating committees was to ensure that German Texans employed by any state agency were loyal to the United States. In January 1918, the Central Investigating Committees performed their investigation of the Texas State Library, the Texas Library and Historic Commission, and the Legislative Reference Library. Among those questioned to determine his loyalty to the United States was Christian Klaerner, the state librarian.[141]

The German-born Klaerner had been appointed to the librarian position in April 1915 during the Ferguson administration. Prior to that, Klaerner worked as a teacher, choral director, and county superintendent of Washington County. During the investigation, Klaerner stated that he was fifty-six years old, had lived in Texas for thirty-seven years, and had ten children. Much to the investigating committee's dismay Klaerner had only become an American citizen in 1914, a year prior to his appointment as state librarian. The investigators seemed most interested in Klaerner's views on Germany. He admitted he had a brother in the German army. They asked Klaerner, an antiprohibitionist, if he believed a vote for whiskey was a vote for the Kaiser. To which he replied, "I ran away from the Kaiser thirty-seven years ago and I have no cause whatever to vote for him." In addition, Klaerner stated that two of his children had marched in the loyalty parade in Austin in April 1917, one carrying the American flag. Klaerner was a member of the Lutheran church and the Sons of Hermann and claimed it was a loyal organization. In his free time he like to drink beer and have a cigar at various places around Austin, such as the Bismarck and Petri's saloon, headquarters for the pro-German element. Klaerner stopped the library's subscription to *Life* magazine because he felt it was anti-German, but continued to take *Viereck's Weekly* (formerly *The Fatherland*) and the *New Yorker Staats-Zeitung*, two pro-German publications.[142]

The investigating committee believed that the state librarian's job was a "dangerous place to put a dangerous man" and, if Klaerner was disloyal, "he might do great damage to our country." Other employees of the State Library accused Klaerner of being pro-German, ordering books on Germany, possessing "strong German ideas," and having "German characteristics." One employee testified that Klaerner had ordered books promoting German *Kultur* at the expense of other books the library needed. Furthermore, Klaerner would not make available materials that would aid prohibitionists or those calling for Governor Ferguson's impeachment.[143]

The final report of the investigating committee did not find proof of Klaerner's disloyalty, yet the findings made it clear the committee no longer wanted someone of German descent to serve as state librarian. In addition, the committee found in the library several books, papers, and periodicals which were "manifestly written with the view of exploiting Germany's greatness, and in many instances openly antagonistic to America and our Allies." In the committee's judgment, the books "should be destroyed" or at least "interned during our war with Germany." According to the committee, "To encourage the reading of German literature or even to encourage the study of German in our schools . . . is in a measure cooperating with the German plan whose purposes are to Germanize and conquer the world not only with German armies but German ideas, literature, and language." Furthermore, the committee stated, Klaerner's "demeanor and appearance are not those of a representative Texan." The committee found him incompetent and recommended his resignation. Following his dismissal, Klaerner went on to become the director of Austin *Saengerrunde* from 1922 to 1949.[144]

Individual *Vereine* in Texas likewise became targets of federal surveillance and investigation. In March 1918, the Kleberg CCD requested a Department of Justice investigation of the *Germania Gegenseitigen Unterstuzung Verein* (German Mutual Aid Society; today it's known as Germania Farm Mutual Insurance Association) to find out if the society "engaged in any activities detrimental to the government." The aid society was open to any German-speaking property owner, as all transactions were carried out in German. The aid society was "one of the biggest, oldest and most substantial fire and storm insurance companies in the state of Texas" with a membership estimated to be just over six thousand members. The Justice Department determined that the organization was a legitimate fire and storm insurance association with no subversive designs.[145]

Organizations that traditionally had put versions of German ethnic identity on display likewise felt forced to withdraw from public view. The mayor of Austin banned the performance of any German music at municipal concerts. The sentiment against German music, manifest in declining public support, compelled the Beethoven *Maennerchor* to relinquish its concert hall in San Antonio. Many of such organizations were apolitical, while others had taken positive steps to rally support for the American cause, as did the Sons of Hermann in Texas. These factors, however, could not overcome anti-German sentiment. Because the groups were exclusively German, their presence was undesirable in America. They hindered, or so the argument went, the efficient operation of the American melting pot.

The cumulative effect of the anti-German hysteria of 1917 and 1918 resulted in a rapid retreat from public displays of German ethnicity and a swift decline in elements of German culture in Texas. Self-appointed guardians of American democracy demanded that all

German Texans conform to narrowed standards of patriotic behavior, including the abandonment of German language and culture. As pressures to conform built up, the majority of German Texans complied, though not without resentment. Several *Vereine* and German-language newspapers disappeared and public Germanness all but vanished. As a consequence of the anti-German hysteria, several German Texans were ridiculed, harassed, beaten, painted, tarred, and betrayed in the name of American democratic ideals.

Few German Texans had the courage to point out that the war on German culture in Texas left the enemy untouched and that instead of uniting the American people in a time of crisis, it forced an ethnic divide between worthy citizens of German origin and the rest of American society. The Americanizers nonetheless continued their war on all things German in Texas, including the German language itself, which is the subject of the following chapter.

Attacking the German Language in Texas, 1917-1918

The widespread use of the German language became the most visible aspect and the primary target of anti-German hysteria, but through a powerful press the German language was preserved. In 1917, there were 522 German-language periodicals in the United States, including twenty-one in Texas. German social and cultural organizations, public and private schools, and many households used German to a large extent. German also continued to be used extensively in the churches. Approximately, two hundred Roman Catholic parishes in the United States used the German language exclusively and another two thousand partially used it. The use of German was even more widespread among the Lutherans, since they, unlike the Roman Catholics, were able to form ethnically homogenous denominations. On the eve of World War I, although there was a strong trend toward the use of English, approximately half the nation's two million German-American Lutherans worshipped in the German language. German also was widely used among the small German Reformed and Mennonite bodies.[1]

Not only did the use of German upset many of the so-called superpatriots, but the continued use of German by successive generations prevented proper "Americanization" from occurring. During the war, therefore, many superpatriots moved toward the banishment of the German language.[2]

Hostility toward the use of the German language was particularly pronounced in Texas, where large numbers of German Texans lived in closely knit communities that became targets of suspicion and resentment among their Anglo-Texan neighbors. An attorney from Fredericksburg, for example, complained to the Texas State Council of Defense in July 1918, "The German language is the PREVAILING language in this town and county: it is used commercially to the exclusion of the English language between merchant and customer." German was also "used in all conversations on the streets," by "school children on their way home," and in all "religious services." The attorney stated that the English language was seldom heard except among non-Germans, but even "men without any German blood in them use the German language almost entirely." He complained that in the Red Cross workroom, people spoke German everyday. Frustrated over the apparent failure of Fredericksburg citizens to adopt English, the attorney recommended that the state council take steps to "eradicate the German language, or at least to make some order correcting this evil." He warned the council, however, "if any such action is taken in this county, it will not be done by the local authorities, for they are all Germans." Records do not indicate that the state council ever took any action in the Fredericksburg case.[3]

According to many of the Americanizers in Texas, the continued use of the German language posed the gravest danger to the United States. "Any man," the DeWitt County Council of Defense (CCD) wrote, "who desires to perpetuate the language that has so successfully conducted the dirty propaganda throughout the world is not a good American and at heart is a traitor to our country." The council advised that anyone "who cannot speak the English language and expects to continue his residence in this country is to at once take steps to learn it." The Fayette CCD felt the discontinuing of German would "prove to be a boon to the children of the county" and would "lead to the thorough Americanization of our people."[4] The Goliad CCD felt that unless English was spoken by all people on all occasions, "we can not have anything but Germans among our citizens of German descent."[5] The DeWitt CCD even took it upon itself to change the primary mission with which it had been charged: "The Council of Defense was organized primarily to coordinate the industrial and civic forces of our country" but "our conception of our main duty is that our highest mission is the thorough Americanization of this county."[6]

Complaints about the continued use of the German language poured in from across Texas. The chairman of the Llano County Council of Defense called the German language "the foundation stone of most of the existing evil conditions in this country."[7] The Lions Club of Temple, Texas, recommended that the Bell CCD place a ban on the German language by using "what ever steps are necessary to stop this obnoxious practice."[8] Lipscomb County wrote to Governor William P. Hobby about stopping the use of the German language by a group of German Russians "who are not citizens of the U.S. and who persist on talking the German language anywhere and everywhere, and even hold services in German in two different places each Sunday."[9] A member of the Ochiltree CCD wrote to J. F. Carl, Secretary of the Texas State Council of Defense, that "The German language has got to stop in the panhandle even" if "it becomes necessary to resort to extreme measures."[10] The Travis CCD said the German language needed to "be crushed and exterminated" because it was a convenient avenue of German propaganda, it prevented Americanization, kept alive German thought and ideas, and became an "insidious influence."[11] The Bosque CCD had no desire to punish good German citizens, but the situation necessitated taking "strict measures."[12]

In addition to the complaints registered in Texas, objections appeared from other states as well. The Ellis County Council of Defense in Oklahoma asked that the German language be stopped in the border towns of Texas because Germans from Oklahoma were taking their business to Higgins, Texas. The Oklahoma council said the town of Higgins supposedly told the Germans that "they can use all the German language they want to."[13] In response, the local council in Texas guaranteed "that we will either get these [Higgins] people right or make it so damn unpleasant for them that it will be necessary for them to enclose themselves behind a Chinese wall for protection." The Yankton CCD in South Dakota alerted Secretary Carl and the Parmer CCD in Texas to Peter Kaiser of Friona. Kaiser had written to the *Yankton Press and Dakotan* telling them to stop sending him the English-language newspaper because the paper did not "tell the truth . . . about war" and that he did not want "to pay for no more lies."[14]

But the Goliad CCD published the most vicious attack on the German language in a pamphlet with headlines stating "German is the Hateful Language of Our Hateful Enemy" and "The Plots of Zimmermann to Turn Texas Over to Mexico was in the German Language." After listing several reasons why the German language should be discontinued, the council attacked county treasurer Emil Bergmann for saying at a council meeting, "I would rather die tonight, rather be shot tonight, than be denied the right to talk to my mother in German." Furthermore, the council was upset at the fact the Bergmann's German-born mother had lived in the United States for fifty years, raised fifteen children, and yet did not take the time to learn English. Emil Bergmann's refusal to stop speaking German was evidence of a "secret bondage to the Kaiser." According to the council, Bergmann should, before his mother dies, free her of "the bondage of a hateful and infamous German *Kultur*." The council added, "The resident who persists in thinking '*Deustchland Uber Alles*' or 'Fatherland' stuff will come to very great sorrow." A warning followed for those who continued to use German: "He who willfully persists in speaking the German language when requested by recognized authority to stop doing so places himself in the attitude of giving aid and comfort to the enemy." The council insisted it needed to clean up Germanism in Goliad County, suggesting that "there are some who are not loyal and should be shot."[15]

German Texans and German-language newspapers responded to the efforts to eliminate the use of the German language with a variety of viewpoints, some in defiance, others in resignation. William Andreas (W. A.) Trenckmann, the editor of the weekly German-language newspaper *Das Wochenblatt* (Austin), took great pride in the fact that his paper received Permit No. 1 from the postmaster general, Albert Sidney Burleson, exempting it from

GERMAN IS THE HATEFUL LANGUAGE OF OUR HATEFUL ENEMY

"DEUTSCHLAND UBER ALLES" IS CANNED!

"WHERE IS THE GERMAN FATHERLAND? AS FAR AS THE GERMAN TONGUE IS SPOKEN AND GERMAN PRAYER IS SAID."

counties of DeWitt, Colorado, Caldwell and probably other counties in Texas. DeWitt County had granted this petition, and the other counties had rejected the same. The Victoria Council by a vote of twelve to one, rejected this particu-

flaged with a great deal of language about patriotism and loyalty, but just take the batter and the honey out of this "Ground Two" and see what we have left. We find left only a statement that the Trinity Evangelical Lutheran church in the United

The Plots of Zimmermann to Turn Texas Over to Mexico was in the German Language.

LOYAL AMERICANS WILL NOT SPEAK THE GERMAN LANGUAGE.

"WOULD RATHER DIE TONIGHT, RATHER BE SHOT TONIGHT, THAN BE DENIED THE RIGHT TO TALK TO MY MOTHER IN GERMAN."

SO SAYS COUNTY TREASURER EMIL BERGMANN OF GOLIAD COUNTY, AT A MEETING OF GOLIAD COMMUNITY COUNCIL OF DEFENSE

Since the above report of the Bergmann incident was prepared, it has become known, through testimony of reputable citizens of Goliad, that Mrs. Bergmann can talk and carry on conversation in English. This makes the offense of Emil Bergmann all the greater. In the test, when Emil Bergmann has been requested to choose between Americanism and Germanism, Emil Bergmann cast his lot on the side of Germanism. No citizen of Goliad County will be permitted to defy recognized authority in our fight against the Kaiser at home, while our soldier boys are fighting the Kaiser across the seas.

Published and Distributed by Order of

The Goliad County Council of Defense

Clippings from a pamphlet published by the Goliad County Council of Defense, 1918.

censorship imposed on war news and discussion appearing in German publications. Trenckmann, the first valedictorian of Texas A&M University, started the paper in 1891 and edited and published it for over forty-two years. From the time of its first publication, the paper soon became a respected voice in German-Texan communities and beyond, primarily as a means of informing and educating German-speaking immigrants and their descendants about politics, current issues at all levels, and American institutions.[16]

Das Wochenblatt did not yield on the language question. Trenckmann stated, "The demand that I shall not speak the language of my dear mother, thus honoring her, is persecution pure and simple."[17] The *La Grange Zeitung* questioned the assumption that everything spoken or written in German was inherently disloyal regardless of substance. It further rejected the simplistic implication inherent in the anti-German effort that the German language contributed to Prussian militarism.[18] The *Neu-Braunfelser Zeitung*, which had been one of the earliest and strongest supporters of the war after April 1917, ridiculed the notion that eliminating the German language would insure American success in the war. The United States had emerged victorious in both the Revolutionary and Civil Wars despite the fact that American military leaders had used the "language of the enemy." In this war, knowledge of German was a positive good, enabling American soldiers to detect German military intentions.[19] German-Texan Rudolph Kleberg realized the precariousness of the situation and stated that the use of the German language "must not be permitted to succeed, for it means trouble and probably a serious trouble if our friends of German descent persist in their course."[20] The *Katholische Rundschau* (San Antonio) eventually urged its readers to "stop the public use of German" until "sane ideas prevail again."[21]

Das Wochenblatt argued, "No sane man or well-informed man or woman who knows anything of the history of mankind can contend that the suppression of the German language will help win this war, to unify our nation, to make those of German blood still more loyal." On the contrary, such reactionary measures "might create disloyalty where none was found before." If the domestic effects were undesirable, there was greater danger for the military; the paper doubted that German-American soldiers would "fight with better spirit . . . when the information is brought to them that their old fathers and mothers, in violation of the law, are no longer permitted to hear a German sermon in the church in which they were baptized and confirmed."[22]

The *Giddings Deutsches Volksblatt* noted that efforts to ban the German language violated President Woodrow Wilson's instructions. It also perhaps found it annoying that many Texans were selective in their support for the President's policies, but simultaneously attacked the loyalty of German Texans for having failed to support Wilson's foreign policy before 1917.[23]

Throughout the end of 1917 and the first half of 1918, the Texas State Council of Defense gave mixed signals on how to deal with the German-language controversy in the state. The state council finally released its official statement on the use of the German language in Texas in June 1918:

> It is strongly urged by the Council of National Defense and we concur in that suggestion that the English language be made the means of communication in all public matters and in all private conversation, except where it would work a hardship on those who are unable to speak the English language. We recommend that this be brought about, not by force, but by a proper educational campaign in which it should follow as a matter of spontaneous, patriotic duty that the people would speak the English language. Patriotic citizens of German descent will readily appreciate the delicacy of the situation which makes it necessary that the English language be used in this country upon all occasions and by all people except in those instances of a private nature where they are unable to speak the English language.[24]

Despite the state council's official statement, German Texans continued to use the German language. A woman from Gillespie County wrote to Secretary J. F. Carl saying, "We want to have the

German language stopped. Can we do so without the consensus of all the peoples?" The local judge and others "have requested and advised [the Germans] to stop it, but they have not stopped at all, in public, on the phone, or anywhere."[25] Carl responded, "There is no law which compels the discontinuance of the use of the German language, therefore, there is no way, except by appealing to the patriotism of the people to have the use of the German language discontinued."[26] The Karnes CCD explained that it was "at a loss" as to how to stop the use of the German language.[27] Because "the use of languages other than English" had been "abused and in instances treasonable talk indulged in," the Travis County Council of Defense in September 1918 banned the use of foreign languages over the telephone. If an attempt were made to carry on a conversation in a foreign language, and they did not "immediately cease," operators were to sever the connection.[28]

The Goliad CCD stated that the Germans of their county were determined "to absolutely ignore these resolutions." The council had determined that the only way to get rid of German was "through some laws absolutely forbidding the use of it with a penalty attached."[29] Secretary Carl responded that the only way the resolutions concerning the discontinuing of German "can be carried out is by an educational program in which appeals are made to the patriotism of the people." Members of the Home Guard in Pflugerville pledged to enforce a resolution that eliminated the German language in public and private places and over the telephone.[30]

The use of the German language by Lutheran churches and schools particularly aroused the suspicion of nativists because Lutheranism was a principle target of nativist hostility during World War I. As Martin Luther was a German and nearly two-thirds of the population of Germany was at least nominally Lutheran, "German" and "Lutheran" were virtually inseparable terms to many people, even though only half the world's Lutherans were German and substantially fewer than half the German Americans were Lutheran. Although there were probably more Roman Catholics than Lutherans among America's Germans, non German Americans did not identify the Roman Catholic church with Germany since Catholicism in the United States and the rest of the world was primarily non-German. Unlike Roman Catholicism, however, American Lutheranism was heavily German.[31]

After the war began, suspicions about lack of patriotism among Lutherans were reinforced by the refusal of many Lutheran clergy to cooperate with patriotic activities, such as the sale of war bonds. Anglo-American Protestants were insulted that Lutheran clergy often refused to sit on the same platforms with clergy from other denominations at patriotic rallies. Anglo-American Protestants also failed to grasp that appeals for the sale of war bonds during church services would have violated Lutheran liturgical propriety. Anglo-American Protestants likewise did not understand that American Lutherans shunned political involvement because many Lutherans, particularly, German Lutherans, had come to the United States in order to escape entanglements between church and state. Despite their initial reluctance to cooperate with the war effort, however, Lutherans recognized the importance of dispelling fears about their lack of patriotism.[32]

Lutherans of German extraction vigorously sought to eliminate the erroneous but widely held belief that their synods maintained official ties to the state churches of Germany and that Kaiser Wilhelm II was a Lutheran. In a pamphlet published in 1918, Theodore Graebner, a professor at the Missouri Synod's seminary in St. Louis and editor of the *Lutheran Witness*, explained that the Missouri Synod opposed unionistic religious policies of the German government and was estranged from many Lutherans in Germany. Graebner emphasized that the Kaiser was a Calvinist and pointed out that some American Presbyterians before the war therefore had proudly counted him within their fold. Although Graebner's editorials in the *Lutheran Witness* pointed out the need for Lutherans to avoid criticism of the war, the *Witness* did not encourage patriotic activism.[33]

In Texas, Lutheran pastors and their congregations that worshipped in the German language created the greatest controversy. The Bosque CCD found that "German preachers caused more trouble by their actions and suggestions than anybody else."³⁴ The Castro CCD wrote to Carl saying "it seems to us that if a man's religion cannot be taught in English there is something wrong with it."³⁵ The Comal CCD said, "The Lutheran preacher is being closely watched, and we almost had him; and we're going to get him yet."³⁶ Reverend August Birnbaum of Vernon, Texas, arrived at his Lutheran church one morning in 1918 and found the windows broken along with a note that read, "If you are wise, you will leave Vernon." As a result of the German-language services, many county councils of defense attempted to ban the use of German in churches. The Fayette CCD adopted a resolution urging German-speaking pastors to "adopt the use of the English tongue" as soon as possible and that the resolution be translated into German and read to the congregations.³⁷ The Bosque CCD instructed a pastor to end German services saying, "people are naturally suspicious of anything German, the mere fact of holding any kind of services in German arouses suspicion which is not good."³⁸ In Fannin County, a German pastor had to request permission to hold a burial service in German.³⁹ The language controversy continued throughout the war and the efforts to eliminate German, in the end, met with only modest success.

The Victoria CCD produced and distributed a pamphlet entitled "Sixty Years of Germany in America." In it, the council defended its reasons for rejecting the petition of Trinity Evangelical Lutheran Church to hold services in German. The council asked, "Who kept these people from reading, speaking, and talking English, and who kept them from attending a church where the English language was preached, prayed and spoken?" An American soldier was buried by their pastor in Victoria, Texas, and "the funeral rites were conducted in German, and a German sermon was preached over his body." The council not only despised the German language but everything German: "It is the German mind, the German heart, and the German tongue, of which we disapprove . . . . We are fighting Germany, German soldiers, German methods, German ideas and everything conceivably German, and there is no compromise in us, and we have just begun to fight." The Victoria CCD saw little hope

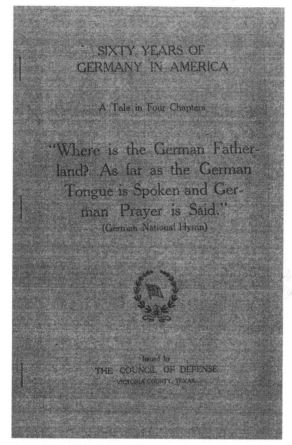

"Sixty Years of Germany in America" – an anti-German pamphlet published by the Victoria County Council of Defense.

for reconciliation between the two sides: "This gulf between America and Germany is too wide ever to be bridged again, and no hands will ever be clasped across it."[40]

The Fayette CCD denied a request by the Evangelical Lutheran Bethlehem Church of Round Top to hold German-language services saying, "To permit the German language as a means of communication is opening the door wide for German propaganda, friction, disorder and disloyalty." The council felt that "The German language is hated by all the peoples who are fighting Germany, because Germany has threatened to conquer and destroy them or put them under German dominion. In fact, everything German is loathed and hated." In its analysis, the Fayette CCD felt the measure "necessary for the protection of the citizens of German extraction." The council wondered, "Have they ever thought how it grates upon the ears of these neighbors when they hear this language, which they cannot understand, in these critical times. . . . It seems to us that while the law does not yet prohibit the use of the enemy language, public sentiment certainly does, and therefore we insist upon the substantial observance of our said resolution." The council concluded by saying, "We trust and feel confident" that all German Texans "in a spirit of patriotism will gladly suspend the use of the German language" during the war and "will speak in the official language of our great and glorious country—the English language."[41]

German Texans soon wrote to state authorities trying to find out what exactly the policy was in relation to the use of the German language in religious services. In response, Secretary of the Texas State Council of Defense J. F. Carl indicated, "I have had quite a number of inquiries from German Lutheran ministers, generally addressed to Governor Hobby and by him referred to me."[42] H. N. Sagebiel wrote to Governor William P. Hobby on behalf of the members of the Lutheran church at Ganado, "all of whom are either of German extraction or emigrants from Germany." Some of the members, mostly older people, "understand the English language very poorly" and as a result, "the members have worshipped in the German language until recently."[43] Sagebiel wanted to know why the German language was singled out. For example, the Bell CCD excluded the German language, but allowed the use of the Bohemian (Czech) language.[44] Hobby forwarded Sagebiel's letter to Secretary Carl who responded, "the Imperial German government is at war with our country and this ought to be a sufficient reply to that inquiry." The use of English was for "the protection of our government against disloyalty and conspiracy." Carl resented the fact that "there are many people in Texas of German extraction or descent who do not speak the English language and have been here a long time." German Texans "ought to be able" to speak English and if they cannot do so, after years of residence it is their own misfortune.

"There never was a war which did not work hardships upon some people. . . . No patriotic man will object to complying with the rule." Carl concluded by saying, "it is not a question of the purposes and loyalty of your Church," but the question "of permitting the use of the language of our enemy in our own country."[45]

Other Lutheran churches in Texas petitioned bans on the German-language to a higher jurisdiction. When the Uvalde CCD ordered the Emmanuel Lutheran Church in Knippa to conduct all services only in English, the German-speaking congregation replied by appealing to the Supreme Court. The Supreme Court ruled favorably and German services resumed with no further interruptions.[46]

The St. John's Evangelical Lutheran Church in Bartlett asked the Bell CCD to consider allowing German language services because the non-English speaking members would be "without any and all spiritual edification." A ban on German would create hardships on mothers and fathers "who have given their sons gladly for our country" and deprive them of "the consolation of God's word in the language" they best know and understand. They concluded in saying that the Evangelical Lutheran Church has nothing to do with the German government.[47] The Bell CCD told the pastor of St. John's, Reverend Theodor Bogisch, that they were "not raising an objection to the worship in church in the German language—although it would probably be prohibited later on by competent authority."[48] Indeed, the county council later issued a resolution forbidding the use of the German language.

In 1895, Bogisch had come to the United States from Germany, having been called to pastor Immanuel Lutheran Church in San Antonio. That same year he joined the First German Evangelical Lutheran Synod of Texas. Bogisch moved to Walburg, Texas, and in 1899 became pastor of St. Peter Lutheran, where he served for seventeen years. While in Walburg in 1914, the First German Evangelical Synod of Texas elected Bogisch president, a position he held for fourteen years. Thus, Bogisch's term as president coincided with World War I. He later wrote, "It would not have been possible for me to serve a large congregation and also serve as president of the Texas Synod, especially during the period of the First World War." In 1916, Bogisch moved to a smaller church, St. John's Lutheran Church in Bartlett. After the United States entered the war in 1917, Bogisch drew considerable interest from the Texas State Council of Defense, not only because he was president of the German Synod, but also due to Bogisch's unwillingness to compromise on the language question.[49] The Bell CCD described Bogisch as a "very head strong. . . . Prussian Preacher" who, when it came to discontinuing the use of German, wanted to fight it out to the bitter end.[50]

In June 1918, the Bell CCD met with Bogisch to discuss German-language services.[51] In response to the Bogisch situation, the Williamson CCD wrote to the chairman of the Bell CCD with its decision to allow discretion in the use of German at churches, saying "I do not believe that it is right for us to deprive these old people the right to worship in German."[52] In response to the advice that they relax the English only resolution for old people who did not understand English, the Bell CCD chairman said, "I have given them no encouragement whatever and refused to authorize any relaxation of our resolution."[53] When he did not receive a sufficient resolution from the council, Bogisch wrote to President Woodrow Wilson, whose office then referred the letter to the Council of National Defense.[54] Bogisch's letter also landed on the desk of the Attorney General of the United States. The Attorney General told Bogisch that there was no federal law prohibiting the use of the German language in religious exercises or elsewhere.[55] Bogisch, delighted, used the response from the highest law enforcement official in the United States to continue to hold German-language services in Bartlett.

The Bosque CCD informed Reverend H. W. Bewie of Clifton that if his church used German in its meetings it was to discontinue the practice immediately.[56] Bewie replied that the older people in his congregation did not understand English and many of them left Germany because they could not "tolerate the Kaiser's rule. . . . Every one of these old German parents have one or more sons in

140

our Army." Bewie wondered if they could get an exemption for the "little German Church in Clifton."[57]

A Lutheran minister told the Goliad CCD that members of his congregation had "tears in their eyes" when learning of the resolution to ban German and asked that he preach at least every other Sunday in German. The minister believed that gradual introduction of English needed to be used in place of an immediate stoppage. The minister concluded that if he discontinued German services, the congregation would ask for his resignation and get someone else "who will preach to them only in German." The Goliad CCD also recommended the prohibition of "German Bibles, Sunday School books, song books, and all other German literature." The council wanted to be able to say that no preacher be permitted to use the German language in sermons, suggesting that parishioners "should either hear English sermons or close their churches. Unless this step is taken there are some people who will go to their grave without making any effort whatever to learn the language of this country."[58]

Lack of a single, cohesive resolution on the German-language question became one of the biggest problems. The German-speaking pastors of Fayette County complained that there was no unity among the state councils. Some states (Iowa, South Dakota, Kansas) were forbidding German, while others (Illinois, Wisconsin, New York, and Pennsylvania) were not hindering the use of German in any way. The pastors also complained about a similar lack of unity in Texas. Some counties (Harris, Austin, Washington, and Lavaca) did nothing to interfere with the preaching in German. Other counties (Bell and Hamilton) had forbidden all German, but now, after mid-1918, it was permitted once or twice a month. Lee County requested at least two "American services" a month. Travis County allowed German in the afternoon for those who did not understand English. Still others (Bastrop, Caldwell, and Victoria) forbid the use of German entirely. In Gillespie County, the council said nothing to adults, but wanted instruction to young people to be in "American." The pastors demanded to know why there was such diversity on such an important issue not only in Texas, but the nation as well. The

141

pastors agreed that English should be the language of the United States, but it could not be "done over night" and it may be "impossible" for certain men to speak to God in any language other than German. "We pastors have a special duty" to "prepare men for eternity" and "Many of our older people know only the German language and will never be able to learn any other." Prayers said in English "are to them only a babbling." The pastors said, "We cannot bear to see" a man in the "December of life" become lost "because the Word of God is taken away from" him. The pastors countered that "the enforced prohibition of a language will retard the Americanization of our country" and provided examples in places in Germany where it was tried and failed.[59]

Other German-speaking pastors were more agreeable. G. H. Biar, pastor of a Lutheran Church-Missouri Synod in Waco, inquired as to how the Texas State Council of Defense felt "towards continuing the study of religion in the German language during the time of war. . . . We are very desirous to cooperate with the council."[60] Secretary Carl told him that the request was simply a "precautionary measure" for the "protection of our German citizens."[61] Later, Reverend Biar worried that if he ended German-language services, members of his congregation would abandon him for a church where German was still used.[62] Biar agreed to comply even though the ban "will work a hardship on our people who know their dear Bible so well in the German language."[63] The DeWitt CCD called the German pastor of the Cuero Lutheran church who agreed to discontinue German "one of the greatest patriots we have ever known" and a "prince among men."[64]

German-language newspapers also responded to the attempts to eliminate the German language from the churches. *Das Wochenblatt* (Austin) wrote that eliminating German-language church services to ensure loyalty was insulting since the United States' armed forces contained thousands of German Lutherans, Catholics, and Methodists, and no traitors had been found among them.[65] The *La Grange Zeitung* found it deplorable that some German congregations and associations claimed it was their patriotic duty to eliminate the use of the German language in their activities.[66] The

Lutherbote für Texas encouraged pastors to learn English, but refused to relinquish the right to use German. The paper stated that Lutherans had to continue to preach in German as long as members were unable to understand English.[67] The Lutheran Synod of Texas established a study plan to assist pastors who wished to learn to preach in English.[68] Interestingly, while German churches in many areas of the country took a defensive stance with positive results in 1918 against the Americanizers, the protests in Texas more often than not led to the intensification of the anti-German efforts. In response to a group of Lutheran ministers who stated that there was no law against the use of the German language, for example, someone replied, "There may be no law against, but there might be a rope."[69]

In July 1918, Secretary Carl of the Texas State Council of Defense telegrammed the Council of National Defense in Washington, D. C., in a near panic. "Some German communities refuse to comply with request to discontinue the use of the German language in public gatherings," he wrote. "This is particularly true of German Lutheran ministers. What means have we of enforcing this rule? Give details today as it is pressing."[70] Section chief Arthur H. Fleming replied that the only powers to discontinue the use of the German language were influence over public opinion and the war powers of the governor. "It is entirely a question of state law and should be taken up with the [state] attorney general," Fleming replied. "It is not a request of the national government and enforcement must therefore rest on state power."[71] In a follow-up letter the Council of National Defense reiterated the fact that the state council could only recommend that German usage be

Group standing in street outside businesses, Westhoff, Texas, May 31, 1910.
Courtesy of Institute of Texan Cultures at UTSA, 103-0317. Loaned by Robert Oliver.

discontinued, it could not be done by force. The Council believed that force would create "a deep seated hatred of America and American institutions in the minds of these same individuals, which is far worse than the use of the German language."[72]

The Jim Wells CCD indicated that if Germans wanted to worship in the German language they would have to do it "in private homes."[73] After their resolution was ignored by German churches, the Jim Wells CCD wrote to Carl asking for advice since German was still the "means of communication on ALL occasions."[74] Carl replied that "there is no way, at present, to compel him to do so."[75]

A pastor at Westhoff in DeWitt County, who was born and educated in Germany, had two sons fighting for the United States in France and had bought Liberty Bonds and War Savings Stamps. But he could not preach in the English language. He felt he could serve his country as well in German as in English, and he expressed dissatisfaction with the lack of consistency between counties in the ban on German, writing to the Texas State Council of Defense that some counties had banned German entirely and "our people will be without spiritual comfort in this hard time of a struggle and sorrows."[76] Secretary Carl fired back in a letter saying:

> This community at Westhoff contains more cussedness to the square mile, in so far as disloyalty is concerned, than any place that has come to my attention in the state of Texas. They nearly all own good farms, are prosperous and have been there for many years, and we have little patience with a people who want to take all the sweet and none of the sour. They ought to have to make this sacrifice now as a penalty for not learning the English language, for they have certainly had ample opportunity.[77]

Issues over the German language and questions of loyalty spawned a lively and acrimonious debate among Texas Lutherans. Some Lutheran pastors, in the wake of suspicions over the use of the German language in Lutheran churches, felt the need to publicly declare their loyalty. William F. Kraushaar (who would later become president of Texas Lutheran College), through his service as a chaplain at Fort Sam Houston during World War I, came into contact with several Lutheran pastors in Texas. Concerned about loyalty, Kraushaar and a group of about twenty other Lutheran pastors traveled to Houston in early October 1918, debated the issue, and drafted a rather strident resolution:

> We believe America is waging a war for liberty and democracy. We believe in her just cause, therefore we again pledge her our allegiance. All those who do not lend her undivided cooperation are against us and traitors to our country. We will deem it our duty and privilege to have anyone who does not fully endorse the above brought to justice. We are for America first, last, and all the time.[78]

Pastor Bartholomew Schleifer of Kerrville, a Hungarian immigrant and not yet a citizen, served as secretary and spokesman of the group, and he sent the signed resolution to every pastor of the Texas Synod, asking each to sign the resolution. Some pastors signed the resolution eagerly; others dismissed it outright as an insult. The resolution outraged Reverend Theodor Bogisch, president of the First German Evangelical Synod of Texas. He ripped into Schleifer:

> I am always ready to give a clear-cut, 100% American, profession of my unswerving allegiance to my country, the United States, whenever the proper authorities desire such profession. But I positively refuse to do so for self-willed parties who are usurping authority and rights which in no way belong to them. To the mode of your procedure, I firmly protest, since it discloses a woeful lack of the most elementary rudiments of decorum. In your procedure, you purposely ignore both the constitution of your synod and the duly constituted authority, in pitiful arrogance, again usurping authority and jurisdiction nowhere invested in you. For the integrity, honor, and welfare of my synod, I again emphatically protest against your maneuvers, which are obviously originating from a highstrung egotism and defiantly contrary to all precedents and good order within our synodical bounds. I am restraining my protest for the sake of a conscience bound to the word of God which, distinctly, demands to have all things done in an "orderly" manner.[79]

The solicitation of patriotism also offended Carl Weeber, the president of Texas Lutheran College and synod representative. He wrote:

> Unstinted allegiance to and effective cooperation with our government always has been simple, true, and genuine Americanism. These, my sentiments and principles, should be supported by acts and facts rather than vainglorious parading and preemptory solicitation on the part of

irresponsible parties and self-constituted authorities with sinister motives and obscure tendencies. The ill-concealed threat embodied in the dictum I defy from the bottom of my heart with the fervor of an American approached by the vaunting usurpations of an alien would-be inquisitor.[80]

The end of the war overwhelmed the debate over Lutheran patriotism and, with a few exceptions, it quickly diminished. Yet, the discussion made for strange bedfellows. The American-born Kraushaar and his like-minded committee, including the Hungarian-immigrant Schleifer, made up one side. Bogisch and Weeber, both naturalized citizens, made up the other. The heated debate left a lasting legacy over just what the role of patriotism and the German language should be in the Lutheran church in Texas.

Reverend Schleifer, however, continued to stir up trouble. As pastor of the *Deutsche Evangelische Kirche* (now Immanuel Lutheran) in Comfort, Schleifer launched a vigorous program that was made up of regular church services and patriotic programs towards the end of World War I. Schleifer, relatively new to the church, created such a stir that the problems would extend past the end of the conflict. In addition, Schleifer also organized meetings that were directly involved with patriotism and had little connection with the church program. The pastor's patriotic activities angered many of the Germans in the congregation, many of whom still had strong attachments to their former homeland. They felt that Schleifer overstepped his bounds as a pastor and acted as an agent of the United States government. To make matters worse, in October 1918, Reverend Schleifer announced that German-language services would only be held every other service from then on. For many in the congregation, this action became the final straw.[81]

Matilda Faust, a prominent church member, asked Pastor Schleifer to go back to German services only. Additionally, she took offense to a number of comments Schleifer had made. Faust wrote in January 1919, "I must tell you that some people were offended by your Thanksgiving [1918] address because it was too pro-English or pro-Ally. Others made objections to your Christmas address for the same reason." She instructed Schleifer that "a minister must be very discreet, and must especially not encourage those few Americans we have here." Faust further indicated that the Americans in Comfort did nothing to support the war effort but instigate and talk "about the 'Dutch' and 'Huns.'" Rather, "the German women were the ones who did great things." The "others have nothing but gas." Faust hoped that when censorship was lifted, "we shall be able to learn the truth. Now we can hear only [the English] side." Consequently, "a minister who wants to preach in a German town like Comfort ought not to sympathize with that side. The same is the case with Prohibition." Faust told Schleifer the information was for his "guidance in the future . . . even if you should go to preach somewhere else." She then concluded by telling the pastor that he should preach in the town of Waring twice a month.[82]

After receiving this information, Reverend Schleifer reported Faust to the U.S. government as a German spy, despite the fact that she had one son in the secret service and two sons in the U.S. army. The development resulted in the correspondence being turned over to the Kerr CCD and eventually to Secretary Carl of the Texas State Council of Defense. The Kerr CCD indicated that Schleifer believed that "a drastic campaign of education should be waged among the German people." Years later, Faust's son remarked, "She had three sons on the fighting front for the States. I ask you, would she double-cross her own flesh? My mother left the church and never set foot in it again."[83]

Secretary Carl asked Faust to explain the "real meaning" behind the letter she had written to the pastor. Not to be intimidated, Faust continued her attack on Schleifer. Faust called Schleifer an "anarchist . . . posing as a patriot" who had belonged to the "Reds" in Germany and had only been in the United States for six years. Faust concluded by saying, "my three sons volunteered . . . my loyalty should be above question."[84]

Schleifer asked Secretary Carl in March 1919 to return the letter that Faust had written him. "Some people at Comfort accuse me of having insulted the whole community by turning over that letter to the Council of Defense." Indeed, Schleifer had worn out his welcome in Comfort. He quit preaching at the *Deutsche Evangelische Kirche* in May and left the community for good in September 1919. As a result, the church held no services for six months. Schleifer left Texas never to return and eventually left the ministry to work as an interpreter for the U.S. government.[85]

Johannes Martin Bergner, a Lutheran pastor from Arneckeville, a German-speaking village between Cuero and Victoria in DeWitt County, paid a severe toll for his reluctance to speak the English language. Born in Germany, Bergner received seminary training in Switzerland. Following the completion of his studies, Bergner volunteered to go to Texas. He arrived in 1909 and became the pastor of Zion Lutheran in Arneckeville. When war in Europe began, Bergner had not completed the process to become an American citizen. The German government cancelled his foreign missionary status and ordered him to return to Germany to fulfill his military service. Injured during a battle, Bergner nonetheless completed his military service and made his way back to Texas shortly before the United States entered the war. In 1918, the DeWitt CCD prohibited the use of the German language in church services. Bergner attempted to preach in English even though his proficiency in that language was marginal. At the same time, tensions between Germans and non-Germans in DeWitt County continued to escalate. When Bergner found out that a Lutheran pastor in Cuero, A. A. Hahn, had cooperated with the local council's ban and encouraged hatred against the Germans, including burning the Kaiser in effigy, Bergner went about the community letting it be known that hatred and bigotry were not the Lutheran thing to do. Bergner protested in German and authorities soon reported him to governmental authorities. United States agents then picked him up and a federal judge sentenced him to an internment camp for citizens and alien enemies "for his own safety." The German government paid for his expenses. Bergner remained a prisoner of the camp for half a year and served there as chaplain. After his release, Bergner joked: "That was one of the best vacations I've ever had." He spent the rest of his life as a Lutheran pastor in Texas.[86]

A. A. Hahn, the pastor of St. Mark's Lutheran Church in Cuero and a signatory to the Houston Resolution of 1918, felt the First German Lutheran Synod of Texas was too pro-German and he led his church to withdraw from the synod. Hahn claimed he had been slandered and vilified by neighboring pastors and by the synod for his patriotic activities. The members of the St. Mark's congregation, however, believed that Hahn "was the only 100% patriot in the whole Synod" and gave him their full support saying that his accusers were "disloyal and pro-German individuals." Following a unanimous vote, the congregation in December 1918 withdrew from the synod "in the firm belief of Justice according to American ideals and not German ideas." Hahn wrote to Bogisch, the synod president, indicating he had taken the step for "patriotic and loyal reasons."[87]

Not only did the German language come under fire during the war, but also some county councils questioned the use of the Spanish language as well. The Jim Hogg CCD reported to the Texas State Council of Defense that a private school for children of Mexican residents was "conducted entirely in the Spanish language and Mexican patriotism and Mexican ideas are taught." The faculty of the school retained "their citizenship to Mexico" and were "endeavoring to raise their children to be loyal citizens of that country." The county council wanted to "close up this Mexican school." Secretary Carl of the state organization, in his response to the letter, urged the Jim Hogg CCD to not take any drastic steps, but to educate the people of the school to use the English language "on the basis of the courtesy shown to the country in which they are living." Carl hoped this would suffice, but added, "more drastic measures may follow the refusal to comply."[88]

It was also the use of German in the parochial schools that aroused the ire of self-styled patriots. The more realistic proponents of Americanization recognized that there was little they could do to eradicate the use of German among adults, but they hoped that the schools would break the German language cycle. The Americanizers particularly feared that children could not properly absorb American values and become good citizens unless they received instruction in the English language. The Wichita CCD complained that a number of communities had private schools that were teaching "more or less in the German language" and the chairman wanted the schools closed. In addition the council recommended that "the State Council of Defense take action to close all schools of public instruction which are teaching or using the German language."[89] The Fayette CCD passed a unanimous motion to "ascertain if the teaching of any foreign language in grammar grades of parochial schools can be prohibited and how it pertains to the German language at this time."[90] Secretary Carl responded, "there is no law, either federal or state, which prohibits the teaching of any foreign language in any school."[91]

Critics of German-language education also contended that the German-language schools undermined the quality of public education. The alleged opposition of German Texans toward tax increases and bond issues for the support of public education particularly inspired resentment. The Bosque CCD urged closing of all parochial schools and for all students to be educated in public schools. The council remarked that the foreign element of the county fought the public schools and bond issues. Additionally, banks and businesses in the county gave preferences to Germans or Norwegians as they spoke foreign languages. The council indicated that this "puts an American boy at a disadvantage, which we feel should be done away with."[92] In areas where Germans comprised a large segment of the population, supporters of public education complained bitterly about Germans who erected fine new parochial school buildings after helping to vote down revenue measures for the improvement of public schools. By keeping students away from the public schools, the private schools also reduced the number of public schools that the states could maintain. Private schools posed a special problem in rural areas, where a reduction in the number of public schools might force public school children to travel a long distance to school.

Amidst the furor to eliminate German from the curriculum of Texas schools, the *Fredericksburger Wochenblatt* noted that despite the war France continued to require the study of the German language in its elementary schools.[93] The *Neu-Braunfelser Zeitung* argued that knowledge of foreign languages was essential to the development of any country.[94] The *Lutherbote für Texas* criticized the decision of some school boards to eliminate the teaching of all foreign languages from elementary schools.[95] Nevertheless, the Lutheran College in Clifton, Texas, discontinued instruction in German after being pressured by the Bosque CCD.[96]

When it was reported to the Bell CCD that Reverend Theodor Bogisch was going to have a summer school near Bartlett taught in the German language, the council took action. The council said to Bogisch, "it should have occurred to you, if you are loyal to our government, that it is extremely out of place and calculated to be destructive of good order for the German language to be longer taught to the youth of our country." Continuing to scold Bogisch the council noted: "You, perhaps, do not realize the utter impropriety of such a course <u>at this time</u> or that the people will not tolerate such things under existing conditions."[97] Bogisch responded that the school was a religious school and its goal was to teach religion to the children and he had the right to teach religion in the German language to the children of his congregation. The council told Bogisch "to teach in the German language is treading on dangerous ground." Bogisch responded by saying he would take this issue up with the governor.[98] Governor Hobby replied that there was "probably no law which would prevent the action of Rev. Bogisch in conducting a private school for religious purposes."[99]

Opponents of the use of the German language also attempted to eliminate German from public schools. For example, the Austin CCD complained that "the German language is used as a medium of communication between the student and pupil in the teaching of all subjects." Furthermore, the German language was used by "school children upon the play grounds of the school."[100] At the onset of the war, German instruction was not widespread in public elementary schools. The use of German was much more common in the high schools. After America entered the war, German-language instruction in the public schools became highly controversial. Some opponents of the continuation of German-language instruction contended there was a close correlation between language and thought patterns and that students who learned to speak German therefore would tend to think like Germans. Opponents also expressed fear that instruction in German would subconsciously encourage admiration of German culture and society. They claimed, moreover that instruction in German provided a means for German propagandists to infiltrate the educational system. Secretary Carl insisted, "I have received many protests against the teaching of German in the public schools of the state while this war continues."[101]

The anti-German sentiment in Texas affected not only the schools, but the schoolchildren themselves. One rural teacher recalled a young German-Texan student crying on the first day of class. When asked what was wrong, he sobbed, "I'm German! The big boys won't play with me because I'm a German." When asked if he would like his mother to come and walk him home from school, he replied, "She can't come because she's sick, but anyway, she's German too."[102]

Teachers came under scrutiny as well, Secretary Carl of the Texas State Council of Defense wrote to the State Superintendent of Schools alerting him to "a number of teachers in the public schools in Texas, particularly in largely German speaking communities, who are alien enemies." Carl then stated "the teacher above all others it seems ought to be a loyal and patriotic citizen."[103] The State Superintendent responded that any alien enemy teacher would immediately have their certificate cancelled.[104]

The 1918 campaign for superintendent of public instruction exemplified the level to which the anti-German panic had spread. Running for reelection was Superintendent W. F. Doughty, a proven Progressive who in 1918 found himself portrayed as the enemy of Progressivism and wartime patriotism. Doughty was allied to James Ferguson, which entailed opposition to prohibition and the support of German Texans. The connection opened Doughty to charges of disloyalty during the height of World War I paranoia. Doughty's former Progressive supporters abandoned him when he failed to sever his ties to Ferguson publicly.[105]

In 1918, Annie Webb Blanton, then president of the Texas State Teachers' Association, vice president of the National Education Association, and professor of education at North Texas State Normal College, challenged Doughty for the state superintendency. Blanton charged that Doughty's connection with Ferguson meant association with political scandal, conservative South Texas bosses who stole elections with tainted Mexican votes, insufficient patriotism, disloyalty, and anti-prohibition and pro-German support. The race was particularly vicious. Blanton's campaign strategy associated her with Progressive Governor Hobby and cast aspersions on Doughty's fitness for office. She intermingled education policy with potent issues of prohibition, wartime loyalty, anti-Germanism, and anti-communism by charging that Doughty "was on the 'Red' list of breweries . . . allied with the German-American Alliance, whose declared purpose was to control the public schools and Universities in the interest of German *Kultur.*" Blanton then promised to "put the great Public School system of Texas solidly in the 'American' column," as she had "no hyphenated connections."[106]

As Blanton and Doughty campaigned for the Democratic nomination, the Texas legislature responded by passing the state's first truly effective English-only law. In 1918 a legislator introduced a bill into the Thirty-fifth Legislature reminding everyone of the English-speaking heritage of the founding fathers and heroes of the Texas War for Independence. Further, it noted that because "the great Anglo-Saxon races who speak and write the English language—our own mother tongue," should be respected, the English language should be preserved. The "costly and useless luxury of spending thousands of dollars teaching the language of our German foe—the language that is being used in our country in seditious propaganda to undermine the patriotic efforts of our government to secure world-wide democracy" should be abolished. In the ensuing debate, the use of German in the schools became branded as "un-American" and yet another element of German *Kultur.* The English-only bill proposed the total elimination of German from Texas public schools, not only in terms of instruction but even German as a course of study.[107]

W. A. Trenckmann, editor of the *Das Wochenblatt* (Austin), made an appeal on behalf of the German language. Trenckmann declared that nearly all Germans were loyal and that passing a law against German would be "disastrous to Texas." A ban on German would not make German Texans more loyal, but would cause them to doubt if they made "the right choice in seeking this country as a land of freedom of the individual." Trenckmann continued, "If you drive out the German element in this country . . . you will drive out a strong part . . . which has done so much to build up this country." Trenckmann mentioned several German names prominent in American history and concluded, "I am working just as hard as anyone for real Americanism, but that does not require prohibiting the teaching of the German language in our schools."[108]

The English-only law passed that year, although it was watered down on several counts. The original bill targeted only the German language. An amendment to the bill sought to ban all foreign languages, but it failed by a large margin. Instead, a compromise measure that vaguely demanded that "teachers in public free schools . . . conduct school work in the English language exclusively" passed. Criminal penalties were included for violating the law. Foreign languages could be taught but not in lower grades.[109] German-Texan Rudolph Kleberg called the bill one that "goes as far as is constitutionally permissible, and in my opinion would abolish the evil of teaching German exclusively in [private and parochial] schools and make English the paramount language."[110]

The reaction to the issue of curtailing German in the public schools was overwhelmingly favorable. One state senator of San Antonio suggested to his local Americanization board that all immigrants, citizen or not, be made to speak English to prove their Americanism and that such "Americanism should be taught in public schools the same as arithmetic or geography." Seeking reelection, Superintendent Doughty gave the legislation his support, defending his tenure as education chief by stating that he had always supported the singing of "patriotic songs" and class instruction "devoted at intervals to the teaching of loyalty, love of country and State." In a strange twist, Representative J. T. Canales of Brownsville, a maverick

Tejano and Progressive who favored prohibition, heartily supported English-only targeting German. Asked sarcastically by an opponent if he would also support the prohibition of his own Spanish, Canales replied, "If we were at war with Spain, yes."[111]

Annie Webb Blanton's 1918 victory over incumbent W. F. Doughty for the state's top education job resulted partly from her open suspicion of immigrants. Her election was part of a Progressive sweep in 1918 of statewide offices. Blanton became the first woman elected to statewide office in Texas.

German newspapers and other publications were also a concern. The Caldwell CCD recommended a state and national law "forbidding circulation of German printed newspapers and periodicals anywhere in the United States."[112] The Dewitt CCD recommended that a law be passed "prohibiting the printing of German newspapers and periodicals of all kinds." The council believed "that no permanent good can be attained unless the printing of the German language is prohibited."[113] Secretary Carl replied, "there is no law to prohibit the publication of German newspapers and periodicals in the German language at this time."[114]

The Guadalupe CCD accused the *Seguiner Zeitung* of publishing several articles that were critical of President Wilson and the government and urged Secretary Carl to address the situation. The council did not want the paper to cease; council members believed it could be of great benefit in war drives and other patriotic activities. They felt the paper benefited old people who could not read any other language, yet they called the condition "deplorable."[115] Ed Hering, the editor of the *Seguiner Zeitung*, responded that his paper's questionable articles were taken from the *Galveston News*, an English-language newspaper that had never been accused of disloyalty. Hering promised that he would assist with any effort undertaken by the council "in the interest of our common country."[116] Despite the apparent cooperation, people accused the German-language newspaper of writing that the United States was "not as free as Germany."[117]

In addition to pressures from the councils of defense, federal restrictions discouraged German-language newspapers from criticizing the United States. Congressional legislation required all foreign language newspapers to file translations of any articles related to the war with the local postmaster. Some papers obtained exemptions; *Das Wochenblatt* (Austin) proudly noted that it had been the first German-language newspaper in the nation to receive such an exemption. Most German-language newspapers were not as fortunate and they were obligated to provide translations, to carry all war news in English, or to omit war reports entirely. Above each Associate Press article that the *Fredericksburger Wochenblatt* had translated and published in German, the paper displayed the requisite disclaimer that it had filed an English translation with the local postmaster. Because the post office could suspend mail service for incendiary materials, editors would have had additional reasons to conform.[118]

In addition to altering their editorial positions on the war, German papers in Texas changed the slant of their reports by altering their sources. Many papers began to rely on English-language wire service reports, which they had earlier denounced for their pro-British bias. Robert Penniger, editor of the *Fredericksburger Wochenblatt*, began to reprint AP reports rather than preparing the war reports himself from various sources and inserting editorial comments. German-language newspapers further transformed their position by emphasizing the likelihood of an Allied victory instead of stressing the Central Powers' military achievements. Kaiser Wilhelm II also came under attack from German-Texan newspapers. The *La Grange Zeitung* told its readers they had a duty to oppose the Kaiser because he answered to no one.[119]

Many German-language newspapers resigned themselves to becoming a part of the United States propaganda network. The *Neu-Braunfelser Zeitung* acquired the habit of printing the phrase "Buy Liberty Bonds" over and over again. Likewise, the *Giddings Deutsches Volksblatt* and the *Fredericksburger Wochenblatt* printed the slogan "Buy War Savings Stamps." The *Lutherbote für Texas* reminded pastors of their responsibility to promote the sale of Liberty Bonds. Several newspapers headed their editorial pages with a picture of the United States flag. In July 1918, the editor of the *Giddings Deutsches*

Volksblatt, J. A. Proske, added a new slogan to his paper: "This is not a German paper, but an American newspaper published in the German language." Similarly, the *Fredericksburger Wochenblatt* wrote "there are no German newspapers in our country, there are only American papers in the German language."[120]

Nonetheless, many Texans could not accept the sudden change in German-language newspapers to a pro-American position. After all, they reasoned, the German-Texan press appeared to have acquired its loyalty only after it became a convenient means to avoid charges of disloyalty. According to many Americans, the very presence of German-language newspapers in the United States had hindered national unity. The ultimate goal was not to secure the cooperation of such papers, but to eliminate them. Suspicion concerning the loyalty of the German-language press helped to achieve the elimination of some as it discouraged merchants from advertising, and motivated subscribers to find a more acceptable news source. In the United States, the number of German-language newspapers declined by over fifty percent, from 554 to 234, between 1910 and 1920.[121]

German organizations that used the German language also came under fire. In July 1918, the Dewitt CCD launched an investigation of the Hochheim Prairie Mutual Fire and Storm Association. The organization wrote its policies in German and conducted its affairs in the German language. The council found that the "organization was formed in 1891," was "very successful," and had a "remarkable record for efficiency and stability." Nevertheless, the council wanted to require that all further policies be written, and future affairs be conducted, in the English language. The DeWitt CCD also complained that Sons of Hermann lodges in many counties were using the German language and sought to order them to use English exclusively, even though the county council felt it would mean "that some of the old people will be deprived of their lodge fraternity."[122] Secretary Carl encouraged the local council to proceed with this action, implying that it would benefit the lodge because "so far as the public is concerned" the use of German "creates a suspicion against those people."[123]

Many historians labeled the war as the most important single event in promoting the adoption of English-language use by German Americans, but German Texans continued to spend the next two decades struggling with the language issue.[124]   Even though the Americanizers made the elimination of the German language in public, churches, newspapers, societies, and schools a priority, many German Texans continued to uphold the importance of the German language.   Some pastors refused to budge on the language issue, protecting German at all costs.   Each individual change from German to English, whether in church or school or some other institution, created controversy and compromise.   Despite the numerous attacks on the "enemy language" in 1917 and 1918, the German language survived the war in Texas and continued to be used for several more decades.

When the armistice came in November 1918, German Texans naturally hoped to rebuild their culture, resume the use of the German language, and begin again the presence of public Germanness.   The belief, however, would prove optimistic.   For German Texans faced a new period, one in which the focus would shifted from one of anti-Germanism to one that reflected an upsurge of American nativism.   In the resulting xenophobia and drive for "100 percent Americanism" in the 1920s, the Germans of Texas had to deal with the widespread social, political, and economic dislocations that followed the war.   Until the mid-1920s, German Texans remained on the defensive.

7

Assimilation or Survival? Postwar to 1930

On November 11, 1918, World War I came to an end when the warring nations signed an armistice agreement. The Great War was over and everywhere people celebrated. In Seguin, Texas, a German community, the news caused the greatest celebration ever held in the city. Church bells rang, factory whistles and car horns blew, shotguns, pistols, and firecrackers went off, and in fact citizens turned loose everything that could make noise. All stores closed and the celebration continued all day. At about 10:30 in the morning, six carloads of Seguinites "loaded for bear" headed to New Braunfels, another German community, with an effigy of the Kaiser hung to a scaffold in tow. A mock funeral for the Kaiser followed.[1]

Although the war had ended, Germany had been defeated, and Kaiser Wilhelm II had fled to the Netherlands to serve out his exile, a technical state of war continued. For many months in the United States as a result the so-called "Americanizers" kept up their vigilance. Also, despite the end of the war, in the weeks just afterward the Texas State Council of Defense did not disband. The organization stayed intact under the guise of rendering aid to returning soldiers. In actuality, the state council continued to monitor the activities of German Texans, not holding its last meeting until June 7, 1919. Opponents of the use of the German language vowed that they would continue to work for its removal. Two days after the signing of the armistice, for example, the Castro County Council of Defense (CCD) wanted to continue the prohibition on the German language. "We have had considerable trouble [with the Germans]," the council remarked, "and would like to keep the ban on." Following the armistice, an informant turned over the name of a German Texan who in relation to American soldiers had remarked, "I hope every one that goes across to France will be killed." Indeed, the dislocations that followed the war created an ideal climate for the fears and frustrations on which nativism typically feeds.[2]

Other "patriotic" organizations continued to monitor German Americans. On November 29, 1918, the American Defense Society (ADS) wrote to the Hillsboro, Texas, Vigilance Corps reminding them that "the war is not over" and "our war in this country has only just begun." The ADS warned that the forces of "Pacifism, pro-Germanism, Bolshevikism and every other form of unrest" have been unleashed and "not much has happened except that the Kaiser has been dismissed." Among its postwar aims the society listed the "rigid suppression of German propaganda," the "non-teaching of German in schools," and the Americanization of "foreigners and foreign settlements in the United States."[3]

In December 1918, the Council of National Defense addressed the state councils of defense stating, "The termination of hostilities does not in any way end the need for vigorous prosecution of work of Americanization on which you have undertaken." The "great task of assimilation, the work undertaken by the Councils of Defense, is as vital as ever."[4]

The postmaster of Kerrville informed Secretary J. F. Carl of the Texas State Council of Defense of a dispute in December 1918 over the use of the German language. The local council of defense had requested that every place of business in Kerrville post a sign reading, "No German spoken or permitted to be spoken here." The postmaster reported that a German Texan had carried on a conversation in German at C. C. Butt Grocery. When the manager of the store, C. C. Butt, Jr., requested that the use of German be stopped, the German Texan responded that "he would speak German when and where he pleased." The manager then told him to leave the store or bear the consequences. The postmaster wanted to know "if there is any way to get at this class of people under existing laws?"[5]

An incident from Seguin illustrated the difficulties that many German Texans faced in trying to negotiate the immediate postwar period. Authorities there arrested a German Methodist minister and charged him with violating the Espionage Act on account of his "disloyal" remarks. The minister's arrest stemmed from his comments in several speeches and letters, following the signing of the armistice, in which he characterized American goals in the war as capitalistic rather than idealistic. He felt he had proved his loyalty during the war by delivering patriotic speeches and an actively participating in the sale of Liberty Bonds. Additionally, the minister had introduced English-language services to his congregation in Seguin. The unpopular decision likely contributed to the congregation's demand that he resign. After his arrest, the minister became distraught and while released on the bond shot himself.[6]

On December 16, 1918, the Texas State Council of Defense released a bulletin asking the various county councils for their input on the best methods to bring about Americanization. The state council believed that English ought to be the language of the home, school, church, and heart of the patriotic citizen. The country could not be thoroughly American, the state council added, "when its citizenship speaks in forty-two different languages." The country "must and will be made thoroughly American." The state council concluded by asking for "suggestions from all over the State" so that Americanization could take place. In doing so, the state council advised that the county councils should not consider the subject from the "standpoint of the German language alone," but from a broader viewpoint so that all people who claim citizenship of "this country" are "truly and in fact American."[7]

Two days before Christmas 1918, the Travis County Council of Defense wrote to Secretary Carl with their recommendations for bringing about "the complete Americanization of the American people." The council suggested that no charters be granted to societies that fostered "racial traits" and "memories." In addition, societies already in existence should be required to conduct all meetings and keep all records in English and change any foreign names to an English equivalent. Also, the council thought that no foreign languages should be used in public or taught in public schools, "except Latin or ancient Greek." Similarly, private schools "solely teaching any foreign language" should not be permitted. On the issue of naturalization, the council felt no person should be permitted to become an American citizen "unless he can read and write English." The Travis CCD directed its suggestions at Germans since they "have shown a greater indisposition to become Americanized than any other race within our borders" and "are in greater numbers" and "we are still at war with them." The council concluded that the suggestions "be made more applicable [to Germans] . . . than to any others."[8]

Likewise, the Secretary of the Hays County Council of Defense, A. W. Birdwell, wrote to Secretary Carl with suggestions to most effectively bring about Americanization. Birdwell, a history professor at Southwest Texas State Normal School in San Marcos, believed English should be the language of all instruction in public schools, the language of worship in religious services, and the language of all public meetings. Also, he wrote that the ban on teaching German in elementary schools should be enforced since the "law has been deliberately and systematically disregarded."[9]

Similar anti-German sentiments were present. The Goliad CCD recommended to Secretary Carl that the Texas state legislature pass a law against the use of the German language "in schools, churches, lodges, and all public gatherings, and against the publication of all German newspapers and other literature." The council added that the law should only be directed against the German language.[10] The Panola CCD pulled no punches. The council wanted, "An act of Congress declaring the German language extinct or dead."[11] Rather than prohibiting the use of the German language, a member of the Texas legislature introduced a resolution in February 1919 urging the Texas members of Congress to seek federal legislation that would exclude all German immigration for a period of fifty years.[12]

The year 1919 was packed with tragedy. Indeed, it was one of the bleakest in the history of the twentieth century. Famine threatened much of Germany and Eastern Europe, civil war tore apart Russia, and an influenza pandemic claimed tens of millions of lives in every part of the globe. Among Americans, the enthusiasm and idealism of the war period gave way to disillusionment as politicians met in Versailles to redraw a map of the world. The sense of unity and national purpose that had exhilarated many Americans faded as domestic conflicts broke out over such subjects as the rights of labor and the League of Nations. Despite the United States' victory in the war, foreign menaces continued to haunt the United States. The Bolsheviks, for example, were winning the civil war in Russia, and the Communists were making significant inroads in Germany and Hungary. The danger of domestic subversion seemed even greater than it had during the war, as the Communists threatened to export their revolution to America and a multitude of revolutionary organizations seemingly worked to overthrow the United States government.

Meanwhile, Americans continued to suffer from the high inflation that had started during the war, and unemployment and recession began to cover the land as the economic demands of the war disappeared. With President Woodrow Wilson suffering the effects of two strokes, the nation lacked effective leadership. Partly in response, one of the most visible public officials became Attorney General A. Mitchell Palmer, whose raids on radicals and deportations of left-leaning aliens did much to inflame the so-called "Red Scare" of the period and to heighten the public sense of crisis. Conditions appeared so bad that a Dallas man told Secretary J. F. Carl of the Texas State Council of Defense that he loathed to "think of our [Dallas] Council being disbanded." Writing in March 1919, he felt that "the world is in a worse condition today than it was a year ago; that the menace of Bolshevikism is even worse than that of Kaiserism" since it is "more insidious" and "apparently covers the earth."[13]

Nevertheless, some German Texans despite opposition from local councils saw the end of the fighting in Europe as an opportunity to resume the use of the German language. A Lutheran church in Kingsbury, Texas, for example, resumed German-language services in late December 1918 and early January 1919, much to the consternation of the local community council of defense.[14] A pastor from Wichita Falls, Texas, believed a ban on foreign languages would be "unwise and too drastic." Such a law, the pastor stated, "would cause hard feelings" and "many churches would become empty and forsaken." The pastor added, "Our great state still needs immigrants."[15]

By the spring of 1919, some of the councils even appeared to begin easing their restrictions on German language use. In March 1919, Secretary Carl held no objection to a German Lutheran church in Hidalgo County holding German services once a month.[16] The same month, H. C. Gaertner, pastor of Salem's Evangelical Lutheran Church in Bynum, requested that the Hill CCD to lift the ban on the German language. The council responded that the German language could not be separated from the "cause against which we fought," at least not "for many years." The council added that German was the language of conspirators, intriguers, and spies and "must be under the ban."[17] Gaertner responded that because of the ban on German, several elderly members of his church had gone without worship services for the past four months since they could not understand sermons, prayers, and hymns in the English language. As a result, some of the elderly members had driven to Waco or Fort Worth to hear services in German since it was not banned in those cities. The travel, Gaertner remarked, proved very inconvenient to old people or not possible at all. Gaertner again asked the county council to reconsider the ban.[18] In a surprising action, the Hill CCD reconsidered and in late April allowed Gaertner's church to again hold worship services in the German language.[19]

The eventual transition of churches in Texas from German to English proved particularly troublesome in many congregations. In DeWitt County, Saint John Evangelical Lutheran Church in Meyersville had disagreements that lasted long after the war. Throughout 1919 and 1920, the congregation debated over the number of church functions that should be conducted in English or

German. Eventually, in June 1922, the disagreements led to the pastor's resignation. He said, "Above all, the troublesome language question has caused so much bitterness, hate, and enmity among the members and against me, that in spite of all the attempts I have made, could not put aside, so I have the impression that it is best for the congregation as well as for me that I end my work here." In requesting a new pastor from the synod, the congregation, still dead set on using German, asked for a new preacher "fluent in the German language, not only to speak it but be able to conduct all church business in this language and also be able to hold services in German." Conversely, Pastor Friedrich Apfelbach of St. John's Lutheran Church in Prairie Hill resigned in November 1921 because he had difficulty using the English language.[20]

Meanwhile, the United States' entry into World War I removed some of the obstacles, including the National German-American Alliance, to prohibition. Prohibition became a patriotic cause to conserve food, protect the soldiers in training camps, and injure the German-dominated brewing industry. Prohibitionists saw the advent of peace as a signal for the final achievement of their cherished goal. The United States Senate in 1919 held hearings that reflected the nativists' concern over the continued production and use of alcohol. The report on *Brewing and Liquor Interests and German and Bolshevik Propaganda* conveniently lumped together all the forces the nativists feared: brewers, Bolsheviks, and Germans.[21]

In the report, all segments of the German-American community were charged with disloyalty. Brewers, some of the most affluent members of the community, were described as a "vicious interest" that had been "unpatriotic because it had been pro-German in its sympathies and conduct." Almost all brewers were felt to be of "German birth and sympathy" that had supported German-American societies. All of the societies were condemned, as most of them had been affiliated with the National German-American Alliance. In addition, the committee felt that purposes of the *Vereine* were "to preserve the customs and language of Germany."[22]

Both German churches and the German-language press came in for its share of criticism as well. The report stated that some

167

branches of the Lutheran church were "particularly active" in "defending the German cause." The Senate committee felt the German press had conspired to prevent assimilation and had been used for political and propaganda purposes. It recommended controls and regulations on foreign-language publications. With reference to the German element in the United States, the report believed a great number of Germans had "maintained and designedly perpetuated the language, customs, and racial ideas of Germany," as well as "German thought."[23]

Though ratification of the Eighteenth Amendment meant that the nation would be dry after January 1920, prohibitionists wanted a Texas state constitutional amendment to cover the last months of 1919. On May 24, 1919, the prohibition measure passed. Although they were incomplete, election returns show that the ten German counties voted overwhelmingly, eight to one, against prohibition. Comal County cast 1,567 against prohibition and only 61 for it. The remainder of Texas, however, voted four to three in favor of prohibition.[24]

The Volstead Act of 1919 prohibited the manufacture and sale of any beverage with more than 0.5 percent alcohol. Prohibition not only deprived German Texans of what they regarded as a staple of their diet, but also deprived German social life of a basic element. Festivities became almost unthinkable now that they were dry. Pastors had to fill out ridiculous forms requesting their monthly supply of communion wine. German Texans regarded prohibition as another act against them. Their language and *Kultur* and now their beverage were being forbidden. Some German-American leaders believed that the prohibition movement was an expression of Anglo-American Puritanism. They felt that prohibition was being forced on German Americans by those motivated by anti-German bigotry. Moreover, German Americans felt prohibition denied them of their personal liberty, as they felt the government had no right to interfere in such matters.

Prohibition proved impossible to enforce. Legend has it that the Spoetzl Brewery continued to brew Shiner beer for local German and Czech farmers. The Pearl Brewery in San Antonio supposedly

168

produced beer for close friends and sale on the black market. In Galveston, prostitution, gambling halls, and saloons were so prevalent that a prominent law enforcement official shrugged the town off as being outside the United States. In Morris County, Texas, authorities in 1920 uncovered a 130-gallon copper still on the property where dry leader Morris Sheppard was born. The Cat Spring Agricultural Society brazenly recorded the purchase of kegs of beer in its minutes. The demand for liquor created the impetus for illegal distilleries at home and smuggling from Mexico. Bootleggers made fortunes in the underground alcohol industry and, ironically, teamed with prohibitionists to see that the state did not legalize liquor again.[25]

By 1932, when the country had righted itself both with respect to anti-Germanism and its futile anti-liquor efforts, Germans in the congressional delegation from Wisconsin, the nation's most German state on a percentage basis, sponsored federal legislation to repeal the hated Eighteenth Amendment. In 1933, states across the land revoked prohibition and German Texans rejoiced. At one minute after midnight on September 15, the Spoetzl Brewery trucks started rolling again to towns like Praha and Dime Box. Within fifteen minutes of the end of prohibition, one hundred trucks and twenty-five railroad boxcars loaded with Pearl beer headed out of the San Antonio brewery grounds.[26]

Women's suffrage appeared on the same ballot as prohibition and German Texans again became targets. In January 1919, Governor William P. Hobby recommended a constitutional amendment to enfranchise women in all elections, but at the same time, he also proposed that aliens not be allowed to vote until they had completed the naturalization process. At the time, so-called "first paper" aliens who had begun the process were fully enfranchised. The legislature paired the issues so that voters could not give women the vote unless they disenfranchised aliens. To make matters more complicated, women could not vote in the referendum, but aliens could. Also, the two proposals could not be voted upon separately but had to be accepted or rejected as a unit. Thus, in order for women's suffrage to stand a good chance of passing, several "first paper" aliens, many of them German, would have to vote to disenfranchise themselves.[27]

Austin suffragist Jane Y. McCallum directed a vigorous campaign. Naturally, the operation posed the suffragists against the "first paper" aliens. Largely as a result of McCallum's efforts, volumes of letters, press releases, and bulletins deluged the offices of newspaper editors throughout Texas. One bulletin appealed to the men of Texas, asking them to choose between "women" and "alien enemies." McCallum wrote, "the immigrant man acquired suffrage by living here long enough to 'declare his intentions' of some day becoming a citizen," but the Texas woman "acquired suffrage by fighting every inch of the way." On May 24, women's suffrage failed to pass by some 25,000 votes. Anti-suffragists viewed the result as a mandate for their view. The same day McCallum remarked, "Sad day for Texas women, but just what we expected with . . . all the Mexicans, Negroes, Republicans, I.W.Ws, Reds, socialists and 'whatnots' including 'first paper' Huns allowed to vote while loyal American women were not."[28]

A printed flyer distributed by the suffragists attributed the defeat to "Negro and Republican-German votes" organized by "our impeached former governor, James E. Ferguson, and his 'crowd.'" The flyer went on to state, "Comal and Gillespie Counties composed practically entirely of Germans, gave only 242 votes for the Suffrage-Alien Amendment and 2,650 votes against it. That is over ten to one against." The suffragists added, "The male voters of Fayette, Guadalupe, Lavaca, Lee, and Washington counties" with "the same kind of Germans that are in Comal . . . gave 7,539 majority against the Suffrage-Alien Amendment." In Travis County, the ballot box at Germania Hall gave forty-two votes against suffrage and only one for. The flyer estimated that the heavily German counties of Texas combined to give "41,836 anti-suffrage, pro-alien votes." The flyer concluded that, "There are, of course, many progressive, loyal Germans who really believe in democracy and supported Woodrow Wilson and the Democratic Party, but they are evidently not the same ones who made up that 25,000 anti-suffrage, pro-alien majority."[29]

Fortunately for the suffragists, the U.S. Congress in June 1919 submitted a constitutional amendment to the states for the enfranchising of women. Governor Hobby called the legislature into special session immediately, and Texas became the ninth state overall, the first in the South, to ratify the Nineteenth Amendment, granting women the right to vote.[30]

The November 1918 armistice did not end anti-Germanism in higher education. Nearly a year after the fighting had ended in Europe, Eduard Prokosch, a professor of Germanic languages at the University of Texas, unexpectedly found himself the subject of a loyalty probe. Austrian-born, Prokosch had received his Ph.D. in Leipzig, Germany, in 1905, and taught at the University of Wisconsin until he came to Texas in 1913. He had written several texts in elementary German for use in American secondary schools. The former United States ambassador to Germany, James W. Gerard, accused Prokosch of propagandizing for the Kaiser, and his comments prompted the university loyalty probe.[31]

In his *Face to Face with Kaiserism* in 1918, Gerard had condemned the professor for reprinting the German national anthem in a first-year grammar book for American school children. Prokosch also had allegedly compared the German federal union to United States federalism, and maintained the Kaiser was responsible to the *Bundesrath* (parliament). These statements, Gerard maintained, were calculated to give the impression that the Germans' "despotic autocracy" was "ruled in very much the same matter as our own republic."[32]

University officials had successfully protected Prokosch from charges of pro-Germanism during the war. Gerard's accusations, however, aroused a public outcry that extended to the Texas state legislature. In June 1919, a senate committee called for the regents to remove Prokosch from the faculty, although the only concrete indication of disloyalty cited was the decision of New York City to bar his grammar books from its public schools on the grounds that they contained German propaganda. In addition, the senate committee voted five to four to abolish the teaching of German in higher education institutions for the next two years.[33]

Vinson realized the campaign against Prokosch was baseless, and promised Prokosch that the university would contemplate no "specific charge of disloyalty" against him, despite the fact that Vinson told Prokosch the citizens of Texas hardly expect "a man with your antecedents and present connections" to be "whole-heartedly loyal." Inadequacy of evidence, however, did not end the problem for the university. The whole of the matter, Vinson informed Prokosch, was that his "continued presence in the faculty of the University is for the time being and for an indefinite period in the future rather a burden than a help to this institution." Vinson asked, "Would it not be better for you to tender your resignation" than to allow the matter to continue to the point where dismissal was necessary?[34]

Prokosch did not attempt to defend himself and replied that he was willing to resign on one condition. Since it was already mid-summer, he would find it difficult to secure another teaching post for September. Therefore, he pleaded that his resignation not be effective until the end of the fall semester. During that period, he would offer his services as a translator to the university faculty. Prokosch had already consulted the history department and found that they were interested in having him translate the writings of "foreign elements" in the United States, especially ethnic groups from Eastern Europe.[35]

Very much relieved that Prokosch would willingly step down, Vinson agreed to present his proposal to the board of regents at their regular meeting on July 7. The board showed no mercy. Not only did they refuse the professor's special request, but they ordered his position vacated as of August 31. No explanation was given for the action.[36]

The university later agreed to explain its position. In minutes dated November 6, the regents gave the following reasons for Prokosch's dismissal: "constant rumors" regarding the "loyalty of Professor Eduard Prokosch," the "assertions" that "Professor Prokosch's books contained German propaganda," and "circumstances over which neither the Board of Regents nor Mr. Prokosch had any control." The board admitted that the "growth of public opinion in this matter" had created an "intolerable situation."

While it was impossible to prove or disprove "charges of disloyalty against Professor Prokosch," the board thought that the "best interests of the University" demanded an end to his tenure. Prokosch's dismissal had been made "with great regret" because of the board's "high appreciation" for his "scholarship and teaching ability."[37]

With the cordial words the University of Texas neatly disposed of the problem, and Prokosch was forced to find a new position in less than two months. That he was able to go to Bryn Mawr for the fall semester of 1919 (Prokosch later taught at Yale University for ten years) was a testament to the respect with which his colleagues elsewhere regarded him. He left Texas, never to return, at a time when his own department was endangered with extinction. In 1919, Governor Hobby vetoed the entire annual appropriation for the German Department. Upon Vinson's advice that the study of German was of "real value," the legislature overrode the governor's veto and salvaged one academic issue from the era of anti-German hysteria.[38]

In 1920, Texas' German-born population numbered 31,062, a figure considerably smaller than the 48,032 German-born Texans in 1910. Nationally, Germans in 1920 still constituted the largest foreign-born element, 12.1 percent, in the United States. Germans also comprised the highest percentage of those who had already become citizens of the United States, about 74 percent. Some historians speculate that the census data indicates that between 1910 and 1920, the German-born as well as the German stock in the United States moved underground. Some changed their names; "Kaiser" became "King" and "Schmidt" became "Smith." Historian La Vern Rippley believes it is unreasonable to believe that the number of German-born dropped 25.3 percent between 1910 and 1920 when there was a continuing flow of German immigrants into the United States between 1910 and the outbreak of war in the summer of 1914. Rippley speculates that in 1910, persons of German birth readily acknowledged to the census-taker where they had been born. By 1920, however, the stigma of being German appears to have been so severe in certain areas that many Germans, when asked by government officials, denied their origins.   In 1920, German-American activist George Sylvester Viereck wrote that some Germans "would deny the Holy Ghost if He were to approach them in German garb or with a Teutonic accent." Although more research is necessary to explain fully the decline, perhaps it can be linked to the anti-German conditions that prevailed in certain states, including Texas.[39]

By 1930, the number of German-born in Texas had fallen by another 5,000; ten years later it was down to 17,970. The decline was slowed but not halted by a slight upsurge in German immigration to the United States in the 1920s that peaked at mid-decade. The xenophobia of the 1920s led to the passage of laws restricting immigration and, for the first time, the enactment of quotas. Restriction on European immigration had been building since 1910 but did not gain legislative distinction until World War I made such an act feasible. The first Immigration Act to become law passed in 1917, beginning with a literacy test, and expanded in 1921 and again in 1924. The Immigration Act of 1924 and its national origins provision favored northern and western European groups (i.e. German) and severely limited "undesirable" immigrants from southern and eastern Europe. Though given impetus by the anti-German feelings aroused during the war, restrictive laws were not directed against the Germans nor did German immigration suffer because a high German quota had already been established. In fact, over twice as many Germans (386,634 to 174,227) immigrated to the United States in the decade 1920-1930 as had arrived between 1910 and 1920, although few of the new arrivals appear to have had Texas as a destination.[40]

Postwar relief efforts conducted by the German-Texan community on behalf of people suffering in Germany during the years of the Weimar Republic reflected the survival of German culture in the state. Here, as elsewhere, German Americans moved slowly and with caution in emerging from wartime isolation. In the relative privacy of the postal windows, they risked their identities with large-scale donations mailed for suffering families in Germany. Likewise, when orchestrated by the churches in Texas, semipublic postwar collections for hungry people in Germany were highly successful. Members of Salem Lutheran Church in Brenham "felt deep concern for those in dire need in Germany. Many packages of food and clothing were sent off." The Sons of Hermann in Texas responded to appeals from various relief organizations in Germany during the early 1920s. Relatives in the homeland wrote to German Texans requesting money for food, clothing, and emigration purposes. Many times, German Texans responded.[41]

Following the disbandment of the Texas State Council of Defense in June 1919, archivists for posterity's sake asked the discharged local councils for summaries of their wartime activities. In October 1920, the Mills CCD wrote that during the war, the Germans of the county "were naturally in sympathy with the old country in the beginning, but after the United States entered, we found nothing to indicate they were not for us."[42] Two years after the war, the Comal County local board stated that the conditions in that county "were unique" because of its German origins and population. Yet, the Germans in early 1917 rallied to "their obligations as American citizens." The board felt the war had produced a positive change in the city of New Braunfels. Whereas, before the war foreign language, customs, political outlooks, and attitudes prevailed in the town, "now little of this is evident," the board remarked, it is "becoming completely Americanized."[43]

The demobilization of the Texas State Council of Defense in June 1919 eliminated one source of anti-German agitation, but other groups stepped forward attempting to eliminate German-Texan culture. The Ku Klux Klan attracted little attention in Texas before 1921. Reorganized near Stone Mountain, Georgia, in 1915, the Klan declared its opposition to all things foreign, Catholics, Jews, and radicals, and its support for white supremacy, the purity of women, law and order, and 100 percent Americanism. Feeding on disturbed postwar conditions, the Klan in December 1922 claimed 700,000 members nationally and entered state and local politics in Texas with considerable success. The organization, however, hung its hat on violence and intimidation and directed a portion of it at German Texans.[44]

Klan activity was especially pronounced in the Eastern Texas German settlements of Austin, Fayette, and Washington counties. Brenham, in particular, had unresolved loyalty issues dating back to the war and became a hotspot for Klan activity. In 1920, Brenham saw a duly elected legislator, John Neinast of the American Party, denied his seat in the legislature because of trumped-up charges of disloyalty. On May 21, 1921, some four hundred members of the revitalized Houston Ku Klux Klan rode into Brenham on the train and marched in the German *Maifest* celebration. Clad in white flowing robes, pointed caps, white face masks, and a red circle with a cross on their uniforms, the KKK men carried signs that read, "Our fathers were here in '61, and their boys are here in '21," and more to the point, "Speak English or quit speaking on the streets of Brenham."[45] The Klan also threatened a Lutheran church in Berlin, Texas, just west of Brenham, with the warning: "Speak the English language or move out of this city and county."[46]

Shortly thereafter, town leaders in Brenham held a meeting and declared that the German language should be banned. Tensions, however, remained high and the Klan soon turned to physical confrontation to serve as a warning to area citizens who persisted in speaking German. Indeed, an incident occurring a full two-and-a-half years after Armistice Day provided the occasion for a special effort by a gang of Texas patriots to force their version of Americanism upon a defenseless victim. The victim was Dr. R. H. Lenert, a lifelong resident of Brenham, Texas. Remembering charges of disloyalty against Lenert during the war and his persistence in speaking German afterward, a gang of eight unknown men in June 1921 beat and then tarred and feathered Lenert. Afterward the men dumped him in downtown Brenham. Lenert had denied the disloyalty charges, declaring he had purchased $1,800 worth of Liberty Bonds and War Savings Stamps during the war. He was tarred and feathered anyway. The incident had the desired effect on Lenert. He tendered his resignation as a member of the board of trustees of Brenham schools. In addition, Lenert begged for forgiveness and promised to teach all his friends "to be one hundred percent Americans and live as true and loyal Americans." The incident showed that long after the war anti-German passions lingered in the state.[47]

Austin County became the scene of the deadliest Klan-related violence in the state. A shootout on the main street of Sealy in September 1922 left four people dead and one severely wounded. The shootout grew out of an incident at a political barbecue in Cat Spring hosted by the Agricultural Society, where there were speakers in German as well as English. Hostilities spilled over to the evening of September 5, when Klan members shot and killed Fritz Schaffner, his son Robert, seriously wounding his younger son Ernest, and leaving his wife in serious condition from the shock of the death of her husband and son. Two of the assailants also died of bullet wounds and a third was later convicted of murder. A newspaper report claimed disputes over "politics, the Ku Klux Klan, and the German language" were said to be involved.[48]

The Klan also attacked German Texans in other parts of the state. In July 1921, authorities arrested four members of the Klan in connection with the tarring and feathering of a Waco man. Around the victim's neck, police found a placard that bore the inscription painted in red: "This is a sample to evil doers and pro-Germans. Beware. One hundred percent Americans—others must go. Ku Klux Klan."[49] The barns of German-Texan farmers mysteriously burned and went uninvestigated.[50] In March 1922, a band of masked men whipped then tarred and feathered German Catholic priest Joseph M. Keller in Slaton, Texas, near Lubbock. After the attack, several citizens of Slaton signed a petition assuring that the community would welcome a new priest that was "100 percent American in his pastoral duties."[51] A Prairie Hill Lutheran church indicated that it had troubles with the Klan until 1924. One day, members arrived at the church to find a hand-written sign on the door that read, "Speak 100% English or this Church will burn!"[52]

Not all German Texans allowed themselves to become victims of Klan violence. In the Brazos County community of North Zulch, Pastor A. J. Meyer, who in 1920 accepted a call to serve the local Lutheran church, arrived fresh out of seminary with a new bride. The Ku Klux Klan attempted to stop him and horsewhip him at a river crossing called the De Moort Crossing. But, Pastor Meyer whipped his horse and passed through the water safely. Later, he received a written warning from the KKK not to teach parochial school or preach in German. Pastor Meyer would not be dissuaded, though. He stayed for four years, when the Mission Board placed the congregation under the leadership of Pastor A. J. Niemann. Also in the town of Slaton, a German Texan recalled his father being stopped in his wagon by the KKK and told, "Germans not allowed." The German's father proceeded to buggy whip the Klan members by himself. In Corpus Christi, Reverend C. Kurz, pastor of the German Lutheran Church, received an unsigned letter warning him to stop preaching in German and using German books. The last sentence of the letter read, "One hundred percent Americanism is our slogan." Pastor Kurz replied that the letter did not bother him "in the slightest degree." When the Klan threatened to march in Nordheim's Silver Jubilee celebration in 1922 to protest the presence of home brew and gambling, Nordheim Germans forced the Klan to change its plan. Members of the KKK approached a German farmer in Stamford and threatened to tar and feather him because the German had invited an African-American farmhand to dinner at his home. The German farmer refused to stop and told the men if they came back, "I'll have my shotgun ready." Parishioners at the German Catholic church in Olfen came to the rescue of Father Joseph Meiser after a group of anti-German men planned to tar and feather him. Following the election of the anti-Klan candidate, Miriam "Ma" Ferguson, to the governorship in 1924, Klan activities in Texas almost disappeared overnight.[53]

The Red Scare, another potential threat to Germans, never fully materialized in Texas, largely because the state had relatively few of the unionized workers and foreign-born radicals that so frightened Americans elsewhere in the nation. The Red Scare, a fear of communism taking hold in the United States, began as several factors including the emotional environment of the war, the fear of a new international communist movement, and an emerging social and economic discontent, fed into and shaped the postwar period of nativism and reaction. The Bolshevik replaced the Kaiser as the symbol of an outside menace seeking to expand discontent among domestic groups. United States Attorney General A. Mitchell Palmer launched a national campaign of mass arrests and deportations directed against aliens and radicals. German-speaking, if not actually German-born, politicians in the United States led the socialist movement; this made the Red Scare a problem for Germans. Texas, however, had relatively few of the unionized workers and foreign-born radicals that frightened Americans elsewhere in the nation. In addition, Texas' German population resided primarily in small towns and rural areas thus having little impact or influence on urban organized labor.[54]

The new issues of the postwar period, however, struck with sudden intensity in Texas in the state elections of 1920. During World War I, loyalty issues had dominated political rhetoric if not behavior to the near exclusion of other concerns. Two years later loyalty issues were still present but their context had changed. The Texas governor's race of 1920 proved eerily similar to the Hobby-Ferguson race of 1918. The Democratic primary pitted former Senator Joseph Weldon Bailey against Pat M. Neff, a former speaker of the House for the Texas legislature. Bailey's campaign denounced prohibition, women's suffrage, socialism, and the League of Nations, thus drawing criticism from pro-Wilson speakers. Dallas dry leader Thomas B. Love alleged, "Every pro-German is with Bailey . . . every dissatisfied brewer and liquor dealer, every man who resents the great administration of Woodrow Wilson and of William P. Hobby as governor will vote the Bailey ticket. And no doubt the Kaiser agrees with Bailey."[55] Former Attorney General M. M. Crane said, "every German sympathizer, every former saloon owner and every man whose mouth had to be closed by the espionage act during the war is for Bailey."[56] Likewise, Bailey supporters accused Neff of having pro-German sympathies. One Bailey supporter sarcastically remarked in Marlin, "I wonder when my friend Neff ceased to be a Kaiser lover. You may not know it but Pat Neff has German blood in him." Despite the fact that some German-language newspapers endorsed Bailey, the primary generated little interest in the German counties of Texas. Bailey carried seventy percent of the German vote, but lost to

Neff on the state level, garnering only forty percent of the state total.[57]

The most remarkable part of the 1920 election season was the reemergence of former governor James E. Ferguson. In August 1919, he formed the American Party and, because he was banned from holding state offices, announced that he would be a candidate for president the following year. Throughout the rest of his political career, Ferguson received an astonishing amount of support from German Texans. State Senator T. H. McGregor, a Ferguson loyalist, ran for governor in 1920 as the American Party candidate. In the general election, Ferguson finished second in the German counties, only a hundred votes behind Republican Warren G. Harding. Despite nearly carrying the German counties, Ferguson finished a distant third on the state level. More noteworthy was the performance of McGregor in the German counties. Despite also finishing third statewide, McGregor carried the German ballots with over twice as many votes as Neff and Republican Charles A. Culberson, and defeating them both in eight of the ten German counties.[58]

In 1922, Ferguson dissolved the American Party and announced his candidacy for the United States Senate. Three klansmen, the most prominent of which was former state senator Earle B. Mayfield, entered what turned out to be a six-man Democratic primary. Ferguson clearly identified himself as the anti-Klan candidate. He also tried to get a light-wines-and-beer referendum on the primary ballot, but the committee turned it down. Unified Klan backing gave Mayfield a large plurality on July 22, but Ferguson finished second carrying the German counties but falling 30,000 votes behind statewide. Nonetheless, he had forced a runoff. Subsequently, the two candidates locked horns in one of the bitterest political fights in state history. Ferguson's old ties to the brewing industry and to Germans again became fodder for attack. Mayfield asked, "Will you send to the United States Senate a man who favors repealing the Volstead Law?" He added, "I say tonight to James E. Ferguson and his cohorts, prohibition is here to stay and thank God it is here to stay." Mayfield then accused Ferguson of being backed by German brewers: "the Anheusers, the Busches, . . . and the Schlitzes" are the men "who now come forward with German gold bonds purchased with blood money. . . . These are the men behind the candidacy of James E. Ferguson." Mayfield told supporters, "On the twenty-sixth of August the Democrats of Texas are going to give James E. Ferguson and his John Barleycorn a knockout blow."[59]

Ferguson fired back, calling Mayfield a "hypocritical wet pro." Ferguson claimed that Mayfield, "with prohibition sweat still on his forehead," helped "drink a quart of bootleg liquor" in Austin. Furthermore, Ferguson accused Mayfield and former governor William P. Hobby of getting "drunk as boiled owls" and running around naked while camping on the San Gabriel River near Georgetown. In addition, Ferguson found Mayfield "guilty of conduct with the opposite sex that I can not, in decency mention when ladies are present in the audience." Ferguson also attacked his opponent's Klan membership, "I charge that Mayfield is a member of the Klan." Ferguson then furthered chastised its members: "Oh, you Ku Kluxers, I don't blame you for wearing a mask—so people can't see who you are or what kind of company you keep." During the war, "you never did read where there was a damned Ku Klux at the front." In 1856, "they called it the Know Nothing Party. Well, they might as well call it that now. Most of you don't know what you are doing." In Ferguson's opinion, the race boiled down to himself and the "high cockalorum of the Ku Klux Klan in Texas."[60]

On August 12, Mayfield claimed that "3,500 negroes of Bexar County voted in the primary of July 22 for Mr. Ferguson" and an effort was "now being made to get the German Republicans of South Texas to vote for the Bell county man." As to war records, Mayfield accused Ferguson of pro-Germanism reminding the crowd that in July 1914 a member of the National German-American Alliance "spoke in German at Seguin, Texas, in behalf of the candidacy of James E. Ferguson for Governor of Texas." The campaign slowly deteriorated, everyday becoming more acrimonious until the runoff. The two candidates even offered to fight one another.[61]

Ferguson campaigned through the German counties thoroughly while Mayfield made almost two hundred August speeches in the dry counties of North and West Texas, with an occasional visit to such Klan strongholds as Houston. German newspapers urged German Texans, no friends of the KKK, to vote for Ferguson since "Mayfield is the candidate of the Klan." On the day of the runoff, Ferguson trounced Mayfield in the German counties but lost the statewide election by 52,000 votes. In the German counties, Ferguson garnered over three times as many votes as did Mayfield, showing the Germans' opposition to prohibition and the Klan. Mayfield went on to victory in the general election while Ferguson viewed his loss as a silver lining. In 1932, Ferguson told a reporter, "though I didn't win the race I established myself as the anti-Klan candidate and that elected my wife two years later."[62]

Though his impeachment conviction kept him banned from state office, Ferguson in 1924 managed to get the name of his wife, Miriam, on the ballot, campaigning with her and making most of her speeches. "Ma" and "Farmer Jim" Ferguson claimed that Texas voters could get "two governors for the price of one." The Democratic primary turned into a fight between Mrs. Ferguson and Klan candidate, Felix D. Robertson. German Texans again backed the Fergusons, primarily because they were anti-Klan. W. A. Trenckmann wrote in *Das Wochenblatt*: "German votes helped [James E.] Ferguson to two victories, and remained true to him even after his office was taken from him." Though "not a friend of the Germans," he presented "himself as a champion . . . for the people." Trenckmann then expressed that he would "a hundred times" rather vote for "Ma" Ferguson than "Farmer Jim." Oscar R. Schumacher, editor of the *Fredericksburger Wochenblatt*, proved more concise: "We need an anti-Klan governor." In the August primary, "Ma" defeated Robertson by almost 98,000 votes statewide. In the German counties, she crushed Robertson, receiving over five times as many votes as her opponent.[63]

In the general election, Mrs. Ferguson faced Republican candidate, George C. Butte, dean of the University of Texas Law School. Despite a growing tendency on the part of German Texans toward Republicanism, Mrs. Ferguson easily won the ten German counties of Texas and the governorship. She became the first elected female governor in the United States. The *Fredericksburger Wochenblatt* wrote: "Innumerable voters who had never before voted the Democratic ticket saw in their vote for Mrs. Ferguson the only hope of keeping our state government out of the hands of the Klan— and rightly so." Thomas B. Love, leader of the anti-Ferguson forces in Texas, blamed the loss on German and black Texans. "The Republican Germans and negroes (about 75,000 of them) voted solidly for Ferguson. If they had voted for Butte, he would have been elected." Mrs. Ferguson continued to garner significant support for the German counties during her two unsuccessful runs for reelection in 1926 and 1930, as well as her victory in 1932. German Texan support did not fade until 1940 with "Ma" Ferguson's final unsuccessful gubernatorial run.[64]

The German-Texan vote in the presidential race of 1928 provided the only other unusual German political impact of the 1920s. The race came down to Republican Herbert Hoover and Democrat Al Smith, the Catholic governor of New York. The German counties of Texas took more than the usual interest in the presidential campaign. In many ways, the race became of question of prohibition more than anything else. Almost without exception, the most prominent of the state's prohibition leaders and many of its best known church leaders indicated early that they would not support Governor Smith and his wet plank. Progressive Democrats in Texas actively criticized their party's candidate as someone who would repeal national prohibition, whereas they portrayed Hoover as the prohibition candidate. The German-language newspapers also weighed in. The *Neu-Braunfelser Zeitung* wrote that every vote for Hoover would "encourage our fanatics to make more useless laws." A week later it wrote, "More and more influential Texans are taking a stand for Al Smith for President. . . . Those who vote for Smith on the Democratic ticket will, in Texas at least, be on the winning side and know the right and freedom of a service." Other German papers, on the contrary, urged German Texans to vote for Hoover. The returns show a remarkable amount of support for Smith in the

German counties, voting in his favor two-to-one over Hoover. In the statewide returns, most remarkably, Texans for the first time gave their electoral votes to a Republican, as Hoover edged Smith. Because of German-Texan support for the wet candidate Smith, Leonard Withington, director of the Texas Republicans, felt that Republicans "probably lost 50% of our usual German-American vote" and that "the loss was almost entirely due to wet sentiment."[65]

In the early 1920s, Texas' educational planners introduced their plans to eliminate foreign influences in the public school system. Annie Webb Blanton, state superintendent of public instruction from 1919 to 1923, directed the Texas public school system as it undertook an Americanization plan. "The Great War," she wrote, "revealed to America its weakness of unassimilated aliens, native and foreign born . . . who had not caught the vision of America, who knew nothing of its institutions, and who could not even understand its language." Blanton cast herself as the Abraham Lincoln of Texas education by stating, "the nation can [not] endure half-native and half-alien today any more than it could endure half-free and half-slave a generation ago, hence, the timeliness of the movement among public schools of the country to shape their course in such a way as to help in the program of Americanization." Blanton viewed the public school as the melting pot of America. To those who felt the end of the war had ended the need for patriotic activity, Blanton said that "The work of patriotism is never finished; when it lags your country suffers, when it ceases, your country dies."[66]

In an article entitled, "The 'Foreign' Problem in Texas," she wrote, "In certain portions of our state there are communities nearly as foreign now in speech and in the habits and customs which their forefathers brought with them across the seas." Blanton complained about the fact that in many towns in Texas "children are trained in private or parochial schools" and "instruction is in a foreign tongue." How, she asked, "are we to imbue them with the lessons of Texas citizenship" if "these children become adults without having learned to read or write the English language?" Unless children spoke only English in school, Blanton scolded, "you must go back to the country which you prize so highly, and rear your children there." She concluded by asking, "Will there ever be a more favorable time than the present to decree that children reared in Texas shall be Texans in spirit as well as in name?" Rarely in the education curriculum, however, were German Texans, or any other European ethnic groups, singled out after the war as needing special Americanization programs. The recipe for the Americanization of these white, European, ethnic groups, for the most part, consisted of not much more than speaking English—a simple Americanization.[67]

Texas' attack on the German language in schools succeeded. The academic study of German dropped dramatically during and after the war. In 1918, ninety-nine public and private high schools were accredited to teach German in Texas. After the war, in 1921, only ten of them were still accredited to teach the language. In comparison, meanwhile, the number of schools accredited to teach Spanish during the same time more than doubled from 67 to 146. Between the academic years of 1917-1918 and 1921-1922, the total number of high school students enrolled in German decreased from 3,977 to 294. Nationally, likewise, the percentage of high school students studying German decreased drastically. In 1915, nearly 25 percent of all high school students in America studied German. By 1922, less than 1 percent of all American high school students studied German. The elimination of German from schools in Texas caused considerable problems for many German-Texan children entering school in the 1920s since a majority of these students had learned German as a first language in the home. Despite legal restrictions, in the late 1920s, some Texas rural public schools reintroduced the study of the German language.[68]

Parents favoring a German-language education for their children, meanwhile, received a boost from a Supreme Court ruling. Nebraska in 1919 prohibited instruction in any "private, denominational, parochial or public school," except in English. Furthermore, the law prohibited the teaching of any modern foreign language until "after a pupil shall have attained and successfully passed the eighth grade." The law was clearly aimed at Nebraska's large German-American population. In 1920, authorities charged Robert T. Meyer, a teacher in a Lutheran school, with violating this statute by teaching biblical studies in German to ten-year-old children during a special hour-and-a-half recess period that the school had instituted after the adoption of the law. Fined twenty-five dollars and costs, Meyer began a series of appeals that in 1923 reached the United States Supreme Court. In *Meyer v. Nebraska*, the court rejected the law on the grounds that it violated the due process clause of the Fourteenth Amendment, which protected the parents' right to choose the language in which their children were schooled. Prohibiting the teaching of a foreign language was, in this context, unreasonable. The Supreme Court struck down similar legislation from Ohio, Iowa, and Oregon (*Pierce v. Society of Sisters*). Thus, by 1925, German Americans had retained the right to educate their own children and teach them to speak their mother tongue.[69]

Along with language education, the war depleted the German-language press in Texas. At one time, at least thirty-five Texas towns had a German-language newspaper, and some had several. Between 1914 and 1919, the number of German newspapers published in Texas declined from twenty-six to fifteen. Because of anti-German sentiments and government restrictions during the war, many newsstands probably refused to sell German papers and many German Texans cancelled subscriptions, forcing papers out of business. Among those that failed were some of the oldest German papers in Texas: *Katholische Rundschau* (San Antonio, 1897-1918), *Texas Deutsche Zeitung* (Houston, 1873-1917), *Nord-Texas Presse* (Dallas, 1891-1917), *Cuero Deutsche Rundschau* (1891-1918), and *Das Volksbote* (Brenham, 1874-1918). In 1922, the following German language newspapers were still being published: *Neu-Braunfelser Zeitung* (1852), *Freie Presse* (San Antonio, 1865), *Fredericksburger Wochenblatt* (1877), *LaGrange Deutsche Zeitung* (1890), *Das Wochenblatt* (Austin, begun at Bellville, 1891, moved to Austin in 1909), *Waco Post* (1891), *Seguiner Zeitung* (1892), *Der Harold* (Taylor, 1895), *Lavaca County Nachrichten* (Hallettsville, 1896), and *Das Wochenblatt* (Giddings, 1899). Many of the German papers still in existence in the 1920s actually saw an increase in subscriptions, most likely drawing readers from the newspapers that folded during the same period. As late as 1927, Texas counted twelve German-language newspapers operating in the state.[70]

Gradually, the German language returned to good favor in Texas. In 1920, the University of Texas reported an increase in the number of students studying Germanic languages. The board of education for Houston schools voted to return German to the curriculum after an eleven-year absence. The *Dallas Morning News* argued for the return of German to Texas' classrooms saying, "To exclude German is to adopt the policy of cutting off the school nose to spite the curriculum's face. . . . By all means, put German back." The state restored textbooks printed in German to favor in 1929. The measure included a list of multiple books in German for use in high schools and junior high schools.[71]

The retention and use of the German language perhaps provided the best evidence of the preservation of *Deutschtum* in Texas. Joseph Wilson has argued that generations of Texans used the German language exclusively for almost all purposes into the 1930s and even later. Caesar (Dutch) Hohn, a German Texan with Yorktown roots, wrote of how his knowledge of German helped him while working with German farmers as a county agent in Washington County during the late 1920s. Churches, communities, schools, and social clubs operated in German. The Cat Spring Agricultural Society kept their records entirely in German until 1942, likewise, the La Bahia Turn *Verein* until 1946. In addition, German Texans wrote correspondence, documents, and periodicals in the German language. Churches kept their histories (of individual congregations as well as of the church bodies), such as those published on anniversary occasions, in German—not as German translations or parallel versions but as the only forms. The churches also kept "official" documents, such as certificates of baptism (the equivalent of birth certificates) and marriage, and death records in German. Some of the documents are still accepted today by state offices as proof of birth, marriage, or death. Furthermore, the most visible evidence is the fact that many gravestones throughout the state bear German inscriptions, some dating into the 1940s.[72]

The "church Germans" in Texas proved to be the greatest purveyors of the German language. Before the United States entered World War I, 145 Lutheran Church—Missouri Synod and *Deutsche Evangelische Synode* congregations held services in the German language. German-Texan children born between 1920 and 1930 were reared in German-speaking homes and community settings, and some were married in German. Churches often "imported" clergy from Germany bringing up-to-date Standard German to the pulpit. Into the mid-twentieth century, many German Texans were confirmed in German by German-born or German-educated pastors. At the North Texas conference of the Lutheran Church—Missouri Synod in 1925, attendees debated the merits of German versus English-language use. "The chief advantage in the use of German is administering to the older people in times of sickness and death," said Reverend W. F. Klindworth, pastor of the Trinity English Lutheran Church in Dallas. "In times of sorrow and bereavement words of cheer and comfort in the language which they learned the Christian religion at their mother's knee is sweet to their ears." After the war, the number of all-German churches steadily declined, yet the percentage of Missouri Synod churches offering English services did not reach fifty percent until 1930, which placed Texas below the national average as far as English language adoption. In 1940, 12,633 Texas Missouri Synod Lutherans still worshipped in churches where at least half the services were in German.[73]

The churches of the rural and small-town German belt proved most successful in maintaining German. In 1919, all German congregations were located in towns such as Cisco, Warda, Shiner, Loebau, and Dime Box. Of the 37 churches holding German services in 1945, all were located in small towns or rural areas except one in Houston and one near San Antonio. The oldest congregations held on to German longest, some offering services in German for over a hundred years. Among churches founded before 1889, German was still used in half the congregations in the 1950s. In addition, German retreated from a broad geographical base to its core area, similar to the German settlement pattern in Texas during the nineteenth century.[74]

Several individual church histories indicate the use of German for years, even decades, after World War I. In 1932, Pastor A. L. Wolff addressed his congregation in German at the dedication of the new St. John's Lutheran Church in San Antonio. A Lutheran church in Wilson in 1938 offered one service a month in German. Bethlehem Lutheran Church in Round Top until 1940 taught Sunday School classes in German. St. John Lutheran Church in New Ulm kept their church minutes in German until 1942. A Lutheran church in Paige maintained German language services until 1957. St. Paul Lutheran Church in Serbin held congregational meetings in German until 1966. In Fayette County, Holy Cross Lutheran in 1958 worshipped twice a month in the German language. An additional note from Holy Cross' history, dated 1970, indicated that church members tutored a new pastor from California in the German language so he could administer the Lord's Supper fluently.[75]

The "club Germans" in Texas slowly, cautiously, and perhaps less enthusiastically, reentered associational life. The Texas State *Saengerfest* began again in 1921 and has been going ever since, albeit on a much smaller scale than before the war. In 1929, audiences heard the voices of 500 singers at that year's *Saengerfest* in San Antonio. Sinking profits caused by World War I and prohibition forced the *Beethoven Männerchor* in San Antonio out of its historic home. It relocated to the King William District where it still meets, drinks, and conducts public concerts in a *halle und garten*. (Photos in the hall from the World War II era have captions still in German). The Houston *Sängerbund* returned to regular meetings and saw its numbers increase in the early 1920s. Throughout Texas, between 1920 and 1930 Germans formed new singing societies, including the Houston *Liederkranz* in 1924. Thirty-three of the singing groups joined the *Deutsch-Texanischer Sängerbund* (German-Texan Singers' League). Many shooting clubs and athletic clubs continued to use German into the 1930s. In the late 1920s, the State Fair of Texas offered German Day for the first time since 1915. Visitors listened to German singing societies and folksongs, watched German plays, ate German foods, and visited various exhibits and attractions.[76]

After the war, the Sons of Hermann proved to be the strongest German organization in the state. In 1920, the Order of the Sons of Hermann in Texas, which by then was financially stronger and had more members than all of the lodges in the rest of the United States combined, broke away from the national order of the Sons of Hermann and became autonomous and independent of the national group. In 1922, the organization claimed that it had 450 lodges and over 25,000 members, and in 1930, at the grand lodge meeting in Galveston, it possessed a membership of 30,000 with assets totaling over four million dollars. The longest passenger train ever run on the San Antonio and Aransas Pass Railway brought delegates to Fredericksburg for the grand lodge of the Sons of Hermann convention in 1924. The townspeople decorated the entire city in the colors of the order with bunting, flags, and electric lights; a concert band even escorted the visitors. In 1928, the Sons of Hermann in Dallas offered a summer school in German language instruction with Gertrude E. Dietel, a teacher from New Braunfels. Complete transition from the German language to the English language by the Texas order was begun early in the 1930s and completed by 1937. Although the "club Germans" never matched their prewar numbers, their continued existence and activities suggest that World War I did not bring about the end of a German culture in Texas.[77]

During the 1920s, anti-German nativism faded as the previously existing anti-Mexican American sentiment multiplied. A few possible explanations exist for this shift in Lone Star nativism. Historian Walter Kamphoefner writes that most German Americans before World War I maintained the use of the German language in their homes, schools, and churches. By the 1940s, the second generation of German Americans, the children of those who immigrated and who themselves were often raised in the United States, maintained the German tongue to a remarkable degree even though the war decimated classroom German. Kamphoefner argues that German Americans were neither socioeconomically handicapped nor marginalized by German language retention. German Americans had just as much social mobility and even higher rates of economic stability and home ownership than did non-German, English speakers. Preserving German worked for German Americans.[78]

German Texans by the second generation were making the transition from working class to the middle class. Historian Alwyn Barr in a quantitative analysis of economic mobility among blacks, Mexican Americans, and German Texans in San Antonio from 1870 to 1900 found that German immigrants rapidly and substantially gained toward the middle class while Mexican Americans—largely because of race—remained employed in exploitive manual labor. The slight economic mobility of Mexican Americans differed insignificantly from the statistical baseline of inertness provided by the African-American sample. Why did German immigrants to San Antonio, as committed as Mexican Americans to the maintenance of their native tongue, advance, while Mexican Americans did not? Barr believes, "the presence of more distinct ethnic groups such as Negroes and Mexican Americans apparently enhanced the chances for occupational advance by European immigrants and reduced the level of prejudice against them." German Texans made the jump to the middle class and eventually to whiteness, whereas Mexican Americans became racialized—an "other" race with African Americans.[79]

The reasons why the sharp and focused nativism directed against German Texans during the war declined after the war are complex and still not fully understood. By the mid-1920s, certainly, the furor over the Americanization of Germans was over. The Ku Klux Klan's appropriation of the term in the early 1920s, mounting public disillusionment with the World War experience, weariness with prohibition, the end of mass immigration through the acts of 1921 and 1924, discredited the cause and allowed attention to focus on other issues. Historian Russell A. Kazal, in his recent study of Germans in Philadelphia from 1900 to 1930, found that in the postwar years, Germans increasingly identified themselves as Americans—"Old Stock"—to differentiate themselves from African Americans, recent immigrants from southern and eastern Europe, and other minorities. In Texas, likewise, as the postwar hysteria and nativism died out, Germans became accepted as "Anglos." Ethnic groups that could not pass as Anglo American, specifically Mexican

Americans and African Americans, became the focus of discrimination. Germans, like their Anglo neighbors, often ignored the ways of Mexican and African Americans, limiting cultural exchange and understanding.[80]

By 1930 then, German-Texan culture had survived the war. The culture, however, did not go unscathed and significant assimilation took place. The German language disappeared from Texas' classrooms, German newspapers and societies failed, more and more churches adopted English-language services, and public displays of German ethnicity retreated from Texas' streets. Yet, despite a submerged German ethnicity, the Texans of German descent managed to preserve their culture. The war brought a disruption, rather than an elimination of German institutions. The war, therefore, served as a turning point in German-Texan history, and one that culminated in the redefinition of German-Texan ethnicity in the 1920s. The period from 1900 to 1930, consequently, marked not the end of German-Texan culture, but the beginning of a new one. German Texans still constituted one of the largest European immigrant groups in the state. More importantly, Germans still played major roles in Texas' economy, influenced newspapers, politics, and social life in the state, and, thus, had ample strength to assert their ethnicity. It would take several more years and another World War before German-Texan culture would be driven into submission.

Conclusion

Events in the decades after the 1920s did little to revive German culture among German Texans and much to keep the culture on the decline. The 1930s did see the abrupt rise of a second German-American Bund, a Nazi movement that found marginal support in Texas, but the Bund was overwhelmingly an organization of postwar German immigrants. It collapsed even before the United States entered World War II against Germany. World War II did not bring a second anti-German hysteria, but some German individuals experienced harassment due to their ethnic background. The war's revelations of Nazi atrocities, however, contributed to the reluctance of many to advertise their German heritage, a reluctance that continues among a few German Texans to this day.

With its distinctive history of German immigration, its significant German population, and its German contribution to the state's history, early twentieth-century Texas occupied a position of strategic importance within German America. But how does the study of German Texans and World War I compare to that of other states and what characteristics made the Texas case unique? Granted, many of the answers to the two questions are beyond the scope of this work. With a few exceptions, many case studies of German Americans and World War I rarely venture beyond 1920. Yet, some recent scholarship suggests that the Texas experience compares favorably to the states of the Midwest, which have been the focus of a majority of the case studies, despite Texas' relatively small percentage of Germans statewide in comparison to the states of the Midwest.

What then were the unique characteristics in the case of German Texans and World War I? Although Texas' German-born population ranked only thirteenth among all states in 1900, the percentages of Germans within some counties in Texas ranked among the highest in the nation outside of the Midwest. Therefore, if Texas was not a "German state," certain counties clearly were. Because of the high concentration in the German counties, Texas' German population resisted assimilation for a long time. In addition, as it was concentrated in rural areas and small towns, the German population in Texas allowed German-Texan culture to remain even more insular than that of urban Germans. In an article on German-American assimilation, historian Kathleen Neils Conzen argued, "if a real German culture has survived anywhere, it is in the densely German rural areas of the midwest and plains states." Conzen adds that religion, and the "successful adaptation of German customs of family farm operation, and inter-generational land transfer played a large role in maintaining such communities." In a number of ways, the Texas case is similar.[1]

The beginning of the Great War in Europe in 1914 did not prove to be a divisive issue in Texas. Both English-language and German-language newspapers in the state felt free to express opinions both for and against the Allied Powers and Central Powers. Almost all German papers opposed Britain's anti-German propaganda, published letters from relatives in Germany, and did not hesitate to attack President Woodrow Wilson's lack of true neutrality. Likewise, German-American organizations, most specifically the National German-American Alliance, lobbied for pro-German policies. German Texans felt it perfectly natural to want to support their old fatherland in this global conflict. Should the United States enter the war against Germany, the German papers remained confident that the entire country, including its German-American population, would stand behind the president during the national crisis. The public mindset expressed in the German-Texan press acknowledged the dual identity of being German as well as American.

The revelation of the Zimmermann telegram in 1917, however, offering the Mexicans an alliance with the promise of *reconquista*, was a much greater affront to Texans than to other Americans. It brought public indignation and alarm to the state and did for Texans what the sinking of the *Lusitania* had done for the rest of the country. Many in the state felt the U.S. should immediately enter the war and it put German Texans in a extremely precarious position.

Once America intervened in World War I, securing the loyalty of German immigrants to the war effort and eradicating any suspected disloyalty became a primary goal. Whipped up by the Committee of Public Information, the Council of National Defense, the Texas State Council of Defense and its county councils, the anti-German hysteria soon spread throughout Texas. The growing pressure to appear patriotic broke friendships, weakened neighborly relations, and even turned German Texans against each other. A few days before it ceased publication, the Brenham *Texas Volksbote* published a list of some eighty persons who publicly stated they did not support the anti-war American Party (soon carried by the English paper as well). The anti-German hysteria proved to be most intense in the Midwest. Texas experienced the hysteria to a lesser degree, but its path still closely paralleled that of the Midwest. Texas, likewise, witnessed the replacement of German town and street names; bans on the German language; vandalism of German landmarks; elimination of German from public school curricula; the folding of German newspapers and *Vereine*; the arrest of German Texans deemed disloyal; and numerous instances of tarring and feathering, whippings, beatings, and intimidation. German Texans also died, but it is unclear if their deaths were solely the result of anti-German hysteria.

Perhaps the most distinctive quality of the anti-German hysteria in Texas consisted of the fact that the frenzy did not take place evenly. Some areas experienced significant problems, whereas other areas of the state experienced very few difficulties. The large urban areas of Dallas, San Antonio, and Houston, for example, reported very few, if any, cases of violence directed against German

Texans. Metropolitan areas of Texas still appeared to be anti-German, but the pattern did not entail mob action. Each of the large cities sought to conduct its brand of nationalism either under the scope of the law or through public discourse in the urban newspapers. It also seems there was something in the urban experience that made the difference.

A historical examination of Bexar County (San Antonio) from 1880 to 1920 suggests that by approximately 1914, the German-born population had almost vanished. The county's population had grown significantly, while its German-born population decreased by twenty-five percent in the period from 1910 to 1920 alone. By the start of the war, German Texans in urban areas had been forced to assimilate. With the developments taken together, it can be argued that San Antonio's German community deteriorated even before the beginning of the war. Thus, the strength of anti-German hysteria in 1917-18 was merely attacking the last remnants of the once-strong German culture in San Antonio.[2]

Clearly then, most violence and organized intimidation occurred in small towns and rural areas of Texas. Where Germans were very few they tended to be ignored. But where Germans were numerous enough to merit notice, but too few or too divided to effectively defend themselves, is where Germans were subject to the greatest pressures. The citizens of small town and rural Texas often took the elimination of German culture to the extreme. The collective actions of patriotic citizens sought not only to rid the small towns of German propaganda but also to intimidate any pro-German element in the towns. The patriots intended to turn the Germans into loyal Texans.

Intimidation in the small-town setting, however, often did not prove satisfactory for American patriots in many cases. Suspected disloyalty was usually enough to provoke reaction from nativist groups. Local newspapers and county councils helped stir the furor. They encouraged Texans to "Whip the Kaiser" by keeping a watchful eye over the German element. The local county councils proved effective by distributing pamphlets and propaganda and whipping up anti-German sentiment. This appears to be particularly true in the coastal prairie region between Houston and Corpus Christi, which was settled relatively late and may have had more first rather than second generation Germans. The Goliad, Victoria, and DeWitt County Councils of Defense in South Texas, for example, seemed successful in this regard. Many patriots in small towns considered reporting the alleged disloyal remarks insufficient and organized their own brand of collective, vigilant justice. The patriotic elements in the small towns and rural areas, moreover, considered the refusal to purchase Liberty Bonds an immediate affront to their ideals as Americans. The brand of intimidation used against delinquents sought to coerce loyalty, but frequently spilled into violence. A final rationale for the excessive treatment of Germans in small Texas towns may have been the inadequacies of federal and state statutes to deal quickly and harshly with disloyalty. Many small town patriots believed that existing laws would not defeat the pro-German element that had infested their town. They complained that Germans ignored their resolutions, continued to speak German, and participated in elements of German culture. As a result, the patriots felt forced to take the law into their own hands and resort to violent activities.

Another unique feature of the anti-German hysteria in Texas appeared to be the lack of problems reported in the historically German small towns of Texas. The city of Fredericksburg, for example, described almost no instances of violence against German Texans. The city of New Braunfels, in comparison, reported a few possible instances of disloyalty, but again nothing significant. One would naturally assume these cities would be targets for the Americanizers. The facts, however, proved otherwise. Visitors to the German towns often remarked on the number of American flags flying. One visitor to the German towns remarked, "In proportion of population more United States flags are flying in New Braunfels than in Dallas." He went on to say, "Fredericksburg bought great quantities of flags, bunting, and patriotic emblems and had the greatest loyalty demonstration I have seen. It is the same in other towns in that section." A study of two lesser-known German-Texan towns, Muenster and Lindsay, founded by the German Catholic

Flusche brothers in the 1890s, uncovered none of the violent events encountered elsewhere in the state during the war even though the towns were dominated by Germans. (The author attributes it to a tolerant local newspaper editor.) Thus, if German Texans in the German towns held pro-German views, and odds are some did, they disguised those views quite well. Most likely, the fact that the German towns consisted of overwhelming numbers of Texans of German descent also played a role in the lack of problems in the German towns. German Texans usually outnumbered Anglo Texans and the Anglo Texans probably felt that if they undertook any anti-German actions or reported disloyalty, they themselves would become targets. In the historically German towns, Germans protected each other and, therefore, could preserve their culture, even in the face of nationwide anti-Germanism they could not be pushed around. The city of New Braunfels, hardly intimidated, in 1925 named a new elementary school for none other than Carl Schurz: not only a German, but also a Union general and Republican cabinet member.[3]

Anti-German activity in Texas does not appear to have affected the families of prominent German Texans. Highly regarded families of German descent such as the Klebergs, the Guenthers, the Wurzbachs, the Wolters, and the Weinerts experienced little trouble during the war. In fact, Rudolph Kleberg was in great demand as a public speaker and "Four-Minute Man" during World War I. Harry Wurzbach was elected to Congress in 1920 from the San Antonio-Seguin district, and was the first Republican Congressman from the state to be re-elected—to a total of five terms. His successor, Richard Kleberg, who served seven terms, was a Democrat but equally German. This provides additional evidence that Germans were hardly intimidated in areas of Texas where they were heavily concentrated. German-born Max Krueger, a rancher and later manufacturer of oil well equipment, despite having a brother-in-law killed while fighting for the German army, alludes only briefly to World War I in his memoirs. Krueger considered himself a German, yet he did not have divided loyalties, he stood solidly behind the United States. Similarly, even the Texas State Council of Defense called upon the prominent German Texans for advice and help during the war. Apparently, since the families stood firmly entrenched as accepted members of Texas society, the family members' loyalty went without question and none of them appeared to be blatantly pro-German in thought or action.[4]

Another factor at work during the World War I era was psychological. Many German Texans had a "superiority complex" resting in part on their role as the first settlers in places like New Braunfels and particularly Fredericksburg, their Unionism, and their success in agriculture. Lloyd Wenzel, a German Texan who grew up in Seguin during the 1920s, recalled that his paternal grandmother had emigrated from Germany to Texas only shortly after Texas had broke away from Mexico. The Germans who settled near Seguin used the black soil for their farms to grow cotton. Seguin had a big German community, and the Germans called the non-Germans "raggedy." The Germans were very neat and kept their barns and houses painted. Other places, to them at least, looked raggedy compared to their own.[5]

With a majority of the actions taken against German Texans occurring in small towns and rural areas, German settlements likely made up a small part of the area's population. Most likely, the areas consisted of a small clustering of German farms or homes within a larger Anglo-Texan dominated community. The Germans in the rural areas and small towns had higher instances of tighter immigrant communal ties. In less-populated areas, it remained easier to continue local ethnic societies and to maintain cultural heritage. As war hostility intensified, enclaves of Germans practicing their country's customs or frequently using the German language stood out and became easy targets for rising nativist feeling. Unlike the members of well-known German-Texan families, the victims were not the prominent Germans in the state. For the Americanizers in these areas, just the presence of Germans was enough to spark nativism that resulted in collective action, intimidation, or even violence. When such German Texans continued to speak the German language in public, worship in German-language churches, and refused to purchase Liberty Bonds, the result frequently spilled over into threats or violence. The refusal of a German storekeeper to hang a Red Cross poster, for example, was usually enough to provoke action. The local county councils of defense carried out their work with the utmost seriousness and believed that they were helping defeat Germany overseas by attacking German Texans at home. Anti-German parties organized to intimidate the so-called un-American practitioners, likewise, prevailed in the smaller towns and rural areas because groups were easier to gather and organize.

This is not to argue, however, that all German Texans were purely victims of aggressive actions by the Americanizers. Some German Texans proved stubborn, they refused to realize the precariousness of the situation that they faced. They openly supported Germany and flaunted the German language. Pastors refused to budge on language restrictions, created confrontational situations, and made foolish comments. Damning the flag and the country or threatening the life of the president would have caused problems regardless of whether or not the United States was at war with Germany. As they had in the neutrality period, some obstinate German Texans insisted on displaying pictures of Kaiser Wilhelm II or they refused to rise and sing the "Star Spangled Banner" in public gatherings. Caesar (Dutch) Hohn relates about his father who listened in on a conversation between German Texans. They spoke in glowing terms of the Kaiser until Hohn's father could no longer hold his temper. He admonished them to remember that they all left Germany because they were starving there and that the United States had been good to them. If they were so fond of the Kaiser they should go back to Germany. Other German Texans were unwise; certainly they were indiscreet. The Fayetteville Germania Club flew the German flag above its building. Others were tactless or naïve. In Karnes County, an area of Texas that had been reported as being full of pro-German sentiment, a German expressed his hopes for the death of all American soldiers sent to Europe. On the opposite end of the spectrum were German Texans who hoped to shed all marks of German ethnicity and embraced all tenets of superpatriotism. They even reported on their fellow German Texans. Even though they lived in a country believed to exhibit the utmost ideals of democracy and freedom, German Texans failed to grasp the idea that America's entry into World War I would force them to restrict their freedom of speech and that the slightest negative comment or action might be perceived as disloyal.[6]

In retrospect, the anti-German hysteria directed at the Germans of Texas could have been worse. In Great Britain, for example, the British government between 1914 and 1919 forced over 20,000 Anglo Germans (those of German heritage living in England) into Knockaloe internment camp on the Isle of Man for the duration of the war. Although camp life was not particularly punishing, nearly 200 people died during their internment. Historian Frederick C. Luebke argues that the case of German Americans pales in contrast to that of German immigrants in Brazil during the war. There, German Brazilians were the victims of numerous destructive riots. Mobs caused enormous property damage as they destroyed hundreds of residences, German-language newspaper offices, churches, schools, clubhouses, businesses, factories, and warehouses. Following Brazil's declaration of war in October 1917, a second series of riots resulted in more destruction. The Brazilian government declared martial law, forbid all German-language publications, outlawed all German-language worship services, and empowered the president to seize alien enemy property. The Brazilian behavior, therefore, proved to be remarkably violent and repressive compared to the American.[7]

Nor did the end of the war bring quick relief to the plight of German Texans. The dislocations brought on by the end of the war produced an ideal climate for nativism. The resulting xenophobia contributed to the "100 percent American" organizations, such as the Ku Klux Klan. The Klan's activities in Texas, in part, focused on a program of Americanizing foreigners and some of the violence the Klan produced became directed at German Texans. In addition, continued attacks on the German language and proposed immigration restrictions, coupled with Prohibition, ensured continued scrutiny of German Texans. Not until the mid-1920s, did the lives of German Texans appear to normalize again.

Higher concentrations of Germans in small town and rural Texas likely helped fuel a stronger sense of public Germanness in the state after World War I than in other parts of the country. Some German institutions had survived the war by adopting a low-key approach. They kept the use of the German language in public to a minimum, supported the war effort by purchasing Liberty Bonds or raising money, and adopting a pro-American outlook. Some organizations had suspended their activities through the duration of the war.

German Texans did not emerge from the war unscathed; the war clearly submerged their culture. Yet, the continued existence of a German press, the continued use of the German language, the perpetuation of German-language church services, and the presence of numerous German social and cultural organizations prove that German Texans did, indeed, survive the war. Such examples of Germanness in Texas suggest that, contrary to some studies, after World War I German ethnicity did not simply disappear.[8]

The experience in Texas case fits closely with that of the Midwest. Kathleen Neils Conzen states, "Intrafamily assistance and transfer of land to children during the parents' lifetime adapted German goals to American circumstances and fostered an unusual degree of persistence and expansion in many rural ethnic communities." As a result, Conzen adds, "Rural areas of dense German settlement—in Texas, Missouri, Minnesota, and Wisconsin—harbored fifth or even sixth-generation German-speakers."[9]

German-Texan culture survived World War I in many regards only to be further waylaid by World War II. In November 1923, the picture of a Bavarian fascist leader, whose recent coup attempt had failed and led to his arrest, appeared on the front page of the *Dallas Morning News*. Adolf Hitler, a World War I veteran, and his subsequent rise to power, which culminated in his appointment as German chancellor in January 1933, forced another wave of German immigrants to the United States. Numbering about 200,000, the immigrants contained many intellectuals, including scientists, artists, musicians, writers, philosophers, doctors, architects, and actors, many of whom were Jewish. The new arrivals deeply enriched American society from technology to the arts to politics.[10]

Adolf Hitler's emergence on the world's stage once again brought negative attention to German Americans. The creation of pro-Nazi organizations in the United States did not help matters. The most prominent of such organizations was the German-American *Bund* (federation). Formed in 1933 as the Friends of the New Germany, the group in 1936 renamed itself the *Amerikadeutscher Volksbund,* or German-American Bund. The Bund made aggressive use of anti-Semitic Nazi slogans and paramilitary bravado that soon alienated the American public. Even the leaders of the Third Reich distanced themselves from the organization. The Bund recruited its members primarily from recent German immigrants rather than from native German Americans. Its leader, German-born Fritz Kuhn, served as the group's self-appointed "American Führer." The Bund began attracting the attention of the federal government in the summer of 1937 as rumors spread that Kuhn had 200,000 men ready to take up arms. During that summer the Federal Bureau of Investigation conducted a probe of the organization but found no evidence of wrongdoing.[11]

In 1938, Texas congressman Martin Dies of the House Un-American Activities Committee proclaimed that Kuhn had 480,000 followers. Kuhn claimed the organization had 20,000 to 25,000 members and 100,000 unorganized sympathizers. More accurate records show that at the peak of its power the Bund had only 6,500 members and another 15,000 to 20,000 sympathizers, but from time to time the Bund held public rallies. In February 1939, Kuhn and the Bund held their largest rally in Madison Square Garden—ironically, one that marked the beginning of the end for the organization. In front of a crowd of 22,000, flanked by a massive portrait of George Washington, swastikas, and American flags, Kuhn attacked President Franklin D. Roosevelt for being part of a Bolshevik-Jewish conspiracy. After the rally, Kuhn, a naturalized United States citizen, found himself accused of embezzling the group's funds. Despite a conviction, the Bund still held him in high regard. Following America's entry into World War II, the American government sent Kuhn to an internment camp in Kenedy, Texas, where he served out the duration of the war. At one point, Kuhn escaped, but was recaptured. Upon his release in 1946, the government deported Kuhn back to Germany, where he died in 1951.[12]

Although a strong majority of German Texans rejected the activities of the Bund, some evidence suggests a scattering of support in the state for the Third Reich. The *Deutscher Klub* in Dallas displayed side-by-side pictures of Adolf Hitler and Franklin D. Roosevelt. Some Texans rumored that Nazi party organizers from Mexico met with some German Texans. Kuhn claimed the existence of four German-American Bund units in Texas, which were located in the cities of Fort Worth, San Antonio, Taylor, and Austin.[13]

Martin Dies' congressional committee uncovered the presence of the *Kyffhäuser Bund* in Texas, an organization consisting of veterans of the old imperial German army, headquartered in Houston. In fact, the Taylor *Texas Herold* advertised itself on its July 22, 1937 masthead as the official paper of the German veterans' organization. Its articles praised the new regime in Germany, including reprints of Hitler's speeches to the *Reichstag*, and the paper was certainly anti-Semitic. Representatives of the *Kyffhäuser Bund* claimed the group guarded German cultural goods, such as language, music, and literature. Formerly known as *Der Stahlhelm* (steel helmet), the group held loose ties with a national organization in Germany. According to testimony before Dies' committee, a member of the German-American Bund traveled to Houston in an unsuccessful attempt to organize a German-American Bund among the members of the *Kyffhäuser Bund*. Dies' committee also discovered that some money had been collected from German Texans under the guise of charity, but the funds actually aided the German government. The most damaging evidence presented to the committee indicated that agents of the Third Reich had threatened the editors of German-language newspapers in Texas. One of the letters sent by Baron Edgar von Spiegel, German Consul at New Orleans, stated, "German nationalism in Texas is fundamentally only a part of the German nationalism in the whole world." The agent said, "the leaders of German nationals in Texas can justly be proud that they have succeeded in initiating in the last few years such a successful gathering movement" that has thrived because of "the German revival movement of Adolf Hitler" which had "awakened again German nationalism abroad to the consciousness of its racial ties." Letters from Spiegel also alluded to strong ties between the German element in Texas and Germany. After the *Freie Presse für Texas* (San Antonio) had printed articles condemning Nazi Germany, editor G. F. Neuhaeuser received a letter threatening the paper "with all means" since it had printed "propaganda which incites and is untrue." Neuhaeuser considered the letter a direct threat and after his reply he received no more letters from Spiegel.[14]

Despite all such evidence of pro-German sympathies, the activities of the German-American Bund and the Nazis created little support for Germany among the state's German Texans. When questioned about pro-Nazi sympathies among the Sons of Hermann, one of its leaders responded that the fraternal organization steered away from politics. The *Deutsch-Amerikanischer Bund von Dallas*, an organization comprised of several of Dallas' German clubs, created confusion because of the similarity of its name to the German-American Bund. Similar bunds existed in Houston, Galveston, and San Antonio. A. F. "Fritz" Haller, the group's president, proposed to dissolve the organization rather than be associated with Hitler and Nazism. Haller claimed that several of the German consulates in the United States had distributed free books and pamphlets trying to get German Texans to remain loyal to the Third Reich. When the German ambassador, Dr. Hans Luther, visited Haller in Dallas, Luther refused to speak at a dinner in his honor unless the group displayed the Nazi flag. Haller refused to display the emblem but the two eventually worked out a compromise, agreeing to a foot-square flag that was positioned out of view of the audience. Haller vigorously denied the presence of pro-Nazi German Texans attending meetings in the state. "If any such meetings are being held," Haller remarked, it is "not Americans of German extraction. Germans in Texas are not the same as those in other sections," he said. "We have our father's house in Germany, perhaps, but there is no longer a Fatherland." In September 1937, the *Dallas Morning News* wrote, "Texas citizens of German extraction have done well to resent and oppose the efforts of the Nazi party in Germany to obtain allegiance of such Americans to Hitler's dictatorship." The paper added, "There should be no need to disband the social, musical, and other German-American organizations that have done much to promote cultural development in Texas and elsewhere."[15]

The actions of the Third Reich in Europe, from the territorial seizures of the 1930s to the invasion of Poland in 1939 and of the Holocaust in the 1940s, gave Americans of German descent still more incentive to downplay their German heritage. "Hitler was in fact doing the kind of things Allied propagandists had accused the Kaiser of two decades earlier. It was not time to take pride in German heritage," Frederick Luebke wrote.[16]

American intervention in World War II did not bring a repetition of the anti-German backlash of World War I. The FBI did indeed arrest 7,164 German aliens and German Americans, including nearly 300 in Texas. The government sent a number of those arrested to internment camps, the largest of which was located in Crystal City, Texas. Their treatment proved far less harsh than that of Japanese Americans, 100,000 of whom, both native-born citizens and aliens, who experienced internment during the war. And, some Texans of German descent unfortunately encountered anti-German feeling. They received second looks when speaking in German, vandals painted swastikas on German landmarks and homes, and some people described German towns in Texas as being full of "Hitler lovers." Germans cancelled the *Saengerfests* from 1942 to 1944, and the *Houston Sängerbund* changed its name to the *Houston Singing Society* (reversed in 1952).[17]

Nevertheless, no one harbored deep thoughts about the loyalty or disloyalty of German Texans. Several German Texans played important roles in the European theater due to their fluency in the German language. They participated in several crucial battles in their ancestral homeland. Captain Lloyd Wenzel, a P-38 fighter pilot who flew missions out of England into Germany, grew up in Seguin and learned German from his older sister. Wenzel flew alongside Captain Albert Wolfmueller from Fredericksburg and the son of the owner of the Wolfmueller bakery. The fact that the United States

Pacific Fleet Commander, Admiral Chester W. Nimitz, grew up bilingually in the German-Texan town of Fredericksburg helped to ensure that German loyalty did not come into question. In addition, Texas was also the birthplace of another prominent military leader of German name, Supreme Allied Commander Dwight D. Eisenhower.[18]

The perceptions, while conflicting, suggest that anti-German sentiment in Texas was relatively mild during World War II, certainly compared to World War I. The cumulative effect of both conflicts, however, kept German ethnic identity subdued. A member of the *San Antonio Liederkranz*, reflecting on the World War II years, remarked, "We didn't want to have anything to do with anything German. We were young and we were American and we didn't even want to admit that we were of German heritage." The years since 1945 have witnessed little impetus to reverse the German seclusion.[19]

Following World War II, the German-language newspapers in Texas continued to decline. By the end of the war, *Das Wochenblatt* (Austin) and the *Texas Herold* (Taylor) had ceased publication. On October 28, 1945, the *Freie Presse für Texas* (San Antonio) suspended its operations and the *Fredericksburger Wochenblatt* ended its run on January 1, 1946. The development left only two German-language newspapers in Texas after 1946. The *Giddings Deutsches Volksblatt* succumbed on September 15, 1949, leaving only the *Neu-Braunfelser Zeitung* as a German paper in the state. The paper witnessed its one-hundredth anniversary in 1952 and its editor pledged that publication would continue as long as the paper had 1,000 subscribers who read German. By the mid-1950s, the *Zeitung* ran entire editions in English, including advertisements, and by 1957, the number of subscribers slipped well below 1,000. The *Zeitung* dropped German in 1957 and merged with the English paper, the *Herald*, eventually forming the *New Braunfels Herald-Zeitung*. The change thus ended one of the longest running German-language newspapers in the United States.[20]

Remarkably, German-language use among Texans continued. Despite the fact that by 1945, 73.8 percent of Texas Lutherans worshipped in all-English churches and by 1958 Texas no longer had any German-language newspapers, several Texans continued to use German privately. In his study of the 1940 census data on mother tongue, Walter D. Kamphoefner found that 86 percent of second generation German Texans grew up with a German mother tongue. Only Nebraska, with 88 percent, had more second-generation German speakers than Texas. Even more surprisingly, Texas was the only state in which second generation speakers of German were outnumbered by those who were third generation or beyond. In 1960, a New Braunfels radio station still offered fifteen hours of German-language broadcasts weekly, also leading the nation in this category. Clearly, the rural frontier, once considered a great equalizer in terms of Americanization, fostered, if 1940 census data means anything, an opposite reaction. Farming areas of the states of the upper Midwest held on to the German language most tenaciously, and Texas, though not in the Midwest, definitely had a rural German population in 1940.[21]

Especially given the early date of its German settlements, the number of German speakers in Texas is all the more impressive. In 1970, Fredericksburg and its surrounding county still had a German speaking majority of 57 percent a century and a quarter after its founding. It stood alone, but that is not to say that other parts of Texas did not retain German. In fact, there were only nine Texas counties where nobody claimed a German mother tongue, but there were thirteen all told where 15 percent or more of the population did. Colorado, DeWitt, Guadalupe, Lavaca, and Mason counties all ranged between 15 and 20 percent. There were six counties in the 20 to 30 percent range: Fayette (La Grange), Washington (Brenham), Kendall (Boerne, Comfort), Comal (New Braunfels), Blanco (Johnson City), and Austin County. But second in line statewide was Lee County with 35 percent claiming German mother tongue. It is home to a heavy concentration of Wends from a Slavic language island in eastern Germany, who emigrated in 1855 partially to guard their Lutheran faith, but also to escape the pressures of Germanization. But they became Germanized in Texas, switching from the Wendish language to German. Into the twenty-first century the Lutheran churches of Giddings and nearby Serbin offer German services once a month.[22]

In the early 1960s, the estimate of German speakers in Texas numbered 70,000, not far off from the low-end estimate of 75,000 German speakers in 1907. Most of the remaining German speakers passed away during the 1960s and 1970s, however, and left the elimination of Texas German almost complete by the end of the twentieth century. Today, one is more likely to hear Spanish on the streets of New Braunfels or Fredericksburg than German. A 2005 report listed 11,990 Spanish speakers compared to 1,520 German speakers in Comal County (New Braunfels) and 2,860 Spanish speakers compared to 2,270 German speakers in Gillespie County (Fredericksburg). Many German Texans are not happy with this development because they feel many of the Spanish speakers are reluctant to learn English the same way they had to. As such, Spanish has effectively replaced Texas German as the de facto local minority language, which is reflected by the declining number of students who study German in local schools, while classes in Spanish continue to increase in popularity. Yet, researchers are desperately trying to record the last native Texas German speakers, estimated to be less than 8,000. According to the Texas German Dialect Project, the language will be extinct by 2040, ending an over 200-year tradition of the German language in Texas.[23]

Starting about 1950, the United States saw its last major wave of German immigration. Relatives of American servicemen and East German refugees made up a sizable German group to settle in the United States. The post-World War II immigration included a number of German immigrants who made substantial contributions to their adopted homeland, among them numerous scientists and intellectuals. A slight revival in German-American ethnicity followed. German Americans still constituted the United States' largest ethnic group and the emergence of West Germany as a trusted NATO ally led to extensive military and political cooperation. Not only were numerous American troops stationed in Germany, but German troops also trained in the United States, including Texas.

The spirit of cooperation led to the visits of German leaders to Texas. While serving as American vice president, Lyndon B. Johnson invited German Chancellor Konrad Adenauer to his Texas ranch in 1961. Adenauer and his entourage also traveled to Fredericksburg where they met with native-son Admiral Chester W. Nimitz. Later, in 1963, then President Johnson welcomed new German Chancellor Ludwig Erhard to the Texas Hill Country. Erhard was pleased to be able to speak German with some of the German Texans in the area.

The years since, however, have seen little impetus for increased German immigration to the United States. For all practical purposes, German immigration has ended. In the words of historian Kathleen Neils Conzen, "an occasional *Maifest* revival or lecture series on German-American culture signifies that the offspring of immigrants have joined to some extent in the national search for an ethnic heritage, but there is little to suggest the renewal of a viable German-American culture."[24]

More recently, some Texas cities as tourist attractions have promoted large-scale, public celebrations of German ethnicity. These include New Braunfels' Wurstfest, started in 1961, Muenster's Germanfest, which dates to 1975, and Fredericksburg's Oktoberfest, begun in 1981. Here, German ethnicity has been exploited by entrepreneurs of all types—entertainers, restauranteurs, and specialists in tapping tourist dollars. New Braunfels, for example, is almost as well known for its German-named waterpark, *Schlitterbahn* ("slippery road"), than its German-Texan history. The events are akin to what writer David Syring calls the "devil of heritage tourism." One is unlikely to learn much about German-Texan history and culture at the functions, except for the fact that Germans drink beer, eat bratwurst, enjoy music, and wear *lederhosen*.[25]

A few belated efforts have been made, chiefly by academics, to revive the study of German-Texan culture. The German-Texan Heritage Society, formed in 1978, promotes the awareness and preservation of the German cultural heritage in Texas. It operates out of the former German Free School in Austin and publishes the *Journal* several times a year, newsletters, and books detailing various aspects of German influence in Texas from the 1800s to the current day. In addition, it holds an annual meeting with lectures focusing on the unique German heritage and history in Texas. Likewise, the Texas German Society, established in 1983, states its purpose is "to preserve and encourage the German heritage, culture, and language of German-Texans and to continue these through communication, exchange, and good will with our fellow German-Americans and German people in other lands." The fact that the organizations exist and endure is proof to the lasting legacy of German influence in Texas.[26]

Today, almost nine decades after World War I, people willing to look can find traces of the German Texas that was. The town names of New Braunfels, Fredericksburg, Nordheim, Pflugerville, New Berlin, Hochheim, New Ulm, and others reflect the state's German heritage. German festivals still draw large crowds to their events and several Texas cities sponsor Oktoberfest celebrations. Enough singing societies remain to sustain the 60th Texas State *Saengerfest*, most recently held at Beethoven *Maennerchor* in San Antonio during 2006. German-Texan *Vereine*, then, never vanished completely. Yet, what remains of German Texas is but a small fragment of old German America. One fact, however, more than others probably best reflects the changed landscape of German Texas. Today, seven times as many Texas Lutheran churches offer worship services in Spanish than they do in German.[27]

Nonetheless, German Texas never recovered to pre-World War I levels, and the great American experiment in cultural pluralism receded. All the same, Texans, and all Americans of German descent, continued to show some peculiar traits. From the 1920s to as late as the 1970s, they were more likely to be married than the general population, more likely to have three or more children, more likely to reside in male-headed households, more likely to have some higher education, more likely to be employed, more likely to count farmers in their ranks, and more likely to pass the family farm down through the generations. When the U.S. Census Bureau resumed asking citizens about their ethnicity in 1980, some observers were surprised to learn the "Germans" were 50 million strong. By 1990, they were by far the largest ethnic body in the United States at 58 million, and were nearly twice as numerous as those who claimed to be of "English" stock (32.6 million and falling). The map of dominant ethnicity, by county, issued by the bureau showed a great swath of German "blue" across the upper half of the continental U.S. from New Jersey, Pennsylvania, and New York, through the Ohio River Valley into the great Middle West (particularly Missouri, Iowa, Illinois, and Wisconsin), across the Plains states, ending in eastern Oregon and Washington, with pockets in the Carolinas and, of course, Texas. The Texas map showed over forty counties where Germans made up the dominant ethnicity. According to the 2000 census, over two million Texans claimed to be of German ancestry. While the attempts by nativists of the 1910s and early 1920s to turn Germans into Texans had suppressed the more visible cultural attributes of German Texas, the deeper social and familial traits remained—and helped to people a state.[28]

Notes

Chapter 1: Introduction

[1] *La Grange Journal*, Feb. 21, 1918; *Houston Post*, Feb. 15, 1918.

[2] *La Grange Journal*, Feb. 21, 1918.

[3] Ibid.

[4] Ibid.

[5] *La Grange Journal*, Feb. 21, 1918; *Houston Post*, Feb. 15, Mar. 17, 1918.

[6] Carl Wittke, *German-Americans and the World War (With Special Emphasis on Ohio's German-Language Press)* (Columbus: The Ohio State Archaeological and Historical Society, 1936).

[7] John Arkas Hawgood, *The Tragedy of German-America* (New York: G. P. Putnam's Sons, 1940), 297, 301.

[8] David W. Detjen, *Germans in Missouri, 1900-1918: Prohibition, Neutrality, and Assimilation* (Columbia: University of Missouri Press, 1985); Detjen, *The Germans in Missouri*, 184.

[9] Dona Reeves, "An Ethnic Inventory for the German-Texans," *University Forum, Fort Hays State University* 27 (Summer 1982): 3; Joseph Wilson, "The German Language in Central Texas Today," *Rice University Studies* 63, no. 3 (1977): 51; Glen E. Lich, *The German Texans* (San Antonio: The University of Texas Institute of Texas Cultures at San Antonio, 1981), 159, 183; Gilbert J. Jordan, *Yesterday in the Texas Hill Country* (College Station: Texas A&M University Press, 1979), 161.

[10] Kathleen Neils Conzen, "Germans," in *Harvard Encyclopedia of American Ethnic Groups*, eds. Stephan Thernstrom, et al. (Cambridge: Harvard University Press, 1980), 406, 415.

[11] Frederick C. Luebke, *Bonds of Loyalty: German-Americans and World War I* (DeKalb: Northern Illinois University Press, 1974).

[12] Russell A. Kazal, *Becoming Old Stock: The Paradox of German-American Identity* (Princeton: Princeton University Press, 2004).

[13] Ibid., 261.

[14] Terry G. Jordan, "The German Element in Texas: An Overview," *Rice University Studies* 63, no. 3 (1977): 2.

¹⁵ Frederick C. Luebke, "Turnerism, Social History, and the Historiography of European Ethnic Groups in the United States," in *Germans in the New World* (Urbana: University of Illinois Press, 1990), 138-156.

¹⁶ Jürgen Eichhoff, "The German Language in America," in *America and the Germans: An Assessment of a Three-Hundred-Year History*, vol. 1, eds. Frank Trommler and Joseph McVeigh (Philadelphia: University of Pennsylvania Press, 1985), 232; Karl Arndt and May Olson, *German-American Newspapers and Periodicals, 1732-1955*, 2nd ed. (New York: Johnson Reprint, 1965), 614-635.

Chapter 2: German Texans to 1900

¹ Don H. Biggers, *German Pioneers in Texas: A Brief History of Their Hardships, Struggles, and Achievements* (Austin: Eakin, 1983), 8-9.

² Rudolph L. Biesele, "The First German Settlement in Texas," *Southwestern Historical Quarterly* 34 (1930-1931): 334-339.

³ Walter Struve, *Germans and Texans: Commerce, Migration, and Culture in the Days of the Lone Star Republic* (Austin: University of Texas Press, 1996), 45.

⁴ Robert W. Shook, "German Migration to Texas 1830-1850: Causes and Consequences," *Texana* 10 (1972): 230-231.

⁵ Ibid., 232-233.

⁶ Ibid., 234-235.

⁷ Louis Reinhardt, "The Communistic Colony of Bettina," *Texas State Historical Quarterly* 3 (1899): 33-40.

⁸ Terry G. Jordan, "The German Element in Texas: An Overview," *Rice University Studies* 63, no. 3 (1977): 1.

⁹ Ibid.

¹⁰ Michael P. Conzen, "The Clash of Utopias: Sisterdale and the Six-Sided Struggle for the Texas Hill Country," in *Cultural Encounters with the Environment: Enduring and Evolving Geographic Themes*, eds. Alexander B. Murphy and Douglas L. Johnson (Lanham, Maryland: Rowman & Littlefield Publishers, Inc., 2000), 45.

¹¹ Ibid., 46-47.

¹² Ibid., 52-53; Rudolph L. Biesele, "The Texas State Convention of Germans in 1854," *Southwestern Historical Quarterly* 33, no. 4 (April 1930): 247-261.

¹³ Walter D. Kamphoefner, "New Perspectives on Texas Germans and the Confederacy," *Southwestern Historical Quarterly* 102, no. 4 (April 1999): 442.

¹⁴ Walter L. Buenger, "Secession and the Texas German Community: Editor Lindheimer vs. Editor Flake," *Southwestern Historical Quarterly* 82 (April 1979): 379-402; Justine Davis Randers-Pehrson, *Adolf Douai, 1819-1888: The Turbulent Life of a German Forty-Eighter in the Homeland and in the United States* (New York: Peter Lang, 2000).

¹⁵ Kamphoefner, "New Perspectives," 444-447.

[16] Claude Elliott, "Union Sentiment in Texas, 1861-1865," *Southwestern Historical Quarterly* 50 (1946-47): 464-467; Robert W. Shook, "The Battle of Nueces, August 10, 1862," *Southwestern Historical Quarterly* 66 (1962): 31-42.

[17] Terry G. Jordan, "The German Settlement of Texas After 1865," *Southwestern Historical Quarterly* 73, no. 2 (Oct. 1969): 197.

[18] Ibid., 199, 201, 203-204.

[19] Ibid., 204-205.

[20] Ibid., 205.

[21] Ibid., 207.

[22] Kathleen Neils Conzen, "Germans," in *Harvard Encyclopedia of American Ethnic Groups*, eds. Stephan Thernstrom, et al. (Cambridge: Harvard University Press, 1980), 406; Terry G. Jordan, *German Seed in Texas Soil: Immigrant Farmers in Nineteenth-Century Texas* (Austin: University of Texas Press, 1966), 192-203.

[23] Jordan, *German Seed in Texas Soil*, 192-203.

[24] Jordan, "The German Settlement of Texas After 1865," 211.

[25] Conzen, "Germans," 415-416.

[26] Ibid., 421.

[27] Frederick C. Luebke, "German Immigrants and American Politics: Problems of Leadership, Parties, and Issues," in *Germans in the New World: Essays in the History of Immigration* (Urbana: University of Illinois Press, 1990), 81-84.

[28] Luebke, "German Immigrants and American Politics," 85-86.

[29] Joe B. Frantz, "Ethnicity and Politics in Texas," in *German Culture in Texas*, eds. Glen E. Lich and Dona B. Reeves (Boston: Twayne, 1980), 191-202; *Dallas Morning News*, Sept. 26, 1887.

[30] Carlos Kevin Blanton, *The Strange Career of Bilingual Education in Texas, 1836-1981* (College Station: Texas A&M University Press, 2004), 32-33.

[31] Ibid., 33.

[32] Ibid., 35.

[33] Ibid., 34.

[34] Ibid., 34-35, 49-50, 52-53; R.B. Cousins, *Sixteenth Biennial Report of the State Superintendent of Public Instruction for the Years Ending August 31, 1907 and August 31, 1908* (Austin: Von Boeckmann-Jones, 1909), 19; Joseph Wilson, "Texas German and Other Immigrant Languages: Problems and Prospects," in *Eagle in the New World: German Immigration to Texas and America*, eds. Theodore Gish and Richard Spuler (College Station: Texas A&M University Press, 1986), 233.

[35] James D. Ivy, *No Saloon in the Valley: The Southern Strategy of Texas Prohibitionists in the 1880s* (Waco: Baylor University Press, 2003), 63.

[36] Ibid.; *Dallas Morning News*, Aug. 21, 1887.

[37] Ivy, *No Saloon in the Valley*, 92; *Dallas Morning News*, Aug. 13, 1887, Aug. 21, 1887, Sept. 26, 1887, Sept. 30, 1887.

[38] Hans Trefousse, "German-American Immigrants and the Newly Founded Reich," in *America and the Germans: An Assessment of a Three-Hundred-Year*

History, eds. Frank Trommler and Joseph McVeigh, vol. 1 (Philadelphia: University of Pennsylvania Press, 1985), 160-162.

[39] La Vern Rippley, *The German-Americans* (Lanham, Maryland: University Press of America, 1976), 85-86.

[40] Ibid, 87-93.

[41] Judith Berg Sobré, *San Antonio on Parade: Six Historic Festivals* (College Station: Texas A&M University Press, 2003), 136; Glen E. Lich, *The German Texans* (San Antonio: The University of Texas Institute of Texas Cultures at San Antonio, 1981), 99-100.

[42] Conzen, "Germans," 406.

Chapter 3: *Deutschtum* and the Impending Crisis, 1900-1914

[1] Terry G. Jordan, "The German Element in Texas: An Overview," *Rice University Studies* 63, no. 3 (1977): 2; Kathleen Neils Conzen, "Germans," in *Harvard Encyclopedia of American Ethnic Groups*, eds. Stephan Thernstrom, et al. (Cambridge: Harvard University Press, 1980), 410; On the loss of the ability to speak German see Morgan Scott Sosebee, "Henry C. Smith: A Westering Man" (Ph.D. diss., Texas Tech University, 2004), 191-192.

[2] Jordan, "The German Element," 2; Jürgen Eichhoff, "The German Language in America," in *America and the Germans: An Assessment of a Three-Hundred-Year History*, vol. 1, eds. Frank Trommler and Joseph McVeigh (Philadelphia: University of Pennsylvania Press, 1985), 232.

[3] Frederick C. Luebke, *Bonds of Loyalty: German-Americans and World War I* (DeKalb: Northern Illinois University Press, 1974), 27-55; La Vern J. Rippley, *The German-Americans* (Lanham, Maryland: University Press of America, 1976), 99-115.

[4] Luebke, *Bonds of Loyalty*, 34.

[5] Rippley, *The German-Americans*, 99.

[6] Kathleen Neils Conzen, "Germans," in Stephan Thernstrom et al., eds., *Harvard Encyclopedia of American Ethnic Groups* (Cambridge: Harvard University Press, 1980), 418-419.

[7] Conzen, "Germans," 416.

[8] Conzen, "Germans," 416.

[9] Terry G. Jordan, "A Religious Geography of the Hill Country Germans of Texas," in *Ethnicity on the Great Plains*, ed. Frederick C. Luebke (Lincoln: University of Nebraska Press, 1980), 111.

[10] M. Heinrich, *History of the First Evangelical Lutheran Synod of Texas* (Chicago: Wartburg, 1927), 62-63.

[11] William A. Flachmeier, *Lutherans of Texas in Confluence: With Emphasis on the Decade 1951-1961* (Austin: Von Boeckmann-Jones, 1972), 93; Heinrich, *History of the First Evangelical Lutheran Synod of Texas*, 53-54.

216

[12] Judith Berg Sobré, *San Antonio on Parade: Six Historic Festivals* (College Station: Texas A&M University Press, 2003), 110-153.

[13] Glen E. Lich, *The German Texans* (San Antonio: The University of Texas Institute of Texan Cultures, 1981), 143-144.

[14] Lich, *The German Texans*, 163, 166, 169, 171.

[15] Lich, *The German Texans*, 161.

[16] *Dallas Morning News*, Apr. 16, 1907; Lich, *The German Texans*, 160; "Sons of Hermann," vertical file, Center for American History, University of Texas at Austin.

[17] Theodore John Albrecht, "German Singing Societies in Texas" (Ph.D. diss., North Texas State University, 1975), iii-v.

[18] Charles Thomas Johnson, *Culture at Twilight: The National German-American Alliance, 1901-1918* (New York: Peter Lang, 1999), 10-14.

[19] Ibid., 7-9, 14.

[20] Ibid., 5-7.

[21] Ibid., 11.

[22] Clifton James Child, *The German-Americans in Politics, 1914-1917* (Madison: The University of Wisconsin Press, 1939), 13; Johnson, *Culture at Twilight*, 13, 21-22; Luebke, *Bonds of Loyalty*, 98-99.

[23] Since the National German-American Alliance was order disbanded by Congress in 1918, records of the Texas branch of the alliance were most likely destroyed or seized by government officials. The main source for the activities of the Texas branch comes from the Senate testimony of Paul Meerscheidt. See Congress, Senate, Subcommittee of the Committee on the Judiciary, *National German-American Alliance: Hearings Before the Subcommittee of the Committee on the Judiciary*, 65th Cong., 2nd sess. on S. 3529, 23 February–13 April 1918, 186-197; *Dallas Morning News*, Oct. 21, 1909; Albert Godsho, "The National German-American Alliance, and the Washington Convention," *The Penn Germania* 1, no. 3 (March 1912): 212.

[24] Congress, *National German-American Alliance: Hearings*, 186-197.

[25] Congress, *National German-American Alliance: Hearings*, 189-191.

[26] Seth Shepard McKay, *Texas Politics, 1906-1944: With Special Reference to the German Counties* (Lubbock: Texas Tech Press, 1952), 32, 34-35. McKay identifies the ten German counties of Texas as: Austin, Comal, DeWitt, Fayette, Gillespie, Guadalupe, Kendall, Lee, Medina, and Washington.

[27] Lewis L. Gould, *Progressives and Prohibitionists: Texas Democrats in the Wilson Era* (Austin: Texas State Historical Association, 1992), 53-56; McKay, *Texas Politics*, 31.

[28] Seth S. McKay and Odie B. Faulk, *Texas After Spindletop* (Austin: Steck-Vaughn, 1965), 25.

[29] T. Herbert Etzler, "German-American Newspapers in Texas with Special Reference to the Texas Volksblatt, 1877-1879," *Southwestern Historical Quarterly* 58, no. 4 (April 1954): 423, 428; Conzen, "Germans," 420-421.

[30] Jordan, "The German Element," 2; Conzen, "Germans," 410; Historical Census Browser, University of Virginia, Geospatial and Statistical Data Center, http://fisher.lib.virginia.edu/collections/ stats/histcensus/index.html [accessed April 9, 2006]. Percentages for each county were determined by adding the number of persons born in Germany plus those with both parents born in Germany divided by the total population of the county. The percentages did not include those with only one parent born in Germany or some Germans of the second or third generations who met none of the census criteria, which would have, most likely, made the percentage of Germans even higher in those counties.

Chapter 4: German Texans and American Neutrality, 1914-1917

[1] *Fredericksburger Wochenblatt*, Aug. 6, 1914; *Neu-Braunfelser Zeitung*, Aug. 6, 1914; *Giddings Deutsche Volksblatt*, Oct. 29, 1914.

[2] *Dallas Morning News*, Jul. 31, Aug. 21, 22, 25, 28, Sep. 13, Oct. 1, Nov. 30, 1914.

[3] Charles Thomas Johnson, *Culture at Twilight: The National German-American Alliance, 1901-1918* (New York: Peter Lang, 1999), 100-102.

[4] *Dallas Morning News*, Jun. 30, 1916.

[5] *Houston Post*, Aug. 3, 1914; *Dallas Morning News*, Aug. 6, 1914; *San Antonio Express*, Aug. 2, 5, 1914.

[6] *San Antonio Express*, Aug. 16, 1914; *Dallas Morning News*, Aug. 13, 1914.

[7] *Neu-Braunfelser Zeitung*, May 10, 1917; *Fredericksburger Wochenblatt*, Sep. 3, 1914; *Katholische Rundschau*, Oct. 7, 1914.

[8] *San Antonio Express*, Aug. 1, 14, 18, 23, 25, 1914.

[9] *Dallas Morning News*, Aug. 9, 28, 1914.

[10] *Houston Post*, Aug. 12, 24, 1914.

[11] Lewis L. Gould, *Progressives and Prohibitionists: Texas Democrats in the Wilson Era* (Austin: Texas State Historical Association, 1992), 151-161.

[12] Ibid.

[13] Gould, *Progressives and Prohibitionists*, 126-149; Seth Shepard McKay, *Texas Politics, 1906-1944: With Special Reference to the German Counties* (Lubbock: Texas Tech Press, 1952), 54-59.

[14] Gould, *Progressives and Prohibitionists*, 145-146.

[15] Congress, Senate, Subcommittee of the Committee on the Judiciary, *National German-American Alliance: Hearings Before the Subcommittee of the Committee on the Judiciary*, 65th Cong., 2nd sess. on S. 3529, 23 February–13 April 1918, 214, 287-288; *Dallas Morning News*, Nov. 27, 1918.

[16] *Frederickburger Wochenblatt*, Dec. 17, 1914, May 11, 1915; *Katholische Rundschau*, November 18, 1914, Dec. 30, 1914, May 15, 1915.

[17] Frederick C. Luebke, *Bonds of Loyalty: German-Americans and World War I* (DeKalb: Northern Illinois University Press, 1974), 102-106.

[18] Luebke, *Bonds of Loyalty*, 106-111.

[19] Ibid., 104-105.

[20] Frederick C. Luebke, *Bonds of Loyalty: German-Americans and World War I* (DeKalb: Northern Illinois University Press, 1974), 130; Captain Henry Landau, *The Enemy Within: The Inside Story of German Sabotage in America* (New York: G.P. Putnam's Sons, 1937), 3-128.

[21] *Dallas Morning News*, May 9, 11, 1915: *Houston Chronicle*, May 9, 10, 1915; *Houston Post*, May 11, 12, 1915.

[22] *Houston Chronicle*, May 9, 10, 18, 1915; *Houston Post*, May 11, 12, 1915.

[23] *Giddings Deutsches Volksblatt*, Jun. 24, 1915; *Katholische Rundschau*, Jun. 9, 1915.

[24] *San Antonio Express*, Jul. 5, 1915; *Houston Chronicle*, May 20, 1915.

[25] *Das Wochenblatt* (Austin), Sep. 16, 1914, Nov. 11, 1914; *Neu-Braunfelser Zeitung*, Mar. 1, 1917; *Fredericksburger Wochenblatt*, Jul. 13, 1916, Apr. 5, 1917; *Katholische Rundschau*, Jan. 27, 1915; *Lutherbote für Texas*, Aug. 1915.

[26] *Fredericksburger Wochenblatt*, Feb. 1, 1917, Mar. 1, 1917; *Lutherbote für Texas*, August 1915.

[27] *Katholische Rundschau*, Oct. 7, 1914, May 5, 1915, Apr. 12, 1916, Oct. 4, 1916; *Neu-Braunfelser Zeitung*, Feb. 15, 1917; Carl Wittke, *German-Americans and the World War (With Special Emphasis on Ohio's German-Language Press)* (Columbus: The Ohio State Archaeological and Historical Society, 1936), 18-19.

[28] Luebke, *Bonds of Loyalty*, 142, 144.

[29] *Fredericksburger Wochenblatt*, December 9, 1915.

[30] *Dallas Morning News*, July 6, 1915; Higham, *Strangers in the Land*, 199.

[31] *Dallas Morning News*, Jan. 31, Feb. 1, 2, 3, Mar. 9, 1916.

[32] "McLemore (Atkins Jefferson)," vertical file, Center for American History, The University of Texas at Austin.

[33] *New York World*, Apr. 23, 1916; *Dallas Morning News*, Apr. 24, Aug. 13, 1916; John Price Jones and Paul Merrick Hollister, *The German Secret Service in America, 1914-1918* (Boston: Small, Maynard & Co., 1918), 243.

[34] *Dallas Morning News*, Jul. 23, 26, Aug. 1, 1916; Seth Shepard McKay, *Texas Politics, 1906-1944: With Special Reference to the German Counties* (Lubbock: Texas Tech Press, 1952), 70-71.

[35] Congress, Senate, Subcommittee of the Committee on the Judiciary, *National German-American Alliance: Hearings Before the Subcommittee of the Committee on the Judiciary*, 65th Cong., 2nd sess. on S. 3529, 23 February–13 April 1918, 194-196.

[36] McKay, *Texas Politics*, 71-73.

[37] Friedrich Katz, *The Secret War in Mexico: Europe, the United States, and the Mexican Revolution* (Chicago: The University of Chicago Press, 1981).

[38] *Dallas Morning News*, Feb. 28, Mar. 11, 1914; Gould, *Progressives and Prohibitionists*, 116-119.

[39] Barbara W. Tuchman, *The Zimmermann Telegram* (New York: Ballantine Books, 1958), 48-53, 66, 91-92; Katz, *The Secret War in Mexico*, 438; Landau, *The Enemy Within*, 114-128. Witzke was the only German spy sentenced to death in the United States during the war.

[40] Tuchman, *The Zimmermann Telegram*, 92-94.

[41] Tuchman, *The Zimmermann Telegram*, 94-96. La Vern J. Rippley, *The German-Americans* (Lanham, Maryland: University Press of America, 1976), 188.

[42] Katz, *The Secret War in Mexico*, 344-350, 351-367.

[43] *Dallas Morning News*, Mar. 2, 1917.

[44] *Houston Post*, Apr. 7, 9, 1917; *Dallas Morning News*, Apr. 4, 5, 1917.

[45] *Houston Post*, Apr. 9, 1917.

Chapter 5: The Anti-German Hysteria in Texas, 1917-1918

[1] Thomas Fleming, *The Illusion of Victory: America in World War I* (New York: Basic Books, 2003), 30.

[2] John Higham, *Strangers in the Land: Patterns of American Nativism, 1860-1925* (Brunswick: Rutgers University Press, 1955), 204-212.

[3] Frederick C. Luebke, *Bonds of Loyalty: German-Americans and World War I* (DeKalb: Northern Illinois University Press, 1974), 234.

[4] David M. Kennedy, *Over Here: The First World War and American Society* (Oxford: Oxford University Press, 1980), 46, 61-62.

[5] Ibid., 61-62; Luebke, *Bonds of Loyalty*, 208-209, 220; The "Halt the Hun!" poster for the Third Liberty Loan is reproduced in Luebke, *Bonds of Loyalty*, 272; Michael T. Isenberg, *War on Film: The American Cinema and World War I, 1914-1941* (Rutherford: Farleigh Dickinson University Press, 1981), 147-151; Leslie Midkiff DeBauche, *Reel Patriotism: The Movies and World War I* (Madison: The University of Wisconsin Press, 1997), 91-100.

[6] Kennedy, *Over Here*, 14, 26, 75-76, 79-80.

[7] Ibid., 78, 81-82.

[8] Higham, *Strangers in the Land*, 204-205; Luebke, *Bonds of Loyalty*, 215-216, 251.

[9] Luebke, *Bonds of Loyalty*, 3-24, 235-237, 244, 247-248, 252-253, 279.

[10] Kennedy, *Over Here*, 114-117; Luebke, *Bonds of Loyalty*, 214.

[11] Luebke, *Bonds of Loyalty*, 214.

[12] Ibid., 214-215.

[13] Lewis L. Gould, *Progressives and Prohibitionists: Texas Democrats in the Wilson Era* (Austin: Texas State Historical Association, 1992), 225; O. E. Dunlap, biographical file, Center for American History, University of Texas at Austin; *Dallas Morning News*, Oct. 16, 1917; "The Texas State Council of Defense," State Council of Defense Letters, box 2J355, Texas War Records Collection, 1916-1919,

1940-1945, (hereafter cited as TWRC), Center for American History, University of Texas at Austin, (hereafter cited as CAH).

[14] Gould, *Progressives and Prohibitionists*, 225; "Principle Activities of the Texas State Council of Defense," State Council of Defense Letters, box 2J355, TWRC, CAH.

[15] Gould, *Progressives and Prohibitionists*, 225-226; Joe R. Baulch, "Making West Texas Safe for Democracy: The 1917 Farmers and Laborers Protective Association Conspiracy," *West Texas Historical Association Year Book* 62 (1986): 119, 122.

[16] William Hawley Atwell, *Autobiography* (Dallas: Warlick Law Printing Co., 1935), 27, 33; Baulch, "Making West Texas Safe for Democracy," 123.

[17] *Dallas Morning News*, Sep. 30, Oct. 2, 19, 1917; Atwell, *Autobiography*, 32-33; Baulch, "Making West Texas Safe for Democracy," 127.

[18] Seth S. McKay and Odie B. Faulk, *Texas After Spindletop* (Austin: Steck-Vaughn Company, 1965), 52-54; Gould, *Progressives and Prohibitionists*, 215.

[19] McKay and Faulk, *Texas After Spindletop*, 54-55; "Keep Texas Free from the Despoiler," box 3H3, William P. Hobby, Sr. Family Papers, 1914-1997, CAH.

[20] *Dallas Morning News*, Jul. 18, 1918; "'Master of German Viewpoint' Helped Ferguson in Platform," box 3H5, William P. Hobby, Sr. Family Papers, 1914-1997, CAH. Future historian Walter Prescott Webb took two classes from Keasbey while a student at the University of Texas. Webb claimed the Keasbey was the best professor he ever had and he learned more from Keasbey than all his other professors combined.

[21] McKay and Faulk, *Texas After Spindletop*, 68; "S.O.S. Call to Texas Women," Texas Women's Democratic League, TWRC, CAH; *Dallas Morning News*, Jun. 30, 1918; *The Ferguson Forum*, Sep. 19, 1918.

[22] *Houston Post*, Jun. 19, 1918; *Dallas Morning News*, Jun. 21, 1918.

[23] *Dallas Morning News*, Jul. 19, 21, 25 1918.

[24] Seth Shepard McKay, *Texas Politics, 1906-1944: With Special Reference to the German Counties* (Lubbock: Texas Tech Press, 1952), 81-82; McKay and Faulk, *Texas After Spindletop*, 69.

[25] *Katholische Rundschau*, Apr. 25, 1917,

[26] *Neu-Braunfelser Zeitung*, Apr. 12, 1917.

[27] *Giddings Deutsches Volksblatt*, Apr. 19, 26, 1917.

[28] *Fredericksburger Wochenblatt*, Apr. 26, 1917.

[29] *San Antonio Express*, Apr. 10, 1917.

[30] *Neu-Braunfelser Zeitung*, May 3, 1917; *Fredericksburger Wochenblatt*, May 17, 1917.

[31] *Das Wochenblatt*, Dec. 24, 1917.

[32] Annie Greener, interview by Betty Cox, Jun. 15, 21, 1980, Levelland, Texas, Oral History Collection, Southwest Collection, Texas Tech University, Lubbock, Texas.

[33] *Dallas Morning News*, Mar. 10, 12, 1918.

[34] C. A. Goeth to J. F. Carl, Apr. 9, 1918, County Correspondence, box 2J394, TWRC, CAH.

[35] William A. Wurzbach to J. F. Carl, Apr. 2, 1918, County Correspondence, box 2J394, TWRC, CAH.

[36] E. E. Fischer to J. F. Carl, Sep. 15, 1917, County Correspondence, box 2J369, TWRC, CAH.

[37] J. F. Carl to E. E. Fischer, Sep. 17, 1917, County Correspondence, box 2J369, TWRC, CAH.

[38] The Organization of the Victoria County Council of Defense and Its Objects, County Correspondence, box 2J373, TWRC, CAH.

[39] Unknown to E. S. Parks, Apr. 7, 1918, County Correspondence, box 2J367, TWRC, CAH.

[40] Geo. W. Tyler to J. F. Carl, Sep. 10, 1917, County Correspondence, box 2J367, TWRC, CAH.

[41] Ed. W. Knesek to J. F. Carl, Dec. 18, 1917, County Correspondence, box 2J388, TWRC, CAH; Council of National Defense to State Council of Defense, Jul. 31, 1918, County Correspondence, box 2J388, TWRC, CAH; *La Grange Journal*, Feb. 21, 1918. See also Jonathan Zimmerman, "Ethnics Against Ethnicity: European Immigrants and Foreign-Language Instruction, 1890-1940." *The Journal of American History* 88, no. 4 (Mar. 2002): 1383-1404.

[42] W. H. Whitmore to the Honorable Local Board of National Defense, Sep. 19, 1917, County Correspondence, box 2J383, TWRC, CAH; *Texas Monthly*, July 2006.

[43] Bosque County Council of Defense Minutes, Mar. 11, 1918, County Correspondence, box 2J367, TWRC, CAH.

[44] C. B. Kilgore to J. F. Carl, Dec. 24, 1918, County Correspondence, box 2J357, TWRC, CAH.

[45] *Dallas Morning News*, Dec. 22, 1917.

[46] *Dallas Morning News*, Apr. 19, 1918.

[47] J. T. Murray to J. F. Carl, Dec. 29, 1917, County Correspondence, box 2J371, TWRC, CAH.

[48] Bosque County Council of Defense Minutes, Mar. 11, 1918, County Correspondence, box 2J367, TWRC, CAH.

[49] W. D. Crothers to J. F. Carl, Mar. 23, 1918, County Correspondence, box 2J372, TWRC, CAH.

[50] A. P. Engelking to James A. Harley, Feb. 4, 1918, folder 25, box 401-573, Correspondence, Departmental correspondence, Texas Adjutant General's Department, Archives and Information Services Division, Texas State Library and Archives Commission.

[51] W. M. Hanson to Jas. A. Harley, Feb. 4, 1918, folder 24, box 401-573, Correspondence, Departmental correspondence, Texas Adjutant General's

Department, Archives and Information Services Division, Texas State Library and Archives Commission.

[52] Karnes County Council of Defense, Mar. 9, 1918, County Correspondence, box 2J371, TWRC, CAH.

[53] County Food Administrator to Albert Neinhoffer, Apr. 4, 1918, County Correspondence, box 2J367, TWRC, CAH.

[54] W. H. Baldwin to J. F. Carl, Apr. 22, 1918, County Correspondence, box 2J396, TWRC, CAH; J. C. Mitchell to J. F. Carl, Jun. 14, 1918, County Correspondence, box 2J397, TWRC, CAH.

[55] J. C. McDonald to J. F. Carl, Feb. 11, 1918, County Correspondence, box 2J369, TWRC, CAH.

[56] W. H. Baldwin to J. F. Carl, Jun. 27, 1918, County Correspondence, box 2J396, TWRC, CAH.

[57] L. A. Voigt to J. F. Carl, Feb. 28, 1918, County Correspondence, box 2J383, TWRC, CAH.

[58] Ernst A. Eiband to J. F. Carl, Apr. 4, 1918, County Correspondence, box 2J383, TWRC, CAH.

[59] J. F. Carl to C. E. Breniman, Aug. 13, 1918, State Council of Defense, box 2J358, TWRC, CAH.

[60] M. A. Shumard to J. F. Carl, Jul. 27, 1918, County Correspondence, box 2J371, TWRC, CAH.

[61] M. A. Shumard to J. F. Carl, Oct. 5, 1918, County Correspondence, box 2J371, TWRC, CAH.

[62] N. T. Stubbs to J. F. Carl, Sep. 7, 1918, County Correspondence, box 2J373, TWRC, CAH.

[63] J. H. McLean to Texas State Council of Defense, Jul. 30, 1917, County Correspondence, box 2J372, TWRC, CAH.

[64] E. R. Wolcott to J. F. Carl, Dec. 6, 1917, County Correspondence, box 2J372, TWRC, CAH.

[65] E. R. Wolcott to J. F. Carl, Jan. 18, 1918, County Correspondence, box 2J372, TWRC, CAH.

[66] Perry Dickie to J. F. Carl, Jun. 15, 1918, County Correspondence, box 2J394, TWRC, CAH.

[67] Kenneth Krahl to J. F. Carl, Jun. 24, 1918, State Council of Defense Correspondence, box 2J358, TWRC, CAH.

[68] P. L. Campbell to J. F. Carl, Aug. 26, 1918, County Correspondence, box 2J369, TWRC, CAH.

[69] *Dallas Morning News*, Mar. 30, 1918.

[70] *Dallas Morning News*, Apr. 5, 1918.

[71] *Dallas Morning News*, Apr. 16, 1918.

[72] *Dallas Morning News*, Nov. 23, 1918; *The Ferguson Forum*, Nov. 21, 1918. It should be pointed out that it's very unlikely, or at least atypical, for a German Lutheran to holding a "revival service."

[73] Thad Sitton and Dan K. Utley, *From Can See to Can't: Texas Cotton Farmers on the Southern Prairies* (Austin: University of Texas Press, 1997), 53.

[74] *Dallas Morning News*, Dec. 27, 1917.

[75] *Dallas Morning News*, Oct. 26, 1917.

[76] *Dallas Morning News*, Dec. 29, 1917.

[77] Geo. J. Ivy to J. F. Carl, Mar. 28, 1918, County Correspondence, box 2J395, TWRC, CAH.

[78] C. Douglas Duncan to J. F. Carl, Nov. 7, 1918, County Correspondence, box 2J396, TWRC, CAH.

[79] Mark Sonntag, "Hyphenated Texans: World War I and the German-Americans of Texas" (M.A. thesis, University of Texas at Austin, 1990), 116-118.

[80] C. Douglas Duncan to J. F. Carl, Nov. 7, 1918, County Correspondence, box 2J396, TWRC, CAH.

[81] Luebke, *Bonds of Loyalty*, 283.

[82] John S. Cravens to Texas State Council of Defense, Jun. 8, 1918, County Correspondence, box 2J394, TWRC, CAH.

[83] *Fredericksburger Wochenblatt*, Nov. 1, 1917.

[84] *Das Wochenblatt*, Aug. 29, 1917.

[85] *Das Wochenblatt*, Jun. 5, 1918.

[86] L. L. Nusom to Rudolph Kleberg, Apr. 17, 1917, box 2J45, Rudolph Kleberg Family Papers, 1829-1966, CAH.

[87] R. P. Jeter to Rudolph Kleberg, May 15, 1918, box 2J45, Rudolph Kleberg Family Papers, 1829-1966, CAH.

[88] J. C. Baumgarten to Rudolph Kleberg, Jun. 5, 1918, box 2J45, Rudolph Kleberg Family Papers, 1829-1966, CAH.

[89] F. S. Schleicher to Rudolph Kleberg, May 14, 1918, box 2J45, Rudolph Kleberg Family Papers, 1829-1966, CAH.

[90] John Sharp Williams to Rudolph Kleberg, Dec. 5, 1917, box 2J46, Rudolph Kleberg Family Papers, 1829-1966, CAH.

[91] Rudolph Kleberg to Charles Nagel, Aug. 22, 1916, box 2J46, Rudolph Kleberg Family Papers, 1829-1966, CAH.

[92] R. G. Nowlin to Fred M. Huggins, Apr. 10, 1918, County Correspondence, box 2J367, TWRC, CAH.

[93] J. F. Carl to C. E. Breniman, Jul. 10, 1918, State Council of Defense, box 2J358, TWRC, CAH.

[94] C. Douglas Duncan to J. F. Carl, Nov. 7, 1918, County Correspondence, box 2J396, TWRC, CAH.

[95] *Dallas Morning News*, Jun. 15, 1917.

[96] Seadrift Council of Defense Chairman to Chairman County Council of Defense, Jul. 2, 1918, County Correspondence, box 2J368, TWRC, CAH. Italics added.

[97] *Das Wochenblatt* (Austin), Aug. 28, 1918.

[98] Field Division Council of National Defense to T. J. Ponton, Oct. 30, 1918, County Correspondence, box 2J370, TWRC, CAH.

[99] E. E. Swift to J. F. Carl, Jul. 8, 1918, County Correspondence, box 2J368, TWRC, CAH.

[100] P. L. Campbell to J. F. Carl, Sep. 5, 1918, County Correspondence, box 2J369, TWRC, CAH.

[101] Fred M. Huggins to B. C. Baldwin, Dec. 28, 1917, County Correspondence, box 2J367, TWRC, CAH.

[102] L. E. Tennison to T. L. Gillaspie, Jan. 11, 1918, County Correspondence, box 2J367, TWRC, CAH.

[103] Fred M. Huggins to J. F. Carl, Apr. 12, 1918, County Correspondence, box 2J367, TWRC, CAH.

[104] Council of National Defense, Texas Section, Bosque County Council Questionnaire, n.d., County Correspondence, box 2J367, TWRC, CAH.

[105] E. R. Wolcott to J. F. Carl, Jan. 18, 1918, County Correspondence, box 2J372, TWRC, CAH.

[106] *Dallas Morning News*, Apr. 22, 1918.

[107] Janet G. Humphrey, *A Texas Suffragist: Diaries and Writings of Jane Y. McCallum* (Austin: Ellen C. Temple, 1988), 112.

[108] *Austin American-Statesman*, Jun. 30, 1918.

[109] C. G. Robson to J. F. Carl, Jul. 20, 1918, County Correspondence, box 2J388, TWRC, CAH.

[110] Coral Clark to J. F. Carl, Sep. 23, 1918, County Correspondence, box 2J373, TWRC, CAH.

[111] Herbert R. Wilson to J. F. Carl, Nov. 17, 1917, County Correspondence, box 2J383, TWRC, CAH.

[112] C. A. Bain to J. F. Carl, Aug. 30, 1918, County Correspondence, box 2J385, TWRC, CAH.

[113] Unknown to W. P. Hobby, Oct. 7, 1918, County Correspondence, box 2J372, TWRC, CAH.

[114] J. F. Carl to Robert L. Barnes, Sep. 18, 1917, County Correspondence, box 2J371, TWRC, CAH.

[115] Mina W. Lamb, interview by Marshall L. Pennington and David Oberhelman, Jan. 24, Feb. 21, 1975, Oct. 21, 1981, Lubbock, Texas, Oral History Collection, Southwest Collection, Texas Tech University, Lubbock, Texas.

[116] W. A. Clampitt to J. F. Carl, Feb. 12, 1918, County Correspondence, box 2J371, TWRC, CAH.

[117] Unknown to the Council of Defense, Jul. 3, 1918, State Council of Defense, box 2J358, TWRC, CAH.

[118] J. F. Carl to W. P. Hobby, Feb. 14, 1918, County Correspondence, box 2J394, TWRC, CAH; W. P. Hobby to J. F. Carl, Feb. 21, 1918, County Correspondence, box 2J394, TWRC, CAH.

[119] House Bill No. 15, Mar. 11, 1918, County Correspondence, box 2J373, TWRC, CAH; *Fredericksburg Standard*, Mar. 23, Apr. 6, 1918; Trenckmann's letter dated Aug. 17, 1920, published in the *Fredericksburger Wochenblatt*, Oct. 14, 1920.

[120] "Harley to Appoint Loyalty Rangers," Jun. 12, 1918, folder 4, box 401-576, Correspondence, Departmental correspondence, Texas Adjutant General's Department, Archives and Information Services Division, Texas State Library and Archives Commission; James E. Booth to Adjutant General Harley, Jun. 5, 1918, folder 19, box 401-575, TAGD, TSLAC; E. E. Brazell to Adjutant General, Jun. 3, 1918, folder 19, box 401-575, TAGD, TSLAC; Albert F. Mach to Governor W. P. Hobby, Jun. 11, 1918, folder 27, box 401-575, TAGD, TSLAC.

[121] Higham, *Strangers in the Land*, 214; *Dallas Morning News*, Apr. 20, 1917.

[122] Geo. W. Tyler to Chairman Washington County Council of Defense, Oct. 18, 1918, County Correspondence, box 2J366, TWRC, CAH.

[123] *Dallas Morning News*, Feb. 5, 24, 28, Mar. 23, Aug. 15, 1918.

[124] Annette Waite, *German Immigrants Rudolph and August Tschoepe*, n.p., n.d., CAH, 72-87.

[125] Kennedy, *Over Here*, 311-313.

[126] Texas State Council of Defense to the Various County Councils, Bulletin No. 26, May 31, 1918, County Correspondence, box 2J367, TWRC, CAH.

[127] Geo. W. Tyler to J. F. Carl, Jun. 6, 1918, County Correspondence, box 2J397, TWRC, CAH.

[128] M. A. Shumard to J. F. Carl, Aug. 11, 1918, County Correspondence, box 2J371, TWRC, CAH.

[129] Richard J. Veit, "The Growth and Effects of Anti-German Sentiment in Waco, Texas, 1914-1918" (M.A. thesis, Baylor University, 1980), 29-30.

[130] Veit, "The Growth and Effects of Anti-German Sentiment in Waco," 30-31, 150; "Regarding Germania Gegenseitigen Unterstutzung Verein," Albert Neunhoffer, Mar. 9, 1918, County Correspondence, box 2J371, TWRC, CAH.

[131] *Dallas Morning News*, Mar. 30, Jun. 11, 1918; Conrad William Feuge, papers, The Sophienburg Archives, New Braunfels, Texas.

[132] *Ferguson Forum*, Aug. 8, 1918.

[133] Unknown to W. M. Hanson, Feb. 14, 1918, folder 26, box 401-573, Correspondence, Departmental correspondence, Texas Adjutant General's Department, Archives and Information Services Division, Texas State Library and Archives Commission.

[134] Chas. F. Stevens to Walter F. Woodul, Apr. 6, 1918, folder 17, box 401-574, TAGD, TSLAC.

[135] W. M. Hanson to Jas. A. Harley, Feb. 15, 1918, folder 26, box 401-573, Correspondence, Departmental correspondence, Texas Adjutant General's Department, Archives and Information Services Division, Texas State Library and Archives Commission.

[136] *Ferguson Forum*, Dec. 27, 1917; *Dallas Morning News*, May, 26, Dec. 23, 1917.

[137] W. M. Hanson to Jas. A. Harley, Apr. 1, 1918, folder 18, box 401-574, TAGD, TSLAC.

[138] Chas. F. Stevens to Walter F. Woodul, Apr. 23, 1918, folder 3, box 401-575, TAGD, TSLAC.

[139] Chas. F. Stevens to Walter F. Woodul, May 6, 1918, folder 6, box 401-575, TAGD, TSLAC.

[140] C. W. Hellen to J. F. Carl, Dec. 3, 1917, County Correspondence, box 2J371, TWRC, CAH.

[141] Report of Subcommittee 5 on the Library and Historic Commission, and the Legislative Reference Library, Jan. 9, 1918, box 1963/058-2, Records of Subcommittee 5, 1917-1918, Records of the Central Investigating Committees of the House and Senate, Texas Legislature. Archives and Information Services Division, Texas State Library and Archives Commission.

[142] Testimony before Subcommittee 5 [1917 or 1918], Texas Library and Historical Commission, box 1963/058-2, Records of Subcommittee 5, 1917-1918, Central Investigating Committees, TSLAC.

[143] Testimony before Subcommittee 5 [1917 or 1918], Texas Library and Historical Commission, box 1963/058-2, Records of Subcommittee 5, 1917-1918, Central Investigating Committees, TSLAC.

[144] Report of Subcommittee 5 on the Library and Historic Commission, and the Legislative Reference Library, Jan. 9, 1918, box 1963/058-2, Records of Subcommittee 5, 1917-1918, Central Investigating Committees, TSLAC.

[145] "Regarding Germania Gegenseitigen Unterstutzung Verein," Albert Neunhoffer, Mar. 9, 1918, County Correspondence, box 2J371, TWRC, CAH.

Chapter 6: Attacking the German Language in Texas, 1917-1918

[1] Frederick C. Luebke, *Bonds of Loyalty: German-Americans and World War I* (DeKalb: Northern Illinois University Press, 1974), 271; T. Herbert Etzler, "German-American Newspapers in Texas with Special Reference to the Texas Volksblatt, 1877-1879," *Southwestern Historical Quarterly* 58, no. 4 (April 1954): 428; Frederick Nohl, "The Lutheran Church—Missouri Synod Reacts to United States Anti-Germanism During World War I," *Concordia Historical Institute Quarterly* 35, no. 2 (July 1962): 52.

[2] Nohl, "The Lutheran Church—Missouri Synod Reacts," 56.

[3] Rebel L. Robertson to J. F. Carl, Jul. 24, 1918, County Correspondence, box 2J370, Texas War Records Collection, 1916-1919, 1940-1945, (hereafter cited as TWRC), Center for American History, University of Texas at Austin, (hereafter cited as CAH).

[4] Fayette County Council of Defense, Oct. 8, 1918, County Correspondence, box 2J388, TWRC, CAH.

[5] P. L. Campbell to J. F. Carl, Aug. 19, 1918, County Correspondence, box 2J369, TWRC, CAH.

[6] Alex Hamilton to Various Community Councils of Defense, Jul. 13, 1918, County Correspondence, box 2J384, TWRC, CAH.

[7] J. H. McLean to J. F. Carl, Jun 5, 1918, County Correspondence, box 2J372, TWRC, CAH.

[8] Lions Club of Temple, Texas Resolution, n.d., County Correspondence, box 2J366, TWRC, CAH.

[9] Unknown to Gov. Hobby, Oct. 7, 1918, County Correspondence, box 2J372, TWRC, CAH.

[10] H. C. Coffee to J. F. Carl, May 23, 1918, County Correspondence, box 2J375, TWRC, CAH.

[11] Travis County Council of Defense, Aug. 28, 1918, County Correspondence, box 2J375, TWRC, CAH.

[12] Fred M. Huggins to J. W. Butler, May 28, 1918, County Correspondence, box 2J367, TWRC, CAH.

[13] Wilson J. Parrill to Chairman National Council of Defense, May 10, 1918, County Correspondence, box 2J375, TWRC, CAH.

[14] H. C. Coffee to J. F. Carl, May 23, 1918, County Correspondence, box 2J375, TWRC, CAH; Peter Kaiser to the *Yankton Press and Dakotan*, Jan. 24, 1918, County Correspondence, box 2J375, TWRC, CAH; W. O. Nelsen to J. F. Carl, Jan. 29, 1918, County Correspondence, box 2J375, TWRC, CAH; J. F. Carl to Mrs. F. W. Jersig, Feb. 6, 1918, County Correspondence, box 2J375, TWRC, CAH.

[15] "'*Deutschland Uber Alles*' is Canned!," J. A. White, Chairman, Publicity Committee, Goliad County Council of Defense, Sep. 15, 1918, reprinted in *The Journal of the German-Texan Heritage Society* 26, no. 1 (Spring 2004): 39-47.

[16] "Trenckmann, William Andreas," *Handbook of Texas Online*, http://www.tshaonline.org/handbook/online/articles/TT/ftr8.html [accessed November 17, 2009]. Trenckmann had grown up in Austin County and had started his paper in Bellville as the *Bellville Wochenblatt* before moving it to Austin in 1909 (after his election to the legislature in 1905).

[17] *Das Wochenblatt* (Austin), Sep. 4, 1918.

[18] *La Grange Zeitung*, Jun. 27, 1918.

[19] *Neu-Braunfelser Zeitung*, Aug. 8, 1918.

[20] Rudolph Kleberg to J. C. Baumgarten, n.d., box 2J46, Rudolph Kleberg Family Papers, 1829-1966, CAH.

[21] *Katholische Rundschau*, Jun. 5, 1918.

[22] *Das Wochenblatt*, Jun. 19, 1918.

[23] *Giddings Deutsches Volksblatt*, Aug. 1, 1918.

[24] Texas State Council of Defense to the Various County Councils of Defense, Bulletin no. 27, Jun. 5, 1918, County Correspondence, box 2J366, TWRC, CAH.

[25] Abbie Cook to J. F. Carl, Oct. 9, 1918, County Correspondence, box 2J370, TWRC, CAH.

[26] J. F. Carl to Abbie Cook, Oct. 14, 1918, County Correspondence, box 2J370, TWRC, CAH.

[27] F. E. Seale to J. F. Carl, Aug. 14, 1918, County Correspondence, box 2J371, TWRC, CAH.

[28] R. G. Crosby to J. F. Carl, Sep. 13, 1918, County Correspondence, box 2J375, TWRC, CAH; R. G. Crosby to J. W. Ezelle, Sep. 5, 1918, County Correspondence, box 2J375, TWRC, CAH.

[29] P. L. Campbell to J. F. Carl, Aug. 19, 1918, County Correspondence, box 2J369, TWRC, CAH.

[30] J. F. Carl to P. L. Campbell, Aug. 21, 1918, County Correspondence, box 2J369, TWRC, CAH; *Dallas Morning News*, Jul. 23, 1918.

[31] Nohl, "The Lutheran Church—Missouri Synod Reacts," 56.

[32] Ibid., 61-64; Alan Graebner, "World War I and Lutheran Union: Documents from the Army and Navy Board, 1917 and 1918," *Concordia Historical Institute Quarterly* 41 (May 1968): 51-64.

[33] Nohl, "The Lutheran Church—Missouri Synod Reacts," 59-60.

[34] Fred M. Huggins to J. F. Carl, Jan. 4, 1919, County Correspondence, box 2J367, TWRC, CAH.

[35] C. B. Kilgore to J. F. Carl, Dec. 24, 1918, Texas State Council of Defense, box 2J357, TWRC, CAH.

[36] Ernst A. Eiband to J. F. Carl, Apr. 4, 1918, County Correspondence, box 2J383, TWRC, CAH.

[37] Fayette County Council of Defense, Oct. 8, 1918, County Correspondence, box 2J388, TWRC, CAH.

[38] Fred M. Huggins to Rev. Pfundt, Jun. 25, 1918, County Correspondence, box 2J367, TWRC, CAH.

[39] Leonard Bailey to J. F. Carl, Nov. 7, 1918, County Correspondence, box 2J383, TWRC, CAH.

[40] "Sixty Years of Germany in America," Victoria County Council of Defense, box 2J373, TWRC, CAH.

[41] Fayette County Council of Defense to the Trustees of Evangelical Lutheran Bethlehem Congregation, Round Top, Texas, Aug. 25, 1918, box 2J46, Rudolph Kleberg Family Papers, 1829-1966, CAH.

[42] J. F. Carl to George W. Tyler, Jul. 22, 1918, County Correspondence, box 2J366, TWRC, CAH.

[43] H. N. Sagebiel to W. P. Hobby, Jul. 10, 1918, County Correspondence, box 2J370, TWRC, CAH.

[44] George W. Tyler to F. W. Chudej, Oct. 2, 1918, County Correspondence, box 2J366, TWRC, CAH.

[45] J. F. Carl to H. N. Sagebiel, Jul. 20, 1918, County Correspondence, box 2J366, TWRC, CAH.

[46] H. N. Sagebiel to W. P. Hobby, Jul. 10, 1918, County Correspondence, box 2J370, TWRC, CAH; Emmanuel Lutheran Church, Knippa, Texas, brief chronological history, Evangelical Lutheran Church in America, Region IV – South Archives, Texas Lutheran University, Seguin, Texas.

[47] Trustees of Evangelical Lutheran St. John's Congregation to Bell County Council of Defense, n.d., County Correspondence, box 2J366, TWRC, CAH.

[48] Bell County Council of Defense Memoranda, Jun. 8, 1918, County Correspondence, box 2J366, TWRC, CAH.

[49] Paul Adolf Theodor Bogisch, biography and autobiography, box 3J243, Lorena Hillyer Fox Papers, CAH.

[50] J. C. Mitchell to George W. Tyler, Sep. 6, 1918, County Correspondence, box 2J366, TWRC, CAH.

[51] Bell County Council of Defense Memoranda, Jun. 26, 1918, County Correspondence, box 2J366, TWRC, CAH.

[52] Stanton Allen to George W. Tyler, Jul. 10, 1918, County Correspondence, box 2J366, TWRC, CAH.

[53] George W. Tyler to J. C. Mitchell, Jul. 24, 1918, County Correspondence, box 2J366, TWRC, CAH.

[54] Arthur H. Fleming to the Trustees of the Evangelical Lutheran Zion's and St. John's Congregation, Aug. 8, 1918, County Correspondence, box 2J366, TWRC, CAH.

[55] United States Attorney to Rev. Theodor Bogisch, Sep. 4, 1918, County Correspondence, box 2J366, TWRC, CAH; Department of Justice to Theodor Bogisch, Sep. 3, 1918, Hugh R. Robertson to Theodor Bogisch, Sep. 4, 1918 in "German Language and Patriotism Issues in Texas circa WWI," Special Collections, Evangelical Lutheran Church in America, Region IV – South Archives, Texas Lutheran University, Seguin, Texas.

[56] Fred M. Huggins to Rev. Bewie, May 14, 1918, County Correspondence, box 2J367, TWRC, CAH.

[57] J. W. Butler to Fred M. Huggins, May 24, 1918, County Correspondence, box 2J367, TWRC, CAH.

[58] P. L. Campbell to J. F. Carl, Aug. 19, 1918, County Correspondence, box 2J369, TWRC, CAH.

[59] German-speaking Protestant Pastors of Fayette County (Rev. H. C. Biermann, et al) to the Fayette County Council of Defense, Nov. 1, 1918, County Correspondence, box 2J388, TWRC, CAH.

[60] G. H. Biar to Texas State Council of Defense, Jun. 19, 1918, State Council of Defense Correspondence, box 2J394, TWRC, CAH.

[61] J. F. Carl to G. H. Biar, Jun. 21, 1918, State Council of Defense Correspondence, box 2J394, TWRC, CAH.

[62] G. H. Biar to J. F. Carl, Jun. 26, 1918, County Correspondence, box 2J372, TWRC, CAH.

[63] G. H. Biar to J. F. Carl, Jun. 26, 1918, County Correspondence, box 2J372, TWRC, CAH.

[64] DeWitt County Council of Defense to Various Community Councils of Defense, n.d., County Correspondence, box 2J384, TWRC, CAH.

[65] *Das Wochenblatt* (Austin), Jun. 19, 1918.

[66] *La Grange Zeitung*, Nov. 21, 1918.

[67] *Lutherbote für Texas*, August 1918.

[68] *Lutherbote für Texas*, June 1918.

[69] J. F. Carl to A. W. Jordan, Sep. 27, 1918, County Correspondence, box 2J383, TWRC, CAH.

[70] J. F. Carl to Arthur H. Fleming telegram, Jul. 16, 1918, State Council of Defense Correspondence, box 2J394, TWRC, CAH.

[71] Arthur H. Fleming to J. F. Carl telegram, Jul. 16, 1918, State Council of Defense Correspondence, box 2J394, TWRC, CAH.

[72] John S. Cravens to Texas State Council of Defense, Jul. 31, 1918, State Council of Defense Correspondence, box 2J394, TWRC, CAH.

[73] "English Language Exclusively" Resolution, Jim Wells County Council of Defense, Aug. 2, 1918, County Correspondence, box 2J371, TWRC, CAH.

[74] Frank J. Blake to J. F. Carl, Aug. 14, 1918, County Correspondence, box 2J371, TWRC, CAH.

[75] J. F. Carl to Frank J. Blake, Aug. 19, 1918, County Correspondence, box 2J371, TWRC, CAH.

[76] Rev. J. F. Christiansen to A. H. Fleming, Aug. 16, 1918, County Correspondence, box 2J384, TWRC, CAH.

[77] J. F. Carl to Arthur H. Fleming, Aug. 24, 1918, County Correspondence, box 2J384, TWRC, CAH.

[78] "Houston Resolution of 1918," in "German Language and Patriotism Issues in Texas circa WWI," Special Collections, Evangelical Lutheran Church in America, Region IV – South Archives, Texas Lutheran University, Seguin, Texas.

[79] Theodor Bogisch to B. Schleifer, n.d., in "German Language and Patriotism Issues in Texas circa WWI," Special Collections, Evangelical Lutheran Church in America, Region IV – South Archives, Texas Lutheran University, Seguin, Texas.

[80] C. Weeber to Whom It May Concern, n.d., in "German Language and Patriotism Issues in Texas circa WWI," Special Collections, Evangelical Lutheran Church in America, Region IV – South Archives, Texas Lutheran University, Seguin, Texas.

[81] Immanuel Lutheran Church, Comfort, Texas, history, Evangelical Lutheran Church in America, Region IV – South Archives, Texas Lutheran University, Seguin, Texas.

[82] Matilda Faust to B. Schleifer, Jan. 19, 1919, County Correspondence, box 2J371, TWRC, CAH.

[83] H. C. Geddie to J. F. Carl, Jan. 31, 1919, County Correspondence, box 2J371, TWRC, CAH; Immanuel Lutheran Church, Comfort, Texas, history, Evangelical Lutheran Church in America, Region IV – South Archives, Texas Lutheran University, Seguin, Texas.

[84] J. F. Carl to Mrs. L. F. Faust, Feb. 25, 1919, County Correspondence, box 2J371, TWRC, CAH; Mrs. L. F. Faust to J. F. Carl, Feb. 26, 1919, County Correspondence, box 2J371, TWRC, CAH.

[85] B. Schleifer to J. F. Carl, Mar. 20, 1919, County Correspondence, box 2J371, TWRC, CAH; Immanuel Lutheran Church, Comfort, Texas, history, Evangelical Lutheran Church in America, Region IV – South Archives, Texas Lutheran University, Seguin, Texas.

[86] Zion Lutheran Church, Arneckeville, Texas, history, Evangelical Lutheran Church in America, Region IV – South Archives, Texas Lutheran University, Seguin, Texas; *Centennial, Zion's Lutheran Church, Arneckeville, Texas, 1868-1968*, 11-14, in William A. Flachmeier Collection, Archives and Information Services Division, Texas State Library and Archives Commission, Austin, Texas.

[87] A. A. Hahn to Theodor Bogisch, Dec. 7, 1918; F. W. Jaeggli to Theodor Bogsich, Dec. 9, 1918; "Report on the Action of St. Mark's Congregation at Cuero, Tex. On Dec. 8, 1918," C. Weeber to Theodor Bogisch, Jan. 16, 1919; all found in "German Language and Patriotism Issues in Texas circa WWI," Special Collections, Evangelical Lutheran Church in America, Region IV – South Archives, Texas Lutheran University, Seguin, Texas.

[88] C. W. Hellen to J. F. Carl, Aug. 31, 1918, County Correspondence, box 2J371, TWRC, CAH; J. F. Carl to C. W. Hellen, Sep. 3, 1918, County Correspondence, box 2J371, TWRC, CAH.

[89] Thomas R. J. Orth to J. F. Carl, Nov. 9, 1918, County Correspondence, box 2J374, TWRC, CAH.

[90] Minutes of the Meeting of Fayette County Council of Defense, Jul. 4, 1918, County Correspondence, box 2J388, TWRC, CAH.

[91] J. F. Carl to C. G. Robson, Jul. 29, 1918, County Correspondence, box 2J388, TWRC, CAH.

[92] Bosque County Council of Defense to J. F. Carl, Jan. 10, 1918, County Correspondence, box 2J383, TWRC, CAH.

[93] *Fredericksburger Wochenblatt*, Feb. 28, 1918.

[94] *Neu-Braunfelser Zeitung*, Aug. 23, 1917.

[95] *Lutherbote für Texas*, Nov. 1918.

[96] E. S. Parks to Fred M. Huggins, Oct. 15, 1918, County Correspondence, box 2J367, TWRC, CAH.

[97] George W. Tyler to Rev. Theodore Bogisch, Jun. 4, 1918, County Correspondence, box 2J397, TWRC, CAH.

[98] George W. Tyler to J. F. Carl, Jun. 8, 1918, County Correspondence, box 2J397, TWRC, CAH.

[99] William P. Hobby to George W. Tyler, Jun. 15, 1918, County Correspondence, box 2J366, TWRC, CAH.

[100] C. N. Shaver to J. F. Carl, Feb. 18, 1918, County Correspondence, box 2J396, TWRC, CAH.

[101] J. F. Carl to W. F. Doughty, Feb. 15, 1918, State Council of Defense Correspondence, box 2J394, TWRC, CAH.

[102] Thad Sitton and Milam C. Rowold, *Ringing the Children In: Texas Country Schools* (College Station: Texas A&M University Press, 1987), 123.

[103] J. F. Carl to W. F. Doughty, Feb. 15, 1918, State Council of Defense Correspondence, box 2J394, TWRC, CAH.

[104] W. F. Doughty to J. F. Carl, Feb. 19, 1918, State Council of Defense Correspondence, box 2J394, TWRC, CAH.

[105] Gould, *Progressives and Prohibitionists*, 185-188; *Houston Post*, Jun. 21, 1918.

[106] Debbie Mauldin Cottrell, *Pioneer Woman Educator in Texas: The Progressive Spirit of Annie Webb Blanton* (College Station: Texas A&M University Press, 1993), 48-49; Annie Webb Blanton, vertical file, CAH.

[107] Texas Legislature, House, *Journal of the House of Representatives of the Fourth Called Session of the Thirty-Fifth Legislature* (Austin: Von Boeckmann-Jones Co., 1918), 86-87.

[108] *Dallas Morning News*, Mar. 6, 1918.

[109] Texas Legislature, House, *Journal of the House of Representatives of the Fourth Called Session of the Thirty-Fifth Legislature*, 295.

[110] Rudolph Kleberg to D. C. Giddings, Mar. 19, 1919, box 2J46, Rudolph Kleberg Family Papers, 1829-1966, CAH.

[111] *Houston Post*, Mar. 6, 1918.

[112] Lea Beaty to J. F. Carl, Dec. 20, n.y., State Council of Defense, box 2J357, TWRC, CAH.

[113] Walter Reiffert to J. F. Carl, Jul. 23, 1918, County Correspondence, box 2J384, TWRC, CAH.

[114] J. F. Carl to Walter Reiffert, Sep. 5, 1918, County Correspondence, box 2J384, TWRC, CAH.

[115] E. E. Fischer to J. F. Carl, Aug. 3, 1918, County Correspondence, box 2J369, TWRC, CAH.

[116] Ed Hering to J. F. Carl, Aug. 6, 1918, County Correspondence, box 2J369, TWRC, CAH.

[117] J. F. Carl to E. E. Fischer, Aug. 19, 1918, County Correspondence, box 2J369, TWRC, CAH.

[118] *Das Wochenblatt*, Oct. 17, 1917.

[119] *Fredericksburger Wochenblatt*, Oct. 11, 1917; *La Grange Zeitung*, Nov. 7, 1918.

[120] *Neu-Braunfelser Zeitung*, Jun. 14, 1917; *Fredericksburger Wochenblatt*, Jul. 5, 1917, Jul. 11, 1918; *Lutherbote für Texas*, Jul. 1918; *Giddings Deutsches Volksblatt*, Jul. 11, Sep. 19, 1918.

[121] Kathleen Neils Conzen, "Germans," in *Harvard Encyclopedia of American Ethnic Groups*, eds. Stephan Thernstrom, et al. (Cambridge: Harvard University Press, 1980), 423.

[122] Walter Reiffert to J. F. Carl, Jul. 20, 1918, County Correspondence, box 2J384, TWRC, CAH.

[123] J. F. Carl to Walter Reiffert, Jul. 26, 1918, County Correspondence, box 2J384, TWRC, CAH.

[124] Luebke, *Bonds of Loyalty*, xv-xvi.

Chapter 7: Assimilation or Survival? Postwar to 1930

[1] *Seguin Enterprise*, Nov. 16, 1918.

[2] C. B. Kilgore to J. F. Carl, Nov. 13, 1918, County Correspondence, box 2J383, Texas War Records Collection, 1916-1919, 1940-1945, (hereafter cited as TWRC), Center for American History, University of Texas at Austin, (hereafter cited as CAH); J. B. Rutledge to State of Texas, County of Bexar, Dec. 21, 1918, County Correspondence, box 2J371, TWRC, CAH.

[3] H. D. Craig to Hillsboro Vigilance Corps, Nov. 29, 1918, County Correspondence, box 2J369, TWRC, CAH.

[4] Grosvenor B. Clarkson to the Several State Councils of Defense and State Divisions of the Woman's Committee, Dec. 21, 1918, County Correspondence, box 2J358, TWRC, CAH.

[5] Wheeler G. Carpenter to J. F. Carl, Dec. 20, 1918, County Correspondence, box 2J371, TWRC, CAH.

[6] Sue Bruns, "Persecution of Germans in Central Texas During World War I" (M.A. thesis, Southwest Texas State University, 1972), 123-126; *Ferguson Forum*, Dec. 19, 1918; *Seguin Enterprise*, Dec. 13, 20, 1918.

[7] Texas State Council of Defense to the Various County Councils of Defense, Bulletin 56, Dec. 16, 1918, County Correspondence, box 2J366, TWRC, CAH.

[8] R. G. Crosby to J. F. Carl, Dec. 23, 1918, County Correspondence, box 2J357, TWRC, CAH.

[9] A. W. Birdwell to J. F. Carl, Dec. 22, 1918, County Correspondence, box 2J357, TWRC, CAH.

[10] P.L. Campbell to J. F. Carl, Jan. 11, 1919, County Correspondence, box 2J358, TWRC, CAH.

[11] James G. Strong to J. F. Carl, Dec. 20, 1918, County Correspondence, box 2J358, TWRC, CAH.

[12] *Dallas Morning News*, Feb. 6, 1919.

[13] Robert E. L. Knight to J. F. Carl, Mar. 27, 1919, County Correspondence, box 2J395, TWRC, CAH.

[14] J. I. Cash to J. F. Carl, Jan. 6, 1919, County Correspondence, box 2J357, TWRC, CAH.

[15] W. Utesch to the Most Honorable State Council of Defense, Dec. 1918, County Correspondence, box 2J358, TWRC, CAH.

[16] J. F. Carl to John H. Shary, Mar. 14, 1919, County Correspondence, box 2J370, TWRC, CAH.

[17] C. W. Macune to H. C. Gaertner, Mar. 8, 1919, County Correspondence, box 2J369, TWRC, CAH.

[18] H. C. Gaertner to C. W. Macune, Mar. 17, 1919, County Correspondence, box 2J369, TWRC, CAH.

[19] H. C. Gaertner to R. M. Vaughan, May 2, 1919, County Correspondence, box 2J369, TWRC, CAH.

[20] *Church on the Coleto* (Meyersville: Saint John Evangelical Lutheran Church of Meyersville, 1978), 179-197; *Centennial History, 1877-1977, St. John's Lutheran, Prairie Hill, Texas*, 12, in William A. Flachmeier Collection, Archives and Information Services Division, Texas State Library and Archives Commission, Austin, Texas.

[21] U.S. Congress, Senate Subcommittee on the Judiciary, *Brewing and Liquor Interests and German and Bolshevik Propaganda*, Report and Hearings of the Subcommittee on the Judiciary, U.S. Senate submitted pursuant to the Senate Res. 307 and 439 in three volumes, 66th Congress, 1st Session, Senate Document No. 62 (Washington, D.C.: Government Printing Office, 1919).

[22] Ibid., 1-2, 6-7.

[23] Ibid., 4-7, 43.

[24] Seth Shepard McKay, *Texas Politics, 1906-1944: With Special Reference to the German Counties* (Lubbock: Texas Tech Press, 1952), 85-86.

[25] Shiner Beers, http://www.shiner.com [accessed September 10, 2006]; Wikipedia contributors, "Pearl Brewing Company," Wikipedia, The Free Encyclopedia, http://en.wikipedia.org/w/index.php?title=Pearl_Brewing_Company&oldid=74587056 [accessed September 10, 2006]; *Dallas Morning News*, Aug. 7, 1920. Cat Spring Agricultural Society, *Century of Agricultural Progress, 1856-1956; Minutes of the Cat Spring Agricultural Society* (Cat Spring, Texas, 1956), 295-296, 298.

[26] Shiner Beers, http://www.shiner.com [accessed September 10, 2006]; Wikipedia contributors, "Pearl Brewing Company," Wikipedia, The Free

Encyclopedia, http://en.wikipedia.org/w/index.php?
title=Pearl_Brewing_Company&oldid=74587056 [accessed September 10, 2006].

[27] Gould, *Progressives and Prohibitionists*, 254-255.

[28] "Men of Texas: The Women of Texas Need Your Help on May 24th," Texas
Equal Suffrage Association, n.d., FP E.4 B #26, (folder 6), Jane Y. McCallum
Papers, Austin History Center, Austin, Texas; Janet G. Humphrey, *A Texas
Suffragist: Diaries and Writings of Jane Y. McCallum* (Austin: Ellen C. Temple,
1988), 130, 134.

[29] "Many Factors Contributed to the Apparent Defeat of Suffrage," printed flyer,
n.d., FP E.4 B3 #5, Jane Y. McCallum Papers, Austin History Center, Austin,
Texas.

[30] Gould, *Progressives and Prohibitionists*, 255-256.

[31] Eduard Prokosch, vertical file, Center for American History, University of
Texas at Austin, Austin, Texas.

[32] James W. Gerard, *Face to Face with Kaiserism* (New York: George H. Doran,
Co., 1918), 285-287.

[33] *Dallas Morning News*, Apr. 20, 1917, Jun. 24, 1919; Eduard Prokosch, vertical
file, CAH.

[34] R. E. Vinson to E. Prokosch, Jun. 17, 1919, Board of Regents Minutes,
University of Texas at Austin, found in Eduard Prokosch, vertical file, CAH.

[35] In his letter, Prokosch listed twenty-six languages he was "more or less
acquainted with." See E. Prokosch to Robert E. Vinson, Jul. 1, 1919, Board of
Regents Minutes, University of Texas at Austin, found in Eduard Prokosch, vertical
file, CAH.

[36] Board of Regents Minutes, University of Texas at Austin, Jul. 7, 1919, found
in Eduard Prokosch, vertical file, CAH.

[37] Board of Regents Minutes, University of Texas at Austin, Nov. 6, 1919, found
in Eduard Prokosch, vertical file, CAH.

[38] Eduard Prokosch, vertical file, CAH; *Dallas Morning News*, Jul. 2, Aug. 8,
1919.

[39] La Vern J. Rippley, "Ameliorated Americanization: The Effect of World War I
on German-Americans in the 1920s," in *America and the Germans: An Assessment of
a Three-Hundred-Year History*, vol. 2, eds. Frank Trommler and Joseph McVeigh
(Philadelphia: University of Pennsylvania Press, 1985), 224; Historical Census
Browser, University of Virginia, Geospatial and Statistical Data Center,
http://fisher.lib.virginia.edu/collections/stats/histcensus/index.html [accessed
August 4, 2006]; Viereck quoted in Luebke, *Bonds of Loyalty*, 281-282.

[40] Historical Census Browser, University of Virginia, Geospatial and Statistical
Data Center, http://fisher.lib.virginia.edu/collections/stats/histcensus/index.html
[accessed August 4, 2006]; Conzen, "Germans," 410; Higham, *Strangers in the
Land*, 308-324.

[41] Jack Autrey Dabbs and Edward C. Breitenkamp, *Records of Salem Lutheran Church, Brenham, Texas, 1850-1940* (Austin: J. A. Dabbs and E. C. Breitenkamp, 1986), 31.

[42] J. V. Cockrum, Oct. 18, 1920, County Correspondence, box 2J212, TWRC, CAH.

[43] Local Board for Comal County, now Discharged to Milton R. Gutsch, Director Texas War Collection, University of Texas, Austin Texas, Nov. 12, 1920, County Correspondence, box 2J212, TWRC, CAH.

[44] Norman D. Brown, *Hood, Bonnet, and Little Brown Jug: Texas Politics, 1921-1928* (College Station: Texas A&M University Press, 1984), 49-87.

[45] *Brenham Daily Banner-Press*, May 19, 1921.

[46] Walter D. Kamphoefner, "The Handwriting on the Wall: The Klan, Language Issues, and Prohibition in the German Settlements of Eastern Texas." *Southwestern Historical Quarterly* 111, no. 1 (July 2008): 52.

[47] *Brenham Daily Banner-Press*, Jun. 8-10, 1921.

[48] *Dallas Morning News*, Sep. 7, 1922; Kamphoefner, "The Handwriting on the Wall," 62-63.

[49] *Dallas Morning News*, Jul. 14, 1921.

[50] Mina W. Lamb, interview by Marshall L. Pennington and David Oberhelman, Jan. 24, Feb. 21, 1975, Oct. 21, 1981, Lubbock, Texas, Oral History Collection, Southwest Collection, Texas Tech University, Lubbock, Texas.

[51] *Dallas Morning News*, Mar. 6, 8, 1922.

[52] *Centennial History, 1877-1977, St. John's Lutheran, Prairie Hill, Texas*, 11, in William A. Flachmeier Collection, Archives and Information Services Division, Texas State Library and Archives Commission, Austin, Texas.

[53] "Centennial Moments, Texas District LCMS, http://100.txdistlcms.org/moment19.html, [accessed Dec., 8, 2009]; Stinson Behlen, interview by James Seuseney, Oct. 28, 1982, Slaton, Texas, Oral History Collection, Southwest Collection, Texas Tech University, Lubbock, Texas; *Dallas Morning News*, Oct. 11, 1922; Mina W. Lamb, interview by Marshall L. Pennington and David Oberhelman, Jan. 24, Feb. 21, 1975, Oct. 21, 1981, Lubbock, Texas, Oral History Collection, Southwest Collection, Texas Tech University, Lubbock, Texas; Brown, *Hood, Bonnet, and Little Brown Jug*, 251-252.

[54] Higham, *Strangers in the Land*, 229-233.

[55] *Dallas Morning News*, Dec. 31, 1919.

[56] *Dallas Morning News*, Apr. 11, 1920.

[57] *Dallas Morning News*, Aug. 20, 1920; McKay, *Texas Politics*, 100.

[58] McKay, *Texas Politics*, 102.

[59] *Dallas Morning News*, Aug. 2, 1922

[60] *Dallas Morning News*, Aug. 4, 10, 11, 1922.

[61] *Dallas Morning News*, Aug. 13, 1922.

[62] *Freie Presse für Texas* (San Antonio), Aug. 16, 1922; McKay, *Texas Politics*, 120; Brown, *Hood, Bonnet, and Little Brown Jug*, 117.

[63] Brown, *Hood, Bonnet, and Little Brown Jug*, 229; *Das Wochenblatt* (Austin), Jun. 19, 1924; *Fredericksburger Wochenblatt*, Jul. 23, 1924; McKay, *Texas Politics*, 137.

[64] *Fredericksburger Wochenblatt*, Oct. 15, 1924; McKay, *Texas Politics*, 141, 156, 209, 239, 335; Brown, *Hood, Bonnet, and Little Brown Jug*, 251.

[65] McKay, *Texas Politics*, 177-180; *Neu-Braunfelser Zeitung*, Oct. 25, Nov. 1, 1928; Brown, *Hood, Bonnet, and Little Brown Jug*, 416.

[66] Annie Webb Blanton and R. L. Ragsdale, *Texas High Schools: History and the Social Sciences, Bulletin 124* (Austin: Department of Education, State of Texas, 1920), 8-9.

[67] Annie Webb Blanton, *A Handbook of Information as to Education in Texas, 1918-1922. Bulletin 157* (Austin: Department of Education, State of Texas, 1923), 22-23.

[68] Ibid., 90; S. M. N. Marrs and Opal Gilstrap, *Texas High Schools: The Teaching of Spanish, German, and French. Bulletin 230* (Austin: State Department of Education, 1927), 81; Marcus Nicolini, *Deutsch in Texas* (Münster: Lit. Verlag, 2004), 132.

[69] William G. Ross, *Forging New Freedoms: Nativism, Education, and the Constitution, 1917-1927* (Lincoln: University of Nebraska Press, 1994), 96-133.

[70] T. Herbert Etzler, "German-American Newspapers in Texas with Special Reference to the Texas Volksblatt, 1877-1879," *Southwestern Historical Quarterly* 58, no. 4 (April 1954): 428-429; Karl Arndt and May Olson, *German-American Newspapers and Periodicals, 1732-1955*, 2nd ed. (New York: Johnson Reprint, 1965), 614-635.

[71] *Dallas Morning News*, Dec. 12, 1920, Jan. 11, Feb. 18, Mar. 15, 1929, May 11, 1930.

[72] Joseph Wilson, "Texas German and Other Immigrant Languages: Problems and Prospects," in *Eagle in the New World: German Immigration to Texas and America*, eds. Theodore Gish and Richard Spuler (College Station: Texas A&M University Press, 1986), 231; Caesar (Dutch) Hohn, *Dutchman on the Brazos: Reminiscences of Caesar (Dutch) Hohn* (Austin: University of Texas Press, 1963), 142.

[73] *Dallas Morning News*, Apr. 17, 1925; Joseph C. Salmons and Felecia A. Lucht, "Standard German in Texas," in *Studies in Contact Linguistics: Essays in Honor of Glenn G. Gilbert*, eds. Linda L. Thornburg and Janet M. Fuller (New York: Peter Lang, 2006), 169-170; Arndt and Olson, *German-American Newspapers and Periodicals*, 614-635.

[74] Salmons and Lucht, "Standard German in Texas," 170-171.

[75] August L. Wolff, *The Story of St. John's Lutheran Church, San Antonio, Texas* (n.p.: P. Anderson Co., 1937), 47-48; *50th Anniversary, St. John Lutheran, Wilson,*

Texas, 6-7, in William A. Flachmeier Collection, Archives and Information Services Division, Texas State Library and Archives Commission, Austin, Texas; Sue Watkins Grasty, *Our God is Marching On: A Centennial History of Bethlehem Lutheran Church, Round Top, Texas* (Austin: Von Boeckmann-Jones, 1966), 46; Harold E. Fehler, *Hundredth Anniversary [1867-1968] of St. John Lutheran Church in New Ulm, Texas* (New Ulm: St. John Lutheran Church, 1968); Doris Goerner Laake, *History of St. John Lutheran Church, Paige, Texas* (Paige: D. Laake, 1979), 11; *Holy Cross Lutheran Church, 1873-1973: 100 Years of God's Blessings* (Flatonia: Flatonia Argus, 1973), 80, 86.

[76] Theodore John Albrecht, "German Singing Societies in Texas" (Ph.D. diss., North Texas State University, 1975), 451-457; *Dallas Morning News*, Oct. 5, 1927, Oct. 8, 1928, May 12, 1929.

[77] Sons of Hermann, vertical file, Center for American History, University of Texas at Austin; *Dallas Morning News*, Jan. 23, 1922, Apr. 16, 1924, May 27, Jun. 21, 1928, Apr. 29, 1930.

[78] Walter D. Kamphoefner, "German-American Bilingualism: *Cui Malo?* Mother Tongue and Socioeconomic Status Among the Second Generation in 1940," *International Migration Review* 28 (Winter 1994): 846-864.

[79] Alwyn Barr, "Occupational and Geographic Mobility in San Antonio, 1870-1900," *Social Science Quarterly* 51 (Sept. 1970): 396-403.

[80] Russell A. Kazal, *Becoming Old Stock: The Paradox of German-American Identity* (Princeton: Princeton University Press, 2004).

Chapter 8: Conclusion

[1] Kathleen Neils Conzen, "The Paradox of German-American Assimilation," *Yearbook of German-American Studies* 16 (1981): 157-158.

[2] Historical Census Browser, University of Virginia, Geospatial and Statistical Data Center, http://fisher.lib.virginia.edu/collections/stats/histcensus/index.html [accessed Aug. 19, 2006]. The German born population of Bexar County between 1880-1920: 1880 – 2,621, 1890 – 4,039, 1910 – 4,423, 1920 – 3,331. Meanwhile, between 1880 and 1920, the total population of Bexar County went from 30,470 in 1880 to 202,096 in 1920. Thus, the overall population of the county grew drastically while the German-born population underwent little change.

[3] *Dallas Morning News*, Jun. 4, 1917; Benjamin Paul Hegi, "'Old Time Good Germans': German-Americans in Cooke County, Texas, during World War I," *Southwestern Historical Quarterly* 109, no. 2 (Oct. 2005): 234-257.

[4] Max Amadeus Paulus Krueger, *Second Fatherland: The Life and Fortunes of a German Immigrant*, ed. Marilyn McAdams Sibley (College Station: Texas A&M University Press, 1976), xvii-xviii.

[5] Wolfgang W. E. Samuel, *American Raiders: The Race to Capture the Luftwaffe's Secrets* (Jackson: University Press of Mississippi, 2004), 403.

[6] Caesar (Dutch) Hohn, *Dutchman on the Brazos: Reminiscences of Caesar (Dutch) Hohn* (Austin: University of Texas Press, 1963), 8-9.

[7] Panikos Panayi, "An Intolerant Act by an Intolerant Society: The Internment of Germans in Britain During the First World War," in *The Internment of Aliens in Twentieth Century Britain*, eds. David Cesarani and Tony Kushner (London: Frank Cass, 1993): 53-78; Frederick C. Luebke, *Germans in Brazil: A Comparative History of Cultural Conflict During World War I* (Baton Rouge: Louisiana State University Press, 1987).

[8] For studies that argue the almost complete assimilation of German Americans after World War I, see Carl Wittke, *German-Americans and the World War (With Special Emphasis on Ohio's German-Language Press)* (Columbus: The Ohio State Archaeological and Historical Society, 1936); John Arkas Hawgood, *The Tragedy of German-America* (New York: G. P. Putnam's Sons, 1940); David W. Detjen, *Germans in Missouri, 1900-1918: Prohibition, Neutrality, and Assimilation* (Columbia: University of Missouri Press, 1985).

[9] Kathleen Neils Conzen, "Germans," in *Harvard Encyclopedia of American Ethnic Groups*, Stephan Thernstrom et al., eds. (Cambridge: Harvard University Press, 1980), 415, 424.

[10] *Dallas Morning News*, Nov. 16, 1923.

[11] Philip Jenkins, *Hoods and Shirts: The Extreme Right in Pennsylvania, 1925-1950* (Chapel Hill: University of North Carolina Press, 1997), 142-143.

[12] *Dallas Morning News*, Aug. 17, 1939; Jenkins, *Hoods and Shirts*, 142-143.

[13] *Dallas Morning News*, Sep. 12, 1937.

[14] *Dallas Morning News*, Aug. 17, 1939, Jul. 10-11, 14, 1940.

[15] *Dallas Morning News*, Sep. 12, 14, 18, 1937.

[16] Frederick C. Luebke, *Bonds of Loyalty: German-Americans and World War I* (DeKalb: Northern Illinois University Press, 1974), 330.

[17] FBI files, Freedom of Information Request #319.288, from Dec. 7, 1941 to Jun. 30, 1945, available at http://foia.fbi.gov/custodet/custode2.pdf [accessed Aug. 16, 2006], 222-231; Theodore G. Gish, *The History of the Houston Sängerbund* (Houston: Institute of Texas-German Studies, University of Houston, 1990), 22.

[18] Glen E. Lich, *The German Texans* (San Antonio: The University of Texas Institute of Texas Cultures at San Antonio, 1981), 111-114. Wolfgang W. E. Samuel, *American Raiders: The Race to Capture the Luftwaffe's Secrets* (Jackson: University Press of Mississippi, 2004), 402-407.

[19] Marcus Nicolini, *Deutsch in Texas* (Münster: Lit. Verlag, 2004), 136.

[20] T. Herbert Etzler, "German-American Newspapers in Texas with Special Reference to the Texas Volksblatt, 1877-1879," *Southwestern Historical Quarterly* 58, no. 4 (April 1954): 429; Joseph C. Salmons and Felecia A. Lucht, "Standard German in Texas," in *Studies in Contact Linguistics: Essays in Honor of Glenn G. Gilbert*, eds. Linda L. Thornburg and Janet M. Fuller (New York: Peter Lang, 2006), 177.

240

[21] Walter D. Kamphoefner, "German-American Bilingualism: *Cui Malo?* Mother Tongue and Socioeconomic Status Among the Second Generation in 1940," *International Migration Review* 28 (Winter 1994): 850-851.

[22] Walter D. Kamphoefner, "German Texans: In the Mainstream or Backwaters of Lone Star Society?" *Yearbook of German-American Studies* 38 (2003): 133-134.

[23] Glenn G. Gilbert, "The German Language in Texas: Some Needed Research," in *German Culture in Texas*, eds. Glen E. Lich and Dona B. Reeves (Boston: Twayne, 1980), 238; Jürgen Eichhoff, "The German Language in America," in *America and the Germans: An Assessment of a Three-Hundred-Year History*, vol. 1, eds. Frank Trommler and Joseph McVeigh (Philadelphia: University of Pennsylvania Press, 1985), 232; MLA Language Map Data Center, http://www.mla.org/map_data&dcwindow=same [accessed Dec. 9, 2009]; Hans C. Boas, *The Like and Death of Texas German* (Durham: American Dialect Society, 2009), 279; On the Texas German Dialect Project, see http://www.tgdp.org [accessed Aug. 16, 2006].

[24] Conzen, "Germans," 425.

[25] See http://www.wurstfest.com http://www.germanfest.net http://www.oktoberfestinfbg.com [all accessed Aug. 16, 2006]; David Syring, *Places in the World a Person Could Walk: Family, Stories, Home, and Place in the Texas Hill Country* (Austin: University of Texas Press, 2000), 109.

[26] For the German-Texan Heritage Society see http://www.germantexans.org [accessed Aug. 20, 2006]; On the Texas German Society see http://www.texasgermansociety.com [accessed Aug. 20, 2006].

[27] Evangelical Lutheran Church in America, http://elca.org [accessed Aug. 20, 2006].

[28] Conzen, "Germans," 410. U.S. Census Bureau data available at: http://factfinder.census.gov [accessed Aug. 20, 2006].

Bibliography

Archival Sources

"Blanton, Annie Webb," vertical file, Center for American History, University of Texas at Austin.

Bogisch, Paul Adolf Theodor, biography and autobiography, box 3J243, Lorena Hillyer Fox Papers, Center for American History, University of Texas at Austin.

Correspondence, Departmental correspondence, Texas Adjutant General's Department, Archives and Information Services Division, Texas State Library and Archives Commission. Austin, Texas. Boxes 401-573, 401-574, 401-575, 401-576.

"Dunlap, O. E.," vertical file, Center for American History, University of Texas at Austin.

Emmanuel Lutheran Church, Knippa, Texas, brief chronological history, Evangelical Lutheran Church in America, Region IV—South Archives, Texas Lutheran University, Seguin, Texas.

"Ferguson, James E.," vertical file, Center for American History, University of Texas at Austin.

Feuge, Conrad William. Papers. The Sophienburg Archives. New Braunfels, Texas.

"German Language and Patriotism Issues in Texas circa WWI," Special Collections, Evangelical Lutheran Church in America, Region IV—South Archives, Texas Lutheran University, Seguin, Texas.

"Germans in Texas," vertical file, Center for American History, University of Texas at Austin.

Hobby, William P., Sr. Family Papers, 1914-1917, Center for American History, University of Texas at Austin. Boxes 3H3, 3H5.

Immanuel Lutheran Church, Comfort, Texas, history, Evangelical Lutheran Church in America, Region IV—South Archives, Texas Lutheran University, Seguin, Texas.

Kleberg, Rudolph, Family Papers, 1829-1966, Center for American History, University of Texas at Austin. Boxes 2J45, 2J46.

McCallum, Jane Y. Papers. Austin History Center, Austin, Texas.

"McLemore, Atkins Jefferson," vertical file, Center for American History, University of Texas at Austin.

"Prokosch, Eduard," vertical file, Center for American History, University of Texas at Austin.

Report of Subcommittee 5 on the Library and Historic Commission, and the Legislative Reference Library, Jan. 9, 1918, box 1963/058-2, Records of Subcommittee 5, 1917-1918, Records of the Central Investigating Committees of the House and Senate, Texas Legislature. Archives and Information Services Division, Texas State Library and Archives Commission. Austin, Texas.

"Sons of Hermann," vertical file, Center for American History, University of Texas at Austin.

Testimony before Subcommittee 5 [1917 or 1918], Texas Library and Historical Commission, box 1963/058-2, Records of Subcommittee 5, 1917-1918, Central Investigating Committees. Archives and Information Services Division, Texas State Library and Archives Commission. Austin, Texas.

Texas War Records Collection, 1916-1919, 1940-1945, Center for American History, University of Texas at Austin. Boxes 2J212, 2J213, 2J355, 2J356, 2J357, 2J358, 2J366, 2J367, 2J368, 2J369, 2J370, 2J371, 2J372, 2J373, 2J374, 2J375, 2J376, 2J377, 2J383, 2J384, 2J385, 2J388, 2J392, 2J393, 2J394, 2J395, 2J396, 2J397, 2J398.

Waite, Annette. "German Immigrants Rudolph and August Tschoepe," n.p., n.d., Center for American History, University of Texas at Austin.

Zion Lutheran Church, Arneckeville, Texas, history, Evangelical Lutheran Church in America, Region IV—South Archives, Texas Lutheran University, Seguin, Texas.

Interviews

Behlen, Stinson, interview by James Seuseney, Oct. 28, 1982, Slaton, Texas, Oral History Collection, Southwest Collection, Texas Tech University, Lubbock, Texas.

Greener, Annie, interview by Betty Cox, Jun. 15, 21, 1980, Levelland, Texas, Oral History Collection, Southwest Collection, Texas Tech University, Lubbock, Texas.

Lamb, Mina W. interview by Marshall L. Pennington and David Oberhelman, Jan. 24, Feb. 21, 1975, Oct. 21, 1981, Lubbock, Texas, Oral History Collection, Southwest Collection, Texas Tech University, Lubbock, Texas.

English Language Newspapers

Austin American-Statesman, 1918.

Brenham Daily Banner-Press, 1921.

Dallas Morning News, 1887, 1907, 1909, 1914-1925, 1927-1930, 1937, 1939-1940.

Ferguson Forum, 1918-1919.

Fredericksburg Standard, 1918.

Houston Chronicle, 1915.
Houston Post, 1914-1915, 1917-1918.
La Grange Journal, 1918.

New York World, 1916.
San Antonio Express, 1914-1915, 1917.
Seguin Enterprise, 1918.

German Language Newspapers
Das Wochenblatt (Austin), 1914, 1917-1918, 1924.
Fredericksburger Wochenblatt, 1914-1918, 1920, 1924.
Giddings Deutsches Volksblatt, 1914-1915, 1917-1918.
Katholische Rundschau (San Antonio), 1914-1918.
La Grange Zeitung, 1914, 1918.
Lutherbote für Texas (La Grange), 1915, 1918.
Neu-Braunfelser Zeitung, 1914, 1917-1918, 1928.
San Antonio Freie Presse für Texas, 1922.

Government Documents
Texas Legislature. House. *Journal of the House of Representatives of the Fourth
   Called Session of the Thirty-Fifth Legislature.* Austin: Von Boeckmann-Jones,
   Co., 1918.
U.S. Congress. Senate. Subcommittee of the Committee on the Judiciary.
   *National German-American Alliance: Hearings Before the Subcommittee of the
   Committee on the Judiciary.* 65th Cong., 2nd sess. on S. 3529, 23 February – 13
   April 1918. Washington, D.C.: Government Printing Office, 1918.
U.S. Congress. Senate. Subcommittee on the Judiciary, *Brewing and Liquor
   Interests and German and Bolshevik Propaganda*, Report and Hearings of the
   Subcommittee on the Judiciary, U.S. Senate submitted pursuant to the Senate
   Res. 307 and 439 in three volumes. 66th Cong., 1st sess., Senate Document No.
   62. Washington, D.C.: Government Printing Office, 1919.

Electronic Documents
Centennial Moments, Texas District LCMS.
   http://100.txdistlcms.org/moment19.html [accessed Dec., 9, 2009].
Evangelical Lutheran Church in America. http://elca.org [accessed Aug. 20, 2006].
FBI files, Freedom of Information Request #319.288, from Dec. 7, 1941 to Jun.
   30, 1945, available at http://foia.fbi.gov/custodet/custode2.pdf [accessed Aug.
   16, 2006], 222-231.
Germanfest. Muenster. http://www.germanfest.net [accessed Aug. 16, 2006].
German-Texan Heritage Society. http://www.germantexans.org [accessed Aug. 20,
   2006].

Historical Census Browser. University of Virginia, Geospatial and Statistical Data Center. http://fisher.lib.virginia.edu/collections/stats/histcensus/index.html [accessed April 9, August 4, 19, 2006].

MLA Language Map Data Center. http://www.mla.org/map_data&dcwindow=same [accessed Dec. 9, 2009].

Oktoberfest. Fredericksburg. http://www.oktoberfestinfbg.com [accessed Aug. 16, 2006].

Shiner Beers. http://www.shiner.com [accessed September 10, 2006].

Texas German Dialect Project. http://www.tgdp.org [accessed Aug. 16, 2006].

Texas German Society. http://www.texasgermansociety.com [accessed Aug. 20, 2006].

"Trenckmann, William Andreas," *Handbook of Texas Online*, http://www.tshaonline.org/handbook/online/articles/TT/ftr8.html [accessed November 17, 2009].

U.S. Census Bureau data. http://factfinder.census.gov [accessed Aug. 20, 2006].

Wikipedia contributors, "Pearl Brewing Company," Wikipedia, The Free Encyclopedia, http://en.wikipedia.org/w/index.php?title=Pearl_Brewing_Company&oldid=745 87056 [accessed September 10, 2006].

Wurstfest. New Braunfels. http://www.wurstfest.com [accessed Aug. 16, 2006].

Theses and Dissertations

Albrecht, Theodore John. "German Singing Societies in Texas." Ph.D. diss., North Texas State University, 1975.

Anderson, Adrian N. "Albert Sidney Burleson: A Southern Politician in the Progressive Era." Ph.D. diss., Texas Tech University, 1967.

Borchardt, Craig William. "German Lutheran Transplants and Methodist Converts in Washington and Austin Counties, Texas, 1860-1930." Ph.D. diss., Texas A&M University, 1996.

Bruns, Sue. "Persecution of Germans in Central Texas During World War I." M.A. thesis, Southwest Texas State University, 1972.

Sonntag, Mark. "Hyphenated Texans: World War I and the German-Americans of Texas." M.A. thesis, University of Texas at Austin, 1990.

Sosebee, Morgan Scott. "Henry C. Smith: A Westering Man." Ph.D. diss., Texas Tech University, 2004.

Veit, Richard J. "The Growth and Effects of Anti-German Sentiment in Waco, Texas, 1914-1918." M.A. thesis, Baylor University, 1980.

Articles

Barr, Alwyn. "Occupational and Geographic Mobility in San Antonio, 1870-1900." *Social Science Quarterly* 51 (Sep. 1970): 396-403.

Baulch, Joe R. "Making West Texas Safe for Democracy: The 1917 Farmers and Laborers Protective Association Conspiracy." *West Texas Historical Association Year Book* 62 (1986): 119-129.

Biesele, Rudolph L. "The First German Settlement in Texas." *Southwestern Historical Quarterly* 34 (1930-1931): 334-339.

_____. "The Texas State Convention of Germans in 1854." *Southwestern Historical Quarterly* 33, no. 4 (April 1930): 247-261.

Buenger, Walter L. "Secession and the Texas German Community: Editor Lindheimer vs. Editor Flake." *Southwestern Historical Quarterly* 82 (April 1979): 379-402.

Conzen, Kathleen Neils. "Germans." In *Harvard Encyclopedia of American Ethnic Groups*, eds. Stephan Thernstrom, et al., 405-425. Cambridge: Harvard University Press, 1980.

_____. "The Paradox of German-American Assimilation." *Yearbook of German-American Studies* 16 (1981): 153-160.

Conzen, Michael P. "The Clash of Utopias: Sisterdale and the Six-Sided Struggle for the Texas Hill Country." In *Cultural Encounters with the Environment: Enduring and Evolving Geographic Themes*, eds. Alexander B. Murphy and Douglas L. Johnson, 39-58. Lanham, Maryland: Rowman & Littlefield Publishers, Inc., 2000.

Cox, Patrick L. "An Enemy Closer to Us Than Any European Power": The Impact of Mexico on Texan Public Opinion before World War I." *Southwestern Historical Quarterly* 105, no. 1 (July 2001): 40-80.

"'*Deutschland Uber Alles*' is Canned!," J. A. White, Chairman, Publicity Committee, Goliad County Council of Defense, Sep. 15, 1918. Reprinted in *The Journal of the German-Texan Heritage Society* 26, no. 1 (Spring 2004): 39-47.

Eichhoff, Jürgen. "The German Language in America." In *America and the Germans: An Assessment of a Three-Hundred-Year History*, vol. 1, eds. Frank Trommler and Joseph McVeigh, 223-240. Philadelphia: University of Pennsylvania Press, 1985.

Elliott, Claude. "Union Sentiment in Texas, 1861-1865." *Southwestern Historical Quarterly* 50 (1946-47): 449-477.

Etzler, T. Herbert. "German-American Newspapers in Texas with Special Reference to the Texas *Volksblatt*, 1877-1879." *Southwestern Historical Quarterly* 58, no. 4 (April 1954): 423-431.

Fiebig-von Hase, Ragnhild. "The United States and Germany in the World Arena, 1900-1917." In *Confrontation and Cooperation: Germany and the United States in the Era of World War I, 1900-1924*, ed. Hans-Jürgen Schröder, 33-68. Providence: Berg, 1993.

Frantz, Joe B. "Ethnicity and Politics in Texas." In *German Culture in Texas*, eds. Glen E. Lich and Dona B. Reeves, 191-202. Boston: Twayne, 1980.

Gilbert, Glenn G. "The German Language in Texas: Some Needed Research." In *German Culture in Texas*, eds. Glen E. Lich and Dona B. Reeves, 229-240. Boston: Twayne, 1980.

Godsho, Albert. "The National German-American Alliance, and the Washington Convention." *The Penn Germania* 1, no. 3 (March 1912): 208-213.

Graebner, Alan. "World War I and the Lutheran Union: Documents from the Army and Navy Board, 1917 and 1918." *Concordia Historical Institute Quarterly* 41 (May 1968): 51-64.

Hegi, Benjamin Paul. "'Old Time Good Germans': German-Americans in Cooke County, Texas, during World War I." *Southwestern Historical Quarterly* 109, no. 2 (Oct. 2005): 234-257.

Jordan, Terry G. "The German Element in Texas: An Overview." *Rice University Studies* 63, no. 3 (1977): 1-11.

_____. "The German Settlement of Texas After 1865." *Southwestern Historical Quarterly* 73, no. 2 (Oct. 1969): 193-212.

_____. "A Religious Geography of the Hill Country Germans of Texas." In *Ethnicity on the Great Plains*, ed. Frederick C. Luebke, 109-128. Lincoln: University of Nebraska Press, 1980.

Kamphoefner, Walter D. "German-American Bilingualism: *Cui Malo?* Mother Tongue and Socioeconomic Status Among the Second Generation in 1940." *International Migration Review* 28 (Winter 1994): 846-864.

_____. "German Texans: In the Mainstream or Backwaters of Lone Star Society?" *Yearbook of German-American Studies* 38 (2003): 119-138.

_____. "The Handwriting on the Wall: The Klan, Language Issues, and Prohibition in the German Settlements of Eastern Texas." *Southwestern Historical Quarterly* 111, no. 1 (July 2008): 52-66.

_____. "New Perspectives on Texas Germans and the Confederacy." *Southwestern Historical Quarterly* 102, no. 4 (April 1999): 441-455.

Luebke, Frederick C. "German Immigrants and American Politics: Problems of Leadership, Parties, and Issues." In *Germans in the New World: Essays in the History of Immigration*. Urbana: University of Illinois Press, 1990.

_____. "Turnerism, Social History, and the Historiography of European Ethnic Groups in the United States." In *Germans in the New World: Essays in the History of Immigration*. Urbana: University of Illinois Press, 1990.

Nohl, Frederick. "The Lutheran Church—Missouri Synod Reacts to United States Anti-Germanism During World War I." *Concordia Historical Institute Quarterly* 35, no. 2 (July 1962): 49-66.

Panayi, Panikos. "An Intolerant Act by an Intolerant Society: The Internment of Germans in Britain During the First World War." In *The Internment of Aliens in Twentieth Century Britain*, eds. David Cesarani and Tony Kushner, 53-78. London: Frank Cass, 1993.

Reeves, Dona. "An Ethnic Inventory for the German-Texans." *University Forum, Fort Hays State University* 27 (Summer 1982): 1-3.

Rippley, La Vern J. "Ameliorated Americanization: The Effect of World War I on German-Americans in the 1920s." In *American and the Germans: An Assessment of a Three-Hundred-Year History*, vol. 2, eds. Frank Trommler and Joseph McVeigh, 217-231. Philadelphia: University of Pennsylvania Press, 1985.

Reinhardt, Louis. "The Communistic Colony of Bettina." *Texas State Historical Quarterly* 3 (1899): 33-40.

Salmons, Joseph C. and Felecia A. Lucht. "Standard German in Texas." In *Studies in Contact Linguistics: Essays in Honor of Glenn G. Gilbert*, eds. Linda L. Thornburg and Janet M. Fuller, 167-188. New York: Peter Lang, 2006.

Shook, Robert W. "The Battle of Nueces, August 10, 1862." *Southwestern Historical Quarterly* 66 (1962): 31-42.

_____. "German Migration to Texas 1830-1850: Causes and Consequences." *Texana* 10 (1972): 226-243.

Trefousse, Hans. "German-American Immigrants and the Newly Founded Reich." In *American and the Germans: An Assessment of a Three-Hundred-Year History*, vol. 1, eds. Frank Trommler and Joseph McVeigh, 160-175. Philadelphia: University of Pennsylvania Press, 1985.

Trommler, Frank. "Inventing the Enemy: German-American Cultural Relations, 1900-1917." In *Confrontation and Cooperation: Germany and the United States in the Era of World War I, 1900-1924*, ed. Hans-Jürgen Schröder, 99-125. Providence: Berg, 1993.

Wilson, Joseph. "The German Language in Central Texas Today." *Rice University Studies* 63, no. 3 (1977): 47-58.

_____. "Texas German and Other Immigrant Languages: Problems and Prospects." In *Eagle in the New World: German Immigration to Texas and America*, eds. Theodore Gish and Richard Spuler, 221-240. College Station: Texas A&M University Press, 1986.

Zimmerman, Jonathan. "Ethnics Against Ethnicity: European Immigrants and Foreign Language Instruction, 1890-1940." *The Journal of American History* 88, no. 4 (Mar. 2002): 1383-1404.

Books

50th Anniversary, St. John Lutheran, Wilson, Texas, 6-7, in William A. Flachmeier Collection, Archives and Information Services Division, Texas State Library and Archives Commission, Austin, Texas.

Arndt, Karl and May Olson. *German-American Newspapers and Periodicals, 1732-1955*, 2nd ed. New York: Johnson Reprint, 1965.

Atwell, William Hawley. *Autobiography*. Dallas: Warlick Law Printing Company, 1935.

Beckett, Ian F. W. *The Great War, 1914-1918*. London: Longman, 2001.

Berg-Sobré, Judith. *San Antonio on Parade: Six Historic Festivals*. College Station: Texas A&M University Press, 2003.

Biesele, Rudolph Leopold. *The History of the German Settlements in Texas, 1831-1861.* Austin: Eakin Press, 1987.

Biggers, Don H. *German Pioneers in Texas: A Brief History of Their Hardships, Struggles, and Achievements.* Austin: Eakin Press, 1983.

Blackbourn, David. *The Long Nineteenth Century: A History of Germany, 1780-1918.* New York: Oxford University Press, 1998.

Blanton, Annie Webb. *A Handbook of Information as to Education in Texas, 1918-1922. Bulletin 157.* Austin: Department of Education, State of Texas, 1923.

Blanton, Annie Webb and R. L. Ragsdale. *Texas High Schools: History and Social Sciences. Bulletin 124.* Austin: Department of Education, State of Texas, 1920.

Blanton, Carlos Kevin. *The Strange Career of Bilingual Education in Texas, 1836-1981.* College Station: Texas A&M University Press, 2004.

Boas, Hans C. *The Life and Death of Texas German.* Durham: American Dialect Society, 2009.

Brown, Norman D. *Hood, Bonnet, and Little Brown Jug: Texas Politics, 1921-1928.* College Station: Texas A&M University Press, 1984.

Campbell, Randolph B. *Gone to Texas: A History of the Lone Star State.* New York: Oxford University Press, 2003.

Cat Spring Agricultural Society. *Century of Agricultural Progress, 1856-1956: Minutes of the Cat Spring Agricultural Society.* Cat Spring, Texas: Cat Spring Agricultural Society, 1956.

Centennial History, 1877-1977, St. John's Lutheran, Prairie Hill, Texas, 12, in William A. Flachmeier Collection, Archives and Information Services Division, Texas State Library and Archives Commission, Austin, Texas.

Centennial, Zion's Lutheran Church, Arneckeville, Texas, 1868-1968, 11-14, in William A. Flachmeier Collection, Archives and Information Services Division, Texas State Library and Archives Commission, Austin, Texas.

Child, Clifton James. *The German-Americans in Politics, 1914-1917.* Madison: The University of Wisconsin Press, 1939.

Church on the Coleto. Meyersville: Saint John Evangelical Lutheran Church of Meyersville, 1978.

Clark, Christopher M. *Kaiser Wilhelm II.* London: Longman, 2000.

Coburn, Carol K. *Life at Four Corners: Religion, Gender, and Education in a German-Lutheran Community, 1868-1945.* Lawrence: University Press of Kansas, 1992.

Conzen, Kathleen Neils. *Germans in Minnesota.* St. Paul: Minnesota Historical Society Press, 2003.

Cottrell, Debbie Mauldin. *Pioneer Woman Educator in Texas: The Progressive Spirit of Annie Webb Blanton.* College Station: Texas A&M University Press, 1993.

Cousins, R. B. *Sixteenth Biennial Report of the State Superintendent of Public Instruction for the Years Ending August 31, 1907 and August 31, 1908.* Austin: Von Boeckmann-Jones, 1909.

Dabbs, Jack Autrey and Edward C. Breitenkamp. *Records of Salem Lutheran Church, Brenham, Texas, 1850-1940.* Austin: J. A. Dabbs and E. C. Breitenkamp, 1986.

DeBauche, Leslie Midkiff. *Reel Patriotism: The Movies and World War I.* Madison: The University of Wisconsin Press, 1997.

Detjen, David. *The Germans in Missouri, 1900-1918: Prohibition, Neutrality, and Assimilation.* Columbia: University of Missouri Press, 1985.

Fehler, Harold E. *Hundredth Anniversary [1867-1968] of St. John Lutheran Church in New Ulm, Texas.* New Ulm: St. John Lutheran Church, 1968.

Flachmeier, William A. *Lutherans of Texas in Confluence: With Emphasis on the Decade 1951-1961.* Austin: Von Boeckmann-Jones, 1972.

Fleming, Thomas. *The Illusion of Victory: America in World War I.* New York: Basic Books, 2003.

Gerard, James W. *Face to Face with Kaiserism.* New York: George H. Doran, Co., 1918.

Gish, Theodore G. *The History of the Houston Sängerbund.* Houston: Institute of Texas-German Studies, University of Houston, 1990.

Gish, Theodore and Richard Spuler, eds. *Eagle in the New World: German Immigration to Texas and America.* College Station: Texas A&M University Press, 1986.

Goeth, Ottilie Fuchs. *Memories of a Texas Pioneer Grandmother.* Translated by Irma Goeth Guenther. Burnet: Eakin Press, 1982.

Goodwyn, Lawrence. *Coming to Terms: The German Hill Country of Texas.* College Station: Texas A&M University Press, 1991.

Gould, Lewis L. *Progressives and Prohibitionists: Texas Democrats in the Wilson Era.* Austin: University of Texas Press, 1973.

Grasty, Sue Watkins. *Our God is Marching On: A Centennial History of Bethlehem Lutheran Church, Round Top, Texas.* Austin: Von Boeckmann-Jones, 1966.

Hawgood, John Arkas. *The Tragedy of German-America.* New York: G. P. Putnam's Sons, 1940.

Heinrich, M. *History of the First Evangelical Lutheran Synod of Texas.* Chicago: Wartburg, 1927.

Higham, John. *Strangers in the Land: Patterns of American Nativism, 1860-1925.* Brunswick: Rutgers University Press, 1955.

Hohn, Caesar. *Dutchman on the Brazos: Reminiscences of Caesar (Dutch) Hohn.* Austin: University of Texas Press, 1963.

Holy Cross Lutheran Church, 1873-1973: 100 Years of God's Blessings. Flatonia: Flatonia Argus, 1973.

How the Outlawed German-American Alliance Sought to Control Affairs in Texas. Dallas: Allied Printing, 1918.

Humphrey, Janet G. *A Texas Suffragist: Diaries and Writings of Jane Y. McCallum.* Austin: Ellen C. Temple, 1988.

Isenberg, Michael T. *War on Film: The America Cinema and World War I, 1914-1941*. Rutherford: Farleigh Dickinson University Press, 1981.

Ivy, James D. *No Saloon in the Valley: The Southern Strategy of Texas Prohibitionists in the 1880s*. Waco: Baylor University Press, 2003.

Jenkins, Philip. *Hoods and Shirts: The Extreme Right in Pennsylvania, 1925-1950*. Chapel Hill: University of North Carolina Press, 1997.

Johnson, Charles Thomas. *Culture at Twilight: The National German-American Alliance, 1901-1918*. New York: Peter Lang, 1999.

Jones, John Price and Paul Merrick Hollister. *The German Secret Service in America, 1914-1918*. Boston: Small, Maynard & Co., 1918.

Jordan, Gilbert J. *Yesterday in the Texas Hill Country*. College Station: Texas A&M University Press, 1979.

Jordan, Terry G. *German Seed in Texas Soil: Immigrant Farmers in Nineteenth-Century Texas*. Austin: University of Texas Press, 1966.

Katz, Friedrich. *The Secret War in Mexico: Europe, the United States, and the Mexican Revolution*. Chicago: The University of Chicago Press, 1981.

Kazal, Russell A. *Becoming Old Stock: The Paradox of German-American Identity*. Princeton: Princeton University Press, 2004.

Keene, Jennifer D. *Doughboys, the Great War, and the Remaking of America*. Baltimore: The Johns Hopkins University Press, 2001.

_____. *The United States and the First World War*. London: Longman, 2000.

Keller, Phyllis. *States of Belonging: German-American Intellectuals and the First World War*. Cambridge: Harvard University Press, 1979.

Kennedy, David M. *Over Here: The First World War and American Society*. New York: Oxford University Press, 1980.

Kirschbaum, Erik. *The Eradication of German Culture in the United States: 1917-1918*. Stuttgart: Hans-Dieter Heinz, 1986.

Krueger, Max Amadeus Paulus. *Second Fatherland: The Life and Fortunes of a German Immigrant*, ed. Marilyn McAdams Sibley. College Station: Texas A&M University Press, 1976.

Laake, Doris Goerner. *History of St. John Lutheran Church, Paige, Texas*. Paige: D. Laake, 1979.

Landau, Captain Henry. *The Enemy Within: The Inside Story of German Sabotage in America*. New York: G.P. Putnam's Sons, 1937.

Lich, Glen E. *The German Texans*. San Antonio: The University of Texas Institute of Texan Cultures at San Antonio, 1981.

Lich, Glen E. and Dona B. Reeves, eds. *German Culture in Texas: A Free Earth; Essays from the 1978 Southwest Symposium*. Boston: Twayne Publishers, 1980.

Luebke, Frederick C. *Bonds of Loyalty: German Americans and the First World War*. DeKalb: Northern Illinois University Press, 1974.

_____. *Germans in Brazil: A Comparative History of Cultural Conflict During World War I*. Baton Rouge: Louisiana State University Press, 1987.

_____. *Germans in the New World: Essays in the History of Immigration.* Urbana: University of Illinois Press, 1990.

Marrs, S. M. N. and Opal Gilstrap. *Texas High Schools: The Teaching of Spanish, German, and French. Bulletin 230.* Austin: State Department of Education, 1927.

Martel, Gordon. *The Origins of the First World War.* London: Longman, 2003.

McKay, Seth S. and Odie B. Faulk. *Texas After Spindletop: The Saga of Texas, 1901-1965.* Austin: Steck-Vaughn Company, 1965.

McKay, Seth Shepard. *Texas Politics, 1906-1944, With Special Reference to the German Counties.* Lubbock: Texas Tech University Press, 1952.

Morgenthaler, Jefferson. *The German Settlement of the Texas Hill Country.* Boerne, Texas: Mockingbird Books, 2007.

_____. *Promised Land: Solms, Castro, and Sam Houston's Colonization Contracts.* College Station: Texas A&M University Press, 2009.

Nelson, William P. *German-American Political Behavior in Nebraska and Wisconsin, 1916-1920.* Lincoln: University of Nebraska-Lincoln Publication, 1972.

Nicolini, Marcus. *Deutsch in Texas.* Münster: Lit. Verlag, 2004.

Penniger, Robert. *Fredericksburg, Texas: The First Fifty Years.* Translated by C.L. Wisseman. Fredericksburg: Fredericksburg Publishing Company, 1971.

Randers-Pehrson, Justine Davis. *Adolf Douai, 1819-1888: The Turbulent Life of a German Forty-Eighter in the Homeland and in the United States.* New York: Peter Lang, 2000.

Rippley, La Vern J. *The German-Americans.* Lanham, Maryland: University Press of America, 1976.

Ross, William G. *Forging New Freedoms: Nativism, Education, and the Constitution, 1917-1927.* Lincoln: University of Nebraska Press, 1994.

Samuel, Wolfgang W. E. *American Raiders: The Race to Capture the Luftwaffe's Secrets.* Jackson: University Press of Mississippi, 2004.

Schieber, Clara Eve. *The Transformation of American Sentiment Toward Germany, 1870-1914.* New York: Russell & Russell, 1973.

Seligmann, Matthew S. and Roderick R. McLean. *Germany from Reich to Republic, 1871-1919: Politics, Hierarchy and Elites.* New York: St. Martin's Press, 2000.

Sitton, Thad and Milam C. Rowold. *Ringing the Children In: Texas Country Schools.* College Station: Texas A&M University Press, 1987.

Sitton, Thad and Dan K. Utley. *From Can See to Can't: Texas Cotton Farmers on the Southern Prairies.* Austin: University of Texas Press, 1997.

Struve, Walter. *Germans and Texans: Commerce, Migration, and Culture in the Days of the Lone Star Republic.* Austin: University of Texas Press, 1996.

Syring, David. *Places in the World a Person Could Walk: Family, Stories, Home, and Place in the Texas Hill Country.* Austin: University of Texas Press, 2000.

Trask, David F., ed. *World War I At Home: Readings on American Life, 1914-1920.* New York: John Wiley & Sons, Inc., 1970.

Bibliography

Traxel, David. *Crusader Nation: The United States in Peace and the Great War, 1898-1920*. New York: Alfred A. Knopf, 2006.

Tuchmann, Barbara. *The Zimmermann Telegram*. New York: MacMillan Company, 1966.

Usher, Roland G. *Pan-Germanism*. Boston: Houghton Mifflin, 1913.

Wittke, Carl. *German Americans and the World War (With Special Emphasis on Ohio's German Language Press)*. Columbus: Ohio State Archaelogical and Historical Society, 1936.

Wolff, August L. *The Story of St. John's Lutheran Church, San Antonio, Texas*. n.p.: P. Anderson Co., 1937.

Wüstenbecker, Katja. *Deutsch-Amerikaner im Ersten Weltkrieg: U.S.-Politik und nationale Identitaten im Mittleren Westen*. Stuttgart: Franz Steinar Verlag, 2007.